Guide #19

WRITING SUCCESSFUL TECHNOLOGY GRANT PROPOSALS

A LITA Guide

Pamela H. MacKellar

Neal-Schuman Publishers, Inc.

New York   London

Published by Neal-Schuman Publishers, Inc.
100 William St., Suite 2004
New York, NY 10038
http://www.neal-schuman.com

Printed and bound in the United States of America.

The paper used in this publication meets the minimum requirements of American National Standard for Information Sciences—Permanence of Paper for Printed Library Materials, ANSI Z39.48-1992.

Library of Congress Cataloging-in-Publication Data

MacKellar, Pamela H.
   Writing successful technology grant proposals : a LITA guide / Pamela H. MacKellar.
      p. cm. — (LITA guide ; #19)
   Includes bibliographical references and index.
   ISBN 978-1-55570-763-7 (alk. paper)
   1. Libraries—Information technology—United States—Finance. 2. Libraries—Automation—United States—Finance. 3. Proposal writing for grants—United States. 4. Proposal writing in library science—United States. I. Title.

Z678.9.A4U648 2012
025.1'1—dc23
                                                              2011046318

This book is dedicated to librarianship,

to librarians,

and to thriving libraries.

Contents

vii

xi

List of Illustrations

Figures

Checklists, Examples, Templates, and Worksheets

Preface

The digital revolution is in full swing, and digital is winning. New information technologies have significantly changed the landscape for librarians, transforming the familiar flow of collecting, acquiring, organizing, synthesizing, retrieving, and disseminating information—the foundational principles of librarianship. The way librarians conduct the basic functions of their jobs has shifted from manual techniques to using technology-based methods in almost every way. Librarians must be diligent to stay informed and explore new technologies, identify the most appropriate technology to help meet the information needs of the people they serve, build an infrastructure to support library technology, hire personnel to implement it, provide staff training on how to use it—and find the money not only to pay for the technology, infrastructure, tech-savvy personnel, and technology training but also to replace the technology when it is obsolete and continue to retrain personnel on utilizing new technologies.

In recent years, the demand for technology in libraries has increased while at the same time library budgets have decreased. The United States is now experiencing some of the most challenging economic conditions in decades. Although opinions differ about whether or not our country is in a recession and headed for more difficult times—or the economy is steadily improving—we can all agree this is not an easy time for libraries. In light of this, it is becoming more and more challenging for librarians in libraries of all kinds to ensure the role of libraries as information centers and to live up to their role of technology leaders among the people they serve. At the same time, librarians must live up to this role if libraries are going to thrive as vital and valuable information centers for the people we serve.

Grants are becoming a more important part of every library's funding strategy and, more specifically, an important resource for funding library technology. *Writing Successful Technology Grant Proposals: A LITA Guide* presents a grant process that librarians can incorporate into their jobs to help them fund library technology. The process presented here stresses the importance of planning before proposal writing and, if followed, will save librarians time and increase their chances of success with grants. This book will show librarians that grant work is within their abilities, and it is something they can do. When readers understand the grant process and build it into their jobs, they will find that when a grant opportunity comes along, writing a proposal is not such a monumental undertaking. The more librarians understand the grant process presented in this book, the easier it will be to write a proposal, and acquiring alternative funding—including grants—will become second nature.

Intended Audience and Purpose

Technology projects of all kinds in libraries of all sizes and types are likely to be eligible for grant funding of some kind. *Writing Successful Technology Grant Proposals: A LITA Guide* is written for anyone who wants to know more about grant work, proposal writing, and how to be successful with library technology grants. It is meant primarily for all kinds of librarians and library staff who work in all types of libraries, small to large, that serve populations of all sizes; library technology staff; and information technology staff in organizations that include libraries. The grant process presented in this book will also assist nonprofit staff who are seeking grants for technology projects.

Readers who will benefit most from this book are those who have been hesitant to venture into the grants arena or have been intimidated by grant work and proposal writing in the past. Those who have approached grant work without planning may have concluded that grant work consumes too much time without any guarantees of a return. This book will dispel some of these common misconceptions about grant work—

- Grant work is too difficult.
- Competition for grants is too stiff.
- Proposal writing is too complicated.
- Small libraries are unlikely to be successful at grants.
- It takes a big staff to write a grant proposal.
- You must know someone at the funding agency or foundation to be successful with grants.
- Taking an expensive grant course is necessary.
- Winning a grant means doing more work.
- Small projects are not eligible or attractive to funders.

—and it will instill confidence by providing a framework for understanding the basic nature of grant work and how to approach it in easy-to-understand language.

Organization

The book covers each phase in the grant process from planning through project implementation and continuing the grant process. Understanding these phases and practicing the steps in this book will show you how to write successful technology grant proposals and continuously do grant work as part of your job.

In Chapter 1, "Phases of the Grant Process," you are introduced to the grant process model used in this book. The model illustrates that grant work involves seven different phases and specifically that proposal writing does not come at the beginning of the grant process. Each phase is summarized here to give readers a framework for understanding grant work. Each phase is discussed in detail in the following chapters.

The planning phase stresses the importance of conducting a needs assessment and having the library's plans in place before moving further into the grant process. Chapter 2, "Planning," outlines the common elements of a technology plan and discusses the core proposal components found within a technology plan. Examples of library technology plans useful for designing grant projects are cited.

A step-by-step method for designing a technology project that may become a grant project is the focus of the project design phase. Chapter 3, "Designing Library Technology Projects and Programs," illustrates that proposal writing actually begins during the project design phase and includes a sample technology project design suitable for a grant proposal.

In the teamwork phase you must first have commitment from the organization before forming a grant team. Chapter 4, "The Grant Team," covers this topic and defines team members' positions and duties, team meetings, and team responsibilities.

The research phase consists of the three steps covered in Chapters 5, 6, and 7. Chapter 5, "Sources for Funding Technology Projects," defines the various government and private grant funding sources and provides information about possible sources for library technology funding. "Resources for Finding Technology Grants," Chapter 6, focuses on the resources—or the tools—used for identifying grants that may fund technology projects. It covers useful print directories, electronic directories, online databases, websites, blogs, print and electronic newsletters, and e-mail discussion groups. The different kinds of grants available are defined in Chapter 7, "Researching Technology Grants," which also provides a step-by-step guide to the research process, outlines how to search some specific sources such as Grants.gov, and gives tips on how to keep your research current.

Chapter 8, "Writing and Submitting Your Proposal," covers the writing phase of the grant process. Topics include common proposal components, kinds of grant proposals, and tips on how to write the common proposal components. Here you will find example proposal components, including comments on what works and what doesn't work in each one. A full proposal is analyzed from beginning to end so that the reader can see the details and features of a winning proposal.

Next steps after winning a grant and the first steps in implementing a technology project are part of the implementation phase. Chapter 9, "Implementing Your Technology Project," gives you some guidance on how to proceed once your project is funded, including informing the community, establishing evaluation baselines, and reviewing the budget.

The review phase is covered in Chapter 10, "Reviewing and Continuing the Grant Process," which explains the importance of identifying where your team excelled, what you can do to improve, what steps in the process need more attention, and what you would do exactly the same way the next time around. This is the time when readers will see how to weave grant work into their jobs, when they can see how grant work becomes second nature and success at winning grants follows. This chapter also covers what to do if your proposal was rejected and keeping plans and assessments up to date.

Chapter 11, "Technology Grant Success Stories," gives readers inspiration and motivates them to seek funding opportunities for their library technology projects by providing some examples of successfully funded library technology projects from public, school, academic, and special libraries.

Perspective

The author's intent is to contribute to the survival of libraries by sharing with librarians a grant process model that will increase their success rate with grants for technology projects. Librarians who incorporate this model into their jobs will be positioned to attract additional alternative funding for technology projects that will help meet the information needs of the people they serve. When information needs are being met using technology, people will value libraries as the information centers where they can use technology to find information or gain knowledge and skills to improve their lives. When people value libraries, they will fund them.

Writing Successful Technology Grant Proposals: A LITA Guide is written from the perspective of someone who has experienced the grant process multiple times in different capacities and different kinds of libraries and who understands the commitment and hard work involved. As an active and current writer of grant proposals, the author has recent "in the trenches" experience utilizing and fine-tuning the grant process model. Her experience as a grant reviewer for state and federal agencies has given her valuable insight on how applying the grant process can help improve an applicant's success rate. Teaching has given her insight about common pitfalls in grant work, and this book is meant to show librarians how to avoid them. There is no substitute for spending the time it takes to learn and apply this grant process. It will pay off in the end.

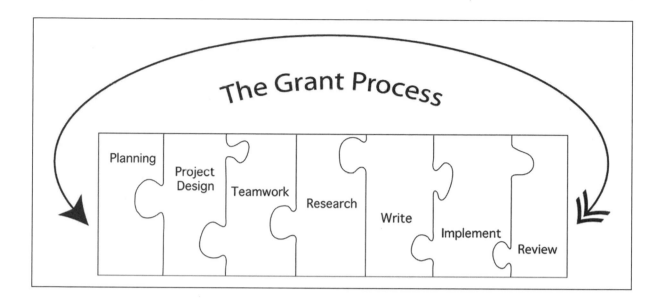

Chapter 1

Phases of the Grant Process

Grant work is a continuous and ongoing process, not a one-time activity. The grant process starts with library plans that are based on meeting the assessed needs of the people who are being served by the library, followed by project design and development; a commitment to the grant process and participation on the grant team by the organization and library staff, partners, collaborators, stakeholders, and community members; researching and selecting the right grant opportunities for your project; writing grant proposals; and project implementation. After you review and debrief at the conclusion of applying for a grant, you are then ready to update the library's plans, project designs, and proposal components in preparation for the next grant opportunity that comes your way.

The illustration of the grant process provided here will help you understand the seven phases in the grant process and visualize how to build grant work into your job. You will benefit the most from this book when you take the time to first understand that grant work is a larger process that includes proposal writing as one step. If you want to be successful at writing grant proposals it is essential that you first understand all phases of the grant process. The grant process is the same whether you are planning to apply for a technology grant or any other kind of grant. Your willingness to embrace this approach will positively affect your future success with technology grants as well as other grants for libraries and other organizations.

Understanding the Grant Process

To be successful with grants, it is important to first understand the grant process and how it works from beginning to end. For many readers, this will be a new paradigm for thinking about grants and proposal writing. If this is a new idea to you, it is well worth the effort to take the time now to understand the whole grant process and where each phase fits into the "bigger picture" of grant work. This understanding will not only increase your chances of success with grants, it will help you build grant work into your job and prepare you for responding to new grant opportunities as they arise. Understanding the process will also give you confidence with grant work and help you avoid the most common pitfalls when applying for grants.

Grant Work and Proposal Writing

As you can see from the illustration at the beginning of the chapter depicting the different phases of the grant process as puzzle pieces, writing grant proposals is only one phase in the grant process—and it is not the first phase. It is a common misconception that grant work begins when you see a great grant opportunity for your library (see Rule #1). It can be very exciting to learn about a grant that could provide the library with needed technology or equipment, additional staff, or more funding for online products and features. The tendency is to rush into writing a proposal by the deadline without completing the necessary preliminary phases in the grant process. When you start grant work with writing the proposal, this places the focus primarily on the money or buying things for the library rather than on meeting the needs of the people the library serves (see Rule #2). This thinking is backwards, and funders will pick up on it right away. Funders want to help people. If they perceive that your primary interest is to get the money without any apparent thought given to how the grant will improve life for the people your library serves, it is an indication to them that your values are not a good match with theirs.

> **Rule #1**
> Grant work starts with planning.

> **Rule #2**
> Grants are about people, not about money or things.

Also, to write a proposal as the first step is a very difficult way to approach grant work. If you take this approach, you are making grant work unnecessarily hard on yourself and your grant team. Grant work can be challenging under the best of circumstances; however, doing it backwards compounds the challenge. Besides being focused on the money rather than on making a difference for people, there is usually a looming deadline against which you are racing to make your library profile, community profile, people's needs, and technology project fit into the funder's criteria. When you work backwards, it produces a lot of stress for you and your team as you search for facts that don't exist to support your proposal.

Attempting to write a proposal without first completing the preliminary steps in their natural order is also likely to end in rejection. After having gone through a very stressful and difficult time writing a proposal tailored to the funder's requirements rather than to the needs of the people you serve, your proposal may not be funded. At this point it is likely that you may be discouraged from writing another grant proposal ever again. You may know librarians who say they don't apply for grants because it is too difficult, too stressful, or too much work. When you inquire further, chances are good that they will tell you they applied for a grant once and writing the proposal was the first thing they did after learning about a grant opportunity. This approach has ruined grant work for many people. Don't let this happen to you.

The Seven Phases of Grant Work

This is the time to pause and take some time to understand the "big picture" of grant work by learning about the seven phases of the grant process. Although this book is about writing successful technology grant proposals, it won't work to go straight to the chapter on proposal writing without reading or understanding the initial phases in the grant process. Focus on understanding this approach and applying it to your situation well in advance of writing a proposal and you will avoid several common pitfalls in grant work. This can be the most challenging part of grant work for some people, because it is human nature to race for the end result in as few steps as possible. Once you understand this process and put it into action, you will be happy you spent time on understanding it. With grant work, as with many other things in life, you can take an approach with a proven success rate or you can cut corners and skip steps. It's your choice; however, when it comes to grants and proposal writing, taking short cuts rarely results in success and often results in rejection, unnecessary stress, and wasted time. Librarians are busy people, and there is no time to waste on writing unsuccessful grant proposals.

An overview of the seven phases of the grant process follows. The remaining chapters in this book will cover each phase in more depth.

Phase 1: Planning

You need to know the real issues or needs in your community (see Definition) or among the people you serve before you design meaningful and relevant technology projects to meet their needs. How can you know the solution until you know the problem?

Community assessment is the systematic collection, organization, analysis, and synthesis of information about a particular community of people. It uses both qualitative and quantitative methodologies. As a research methodology, community assessment is used by a variety of disciplines, agencies, or organizations, including libraries.

Librarians usually assess the needs of the people served by their libraries by conducting a community needs assessment prior to strategic planning and technology planning. A needs assessment, the foundation of library planning, tells you about the needs of all the people your library serves, not just about the people who use the library. The purpose of a library's community assessment is to determine the information needs of the people served by the library and compare them with the goals of programs and services currently being offered by the library. This provides a way to identify gaps in service, and it provides the information necessary to recommend new library programs and services that will satisfy the current needs of the community.

There are many resources librarians can use to plan and design meaningful community needs assessments that will assist them with library planning and decision

> **Definition**
> COMMUNITY: The people served by a library. For a public library this usually means the residents of a geographic area, such as a city, town, village, county, or region. Students, teachers, instructors, lecturers, researchers, faculty, and staff are usually the people served by school, college, or university libraries. The employees of a business or corporation; administration, staff, and members of a museum; residents of a senior living facility; employees, doctors, and staff in a hospital; inmates in a prison; or parents of special needs children visiting a family support center are some examples of people who are served by special libraries.

3

making. The main point is to gather information that will allow you to analyze the specific population your library serves and their unique information needs so you can plan relevant library services and programs to meet those needs. Librarians who distribute generic customer satisfaction surveys to people who visit the library are mistaken to think they are conducting community needs assessments. For effective planning and successful grant proposals, up-to-date community needs assessments are necessary.

In general, it is safe to say technology helps librarians to better serve the information needs of their communities; however, it is important for librarians to select the appropriate technology that will best help meet the specific information needs in their individual communities. Simply adding new library technology does not mean that the technology is helping to meet a community's current information needs (see Rule #3). So, it's not about buying iPads, e-books, equipment for digitizing old photographs, new computers, instituting social networking in your library, or providing computer gaming activities. Rather it is about providing library programs and services that will make a difference for the people you serve by meeting their information needs. To implement those services and programs you may need to purchase technology and equipment or fund staff time to implement the technology projects that will help support successful programs and services. This is the case whether or not you are applying for a grant.

Rule #3
Technology grants fund projects that meet your community's information needs using technology.

Planning is the foundation on which grant proposals are written, and it provides the framework for developing grant projects, including projects that utilize technology. Planning tells librarians where they are, where they are going, and how they will get there. Funders strive to improve life for the people served by libraries, and libraries with plans have much greater prospects for winning grants that fulfill funders' aspirations. Starting with your library's strategic plan and technology plan is proactive, whereas responding to a Request for Proposals (RFP) by writing a proposal as the first step is reactive. Especially in these tough economic times, grants are being awarded to libraries that are proactive, organized, and responsibly and professionally operated. This means libraries that have their strategic plans and technology plans in place, and are focused on meeting the information needs of the people they serve, will have better success with grants.

If your library doesn't have a strategic plan or technology plan, do what you can to make it a priority to undertake these planning processes before writing grant proposals. If you are a library director in a small public or special library, this is likely in your hands; however, if you are working in a large academic library or city public library system where you are not in a leadership position, this can be easier said than done. Lacking a library plan, make plans or suggest making plans for your department or unit within the library. Without plans, it is likely that people's information needs will not be met, poorly designed projects will be created, or technology purchases made only because funding is available. As mentioned earlier, attempting to write your grant proposal before planning puts the focus on getting the money, not on making a difference for people. If you do this, you will end up inventing a project to meet the requirements of the funder. This is not only difficult to do, but it is unlikely to result in a successful grant proposal. On the other hand, if you have already planned technology projects to meet community needs based on your strategic plan and technology plan, you already know these projects were designed to benefit the people you serve.

A big advantage to planning first is that you will inadvertently produce many of your main proposal components while you are planning. For instance, the library's strategic plan itself should minimally provide you with the information you need for these common proposal components:

- Organizational profile and/or Library profile
- Community profile
- Need statement

Plans answer many questions asked by funders in their grant applications, and answers to these questions often help determine grant awards. A library with plans is an organized, responsible applicant with a stated purpose and vision for how to use technology to meet information needs into the future. Including faculty, students, community members, your city's Information Technology (IT) staff, business leaders, and other stakeholders in your library's planning process will help establish relationships with potential project partners or collaborators well in advance of proposal writing.

Phase 2: Project Design

With your strategic plan and technology plan in place, you have what you need to create technology projects that are mission driven and designed to meet the information needs of the people you serve. It is essential that your technology projects emerge from your library's plans, as they are the groundwork you have built to serve your community and its specific needs.

> **Rule #4**
> Designing the technology project and proposal writing are closely linked.

As you design your technology project you will actually be preparing some additional common proposal components (see Rule #4). These may include:

- Technology Project description (including goals, objectives, outcomes, and activities)
- Approach or Methodology
- Timeline
- Budget
- Evaluation plan

When you plan a technology project before writing the proposal, you are ensuring that your project comes from your desire to meet the needs of the people you serve. Likewise, if developed during the planning stages, the goals, objectives and activities, approach or methodology, timeline, budget, and evaluation plan for your project will also come from this same core purpose. You are always on the right track if you are working from your desire to meet needs.

Convene a team of creative thinkers to study the library's technology plan and design projects using the goals, objectives, outcomes, and activities in the plan. It is important to include potential partners in the project planning stages. Their ideas are invaluable as you discover new projects. By including others with similar interests you

5

will decrease the chances of duplicating a project that is already being done in your college or university, school, organization, or community; you will develop new relationships with collaborators, and you will get their perspective and buy-in at an early stage. With partners involved in developing your grant projects, you will have more chances of being successful, the project is more likely to be sustainable, and the project responsibilities can be shared across several organizations.

A solid project design is built on one or more goals, SMART (specific, measurable, achievable, realistic, and time-bound) objectives, outcomes, and the activities required to realize the project. Once a project idea has been developed, research other similar projects that have already been done as well as new and innovative technologies that are appropriate to help meet project goals. You may want to alter your project based on this research, build on what others have done, or incorporate emerging technologies. This research will be part of your project design and is something you'll want to include in your grant proposal later. This lets a funder know that you are well informed about what has been done in the past and what technology is new and emerging and that you are knowledgeable about best practices. It tells them that your project is viable, you know what you are talking about, it is likely to succeed, and it will probably be sustainable because you have learned from past successes and failures. Funders will be assured that their funds will be spent on new and innovative ideas that build on previous experience and are implemented by knowledgeable staff.

The activities you have determined in your project design will provide what you need for a project timeline. Timelines are project-planning tools that are used to represent the timing of tasks required to complete a project. There are many ways to construct timelines, so use the method that is the most straightforward for your project design.

Every project needs a budget. Use the timeline and activities to figure out the personnel and FTE (full-time equivalent) required for your project. Calculate the FTE cost, and add the cost of benefits for your personnel budget. A non-personnel budget includes the other project costs such as hardware, software, equipment, utilities, furniture, marketing, space rental, and supplies. Create your project budget by combining the personnel budget and the non-personnel budget, and adding the costs together to determine the total project cost. When match or in-kind funds are being committed to the project by the library, partners, or other grants, include this information in your project budget. Academic libraries typically must include indirect costs (or overhead) in the project budget. An indirect cost rate is a way to determine what proportion of departmental or organizational administration a project should bear for costs such as heat, light, space rental, and administrative support.

Now determine how you will measure the effectiveness of your project in reaching your stated goals and objectives. Projects are undertaken to have an impact, and evaluation plans show the success of a project's impact as well as point out improvements you can make in your project design during project implementation. The key to writing an evaluation plan is to have objectives that are measurable. With measurable objectives the evaluation plan will be relatively easy to compose, because it is a natural extension of the objectives.

As you see, by the time you have finished designing your technology project, you will have some core proposal components and the foundation you need to write your grant proposal. Now you can understand why strategic planning, technology planning, and project design must come before writing a proposal in the grant process and how you can benefit by approaching grant work this way.

Phase 3: Teamwork

Grant work is a team effort from the planning phase through the project design, research, proposal writing, project implementation, and review phases (see Rule #5). A grant team is necessary so that the library's grant work is supported by the entire library and organization and not driven by only a few people. Also, grant work and proposal writing are much easier when

> **Rule #5**
> Grant work is a team effort.

there is a team of people working on them. No matter the size of your library, it is possible to have a team working on grants. Involve library leadership, faculty, students, staff, board members, business leaders, volunteers, partners, and representatives from your surrounding community. When working on technology grants, make a point of including people who are knowledgeable and energized by technology. For instance, a board member who is adamant about keeping the card catalog furniture and abhors computers may impede your progress on a technology grant.

It is important to appoint a grant coordinator to oversee the grant team, and for large grant projects it may be helpful to include someone to do the research, a proposal writer, an evaluation specialist, or a subject matter expert. Creating a grant team generates ownership, buy-in, and support, and it helps with grant work, project implementation, and the follow-up necessary for successful technology grant projects. It is essential that every decision maker in your organization supports the work of the grant team. A strong commitment from library leadership, grant coordinators, project directors, staff members with responsibilities related to a grant project, and project partners is required.

Grants have benefits, but they also mean your library has obligations to consider (see Rule #6). Everyone must be clear about the responsibilities tied to grant work, and there must be buy-in from everyone involved. These responsibilities include committing resources such as staff time to plan the project, write the proposal, follow up with funders, and perform administrative duties. Space may be needed for the grant team to work, and office support will be necessary for help with editing, proof-

> **Rule #6**
> Grant work requires support from your organization and leadership.

reading, and copying proposals; getting authorized signatures and letters of support; and communicating with potential funders, others in your organization, and partners.

If you are in a large public or academic library or library system, securing commitment from the library director and other leaders in your organization will ensure that you will be allowed sufficient time to do grant work. This often means sharing your day-to-day responsibilities with others or temporarily reducing your daily tasks while you are working on a proposal. Other staff members will need to pitch in to cover for you when you cannot perform your routine duties. This takes advance planning and involvement of leadership. If you will be working with other departments in your organization or partners in your community, support from them as well as library leadership is required to pave the way. If you are a solo librarian in a corporation or a director in a small rural public library, getting commitment from your town administrators or corporate leadership is essential. Likewise, school librarians must find support in their principals, superintendents, or school library system leadership to do grant work. When individuals take on grant work alone without support from their organizations and peers, the chances of success are slim. If you are fortunate enough to win a grant, having buy-in from your peers, support from administration, and cooperation from organizational leaders from the beginning will make project implementation go much more smoothly.

Phase 4: Research

Grant research can be divided into three distinct steps:

1. Understanding the sources of grant funding (see Definition)
2. Understanding the resources for locating a grant (see Definition)
3. Doing the research

> **Definition**
> FUNDING SOURCE: The origin of the funding or grant; the funder or grantor. Funding sources fall into two main categories: government and private.
>
> **Definition**
> GRANT RESOURCE: A tool for locating and identifying grant opportunities; available in a variety of print and electronic formats.

Understanding the Sources

There are two major types of funding sources: government and private. The federal government is the largest source of grant funding in the United States, and each government department, bureau, or office has its own unique priority list and grant guidelines. There are hundreds of federal government grant programs managed by a wide variety of departmental bureaucracies.

Some federal funding is passed directly to states, counties, or local governments for their use or for redistribution through formula grants. In this case a local government will issue an RFP for services or products. State library agencies are one example of a state government source that offers grants to libraries using federal funds received as Library Services and Technology Act (LSTA) funding through the Institute of Museum and Library Services (IMLS).

Foundations, the mainstay of private funding, exist to support the specific ideals that inspired their creation. Corporations offer many opportunities in the form of partnerships, material resources, mentors, expertise, and funds to schools, communities, libraries, and other nonprofits. Corporations often limit grants to the geographic areas in which they operate. Local clubs and organizations and professional associations are additional possible private funding sources for library projects in their areas.

There are many sources for library technology grants, and you must take time to familiarize yourself with both government and private sources from the international to the local level. It is only when you understand the landscape of available sources that you will be able to effectively research the resources and discover the appropriate grant for your technology project.

Understanding the Resources

One resource to start looking for library grants is the *Library Grants Blog* (http://www.librarygrants.blogspot.com/), a free blog that regularly posts new grant opportunities for libraries available nationally. Reading this blog is a great way to get started looking for grants, get a sense for what kinds of grants are out there for libraries, and find out what funders are looking for. Each posting includes the deadline, a short description of the grant, and a link to the full announcement.

Grants.gov (http://www.grants.gov/) is the central storehouse for information on more than 1,000 federal government grant programs, providing access to $500 billion in annual awards. Here you can electronically find and apply for competitive grant opportunities from all 26 federal grant-making agencies.

The Foundation Center (http://foundationcenter.org/) is the largest producer of directories and databases of grant-giving foundations. The Center publishes print and electronic directories by subject, foundation name, geographic region, and grants previously funded. Their subject directories cover a wide range of topics, including libraries and information services and information technology. The Foundation Center's Cooperating Collections (http://foundationcenter.org/collections) are free funding information centers in libraries, community foundations, and other nonprofit resource centers all over the United States that provide a core collection of Foundation Center publications and other materials and services useful for grant seekers.

Corporate websites are good resources for searching grant opportunities offered by corporations and corporate foundations. Look for links on a corporation's main webpage to "community involvement" or "community giving." Many corporations devote entire sections of their websites to explaining what they fund in their communities and how to apply.

Community foundations often have extensive information about local businesses, corporations, and foundations that you may not find in any other single place. Local and regional grant directories; state, regional, and special library associations including divisions, special interest groups, chapters, and library foundations may provide additional resources.

Doing the Research

Librarians have an advantage when it comes to doing grant research, because they are trained to effectively use reference materials and electronic resources to find answers. Here are some specific tips to remember about doing grant research:

- Find keywords in your project plan's goals, objectives, outcomes, and activities.
- Translate your project into the language used by the resources.
- Work from the general to the specific.
- Record what you find.
- Keep your research organized.

Finding a grant to fund your technology project is not all about formulating the right search or using the right search terms. Although this is part of it, to find a funder that wants to fund a project like yours that suits your library and the people you serve, and whose values and purpose match your library's, will take not only online research but also research using print and electronic resources, visiting collections, making phone calls, and talking with funders.

Phase 5: Proposal Writing

It is only after you have completed the first four phases of grant work that are you ready to write the grant proposal. As you have already learned, designing the technology project and proposal writing are closely linked. When you design your technology project in Phase 2 you will actually be preparing some core proposal components, such as the project description (including goals, objectives, outcomes, and activities), approach or methodology, timeline, budget, and evaluation plan. In addition, during the planning stages in Phase 1 you will have already prepared other proposal components, such as the organizational profile and/or library profile, community profile, and need statement. This means that when you reach this phase you have already completed a great deal of work on the grant proposal.

Each proposal will be unique, written to a specific funder and customized to its priorities and designed to meet specific needs in your community. Proposal writing is not a matter of "plugging in" generic components that you have written in the earlier phases of grant work. There is still quite a bit of work to do; however, it is always a relief to know that when you are ready to start writing, you will begin with a solid framework that will provide the information you need to prepare a winning proposal.

The funder's grant guidelines will determine the length, content, and format of the grant proposal that you write—whether it is a letter proposal, form proposal, online proposal, or full proposal. A grant proposal is your chance to make a case for funding your technology project. By crafting the components in a logical way you can capture the readers' attention and lead them to the desired conclusion. Proposals change as you work on them. When you change or fine-tune one section, you will likely have to make changes in another section. If you think of a proposal as a living document it will help you to work with it holistically. No single component exists separately from another. They are all interconnected.

Rule #7
Always follow the application directions and funder's guidelines.

An important aspect of proposal writing is adhering to the guidelines and following directions (see Rule #7). Funders will reject proposals that do not conform to their instructions, including ignoring specified margins and line spacing.

Phase 6: Project Implementation

After you have successfully won a grant there are some preliminary steps to take prior to implementing the project. These include thanking the funder, appointing a project manager, informing the grant team and library administration about your success; getting buy-in and commitment from the organization; informing your community; reviewing the budget; contacting the funder; clarifying the terms of the grant; and reporting requirements.

After completing these preliminary steps, you will want to move forward quickly to implement the project. Technology projects often require budget revisions because prices have likely changed since you submitted the proposal. Baseline data for the project evaluation must be established right away to provide a measure for project success. Timelines must be updated and actual dates included for the purpose of marking progress.

Project implementation begins with naming the project; creating a home for the project; hiring personnel; creating the project team; issuing RFPs for technology; purchasing equipment, supplies, and materials; and staff training. Ongoing project activities include monitoring the project, maintaining flexibility and adaptability, and focusing on the vision.

Phase 7: Review

After hearing from the funder whether or not your project was funded, review the grant process with your team to determine what went well, where you can make improvements, and what you would do exactly the same way next time. There are always lessons to learn from going through the grant process. Don't let the opportunity to learn them pass you by. There is no better time to do this than right after hearing back about your success or rejection. If your proposal was not funded, find out why so you can apply this lesson to your next attempt.

Continuing the Process

Grant work does not stop here; it continues with planning (see Rule #8). Start over in Phase 1 by reviewing and updating your library's assessments and plans, and revisit project designs to make sure they meet current needs. Update your library profile, community profile, and organizational profile, and continue to collect new data about the people you serve. Stay up to date about new grant opportunities, and take advantage of continuing education classes, tutorials, workshops, and webinars about grants and proposal writing. Join fundraising groups, and network with your peers about their fundraising strategies. Seek new partnerships and collaborations, and actively look for new technology projects being implemented in your community.

> **Rule #8**
> Grant work is a continuous process. It does not stop when you hear from the funder about success or rejection.

Summary

Now that you can see the "big picture" of grant work and have a framework for understanding the phases of the grant process covered in this book, it is time to go ahead with an in-depth discussion of Phase 1: Planning. Planning is considered to be the most important part of grant work. You cannot be successful at writing technology grant proposals without planning first.

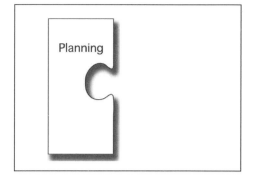

Chapter 2

Planning

This chapter explains the importance of planning, including the essentials of strategic planning and technology plans, how a technology plan aligns with the library's strategic plan, and what library plans have to do with grant work. It will provide pointers about the key elements in your library's plans and important considerations in creating a technology plan that will help you write successful technology grant proposals.

Why Planning Is Essential

"A plan is a strategy for a course of action to get from where you are now to where you want to be" (Bolan and Cullin, 2007: 62). Without a plan, you don't know where you are, where you are going, or how you are going to get there. Planning is necessary before designing a technology project or writing a grant proposal to fund a technology project, because plans provide you with the goals, objectives, outcomes, and activities for library projects that meet needs. Without first developing plans that address the needs of the people your library serves, there is no way to write a grant proposal for funding technology with a purpose. Funders want to know that their grants will contribute to a larger purpose than that of the project itself. By funding a proposal, they want to help a library get to where it needs to go. The strongest proposals illustrate that the project being proposed will help the library accomplish goals that are part of its plans.

A common mistake is to immediately start writing a proposal right after seeing a grant opportunity, without regard to the library's plans. When you approach proposal writing this way, you will find yourself trying to tailor a proposal to a match funder's priorities rather than writing one that proposes a project to meet people's information needs. This is not only a difficult way to write a proposal, but it is highly unlikely that your proposal will be successful. This backward and unnatural way of working will result in stress and frustration as you and your team spend an inordinate amount of time trying to craft a project the funder will find attractive. In the end, even if a proposal written this way is somehow funded, it is unlikely the project will actually meet community needs. In fact, chances are high that a proposal written to please a funder alone will not be a successful one. When you focus on meeting needs and accomplishing

13

the library's mission, your library plans will act as your compass, keeping you headed in the right direction throughout all phases of grant work.

Strategic Planning

Strategic plans provide a foundation for library work and grant work alike. Without a strategic plan you don't know why you are doing what you're doing, because you don't know the goals of the library or where it is headed. If you don't know where the library is headed, there is no way for you to know where you are headed. Working in a library without a strategic plan—or in a library with a "cookie cutter" strategic plan—is like being adrift. Library staff is very busy being busy, but they have no focus that relates to the real needs of the people they serve or the goals of the library. They are usually running around doing "busy work" without a clear direction or purpose. The day is never long enough to do regular job duties, never mind adding grant work to their responsibilities. If you work in a library like this you will probably say you have no time for grant work.

Writing a grant proposal for a library that has no plan means pulling a grant proposal out of thin air. You will have to "invent" things to fill in the vast blank areas, and you will be without some basic core proposal components right from the start. This is very hard work, it is very time-consuming, and in the end it can be fruitless. When you aren't working from a plan designed to meet community needs, funders can tell, and your proposal will not be taken seriously. More important, why would you want grant money to implement a project that isn't part of your plan, your mission and vision, and a way to help the people you serve?

There are many resources available for libraries and other organizations wanting to undertake strategic planning (see Additional Resources at the end of this chapter). If your library does not have a strategic plan, this is the time to create one. It will make running a library go more smoothly and working in a library much more enjoyable; it will give you a purpose, and the people in your community will benefit. Your library will be less chaotic, and there will be fewer misunderstandings or disagreements about what services and programs your library should provide. Coworkers will be on a similar wavelength, and they will be synchronized and calibrated toward meeting the same needs. Planning takes the guesswork out of providing library programs and services, and it reduces the chance that important decisions about what to provide are based on a library director's feelings or personal preferences. Planning objectifies what you do, it points you in the direction of improving your institution or community, it strengthens your ability to justify your work and the importance of the library, and it gives you confidence and empowers you to seek funding from alternative sources in a methodical and informed way.

Planning makes it easier to get buy-in from those who are unsure or technology-shy when the purpose is to serve people rather than to buy the latest technology. Objective thinking overtakes individual wants and desires as well as individual fears and trepidations. With plans, you will accomplish goals and make progress toward your vision. Plans will keep you on track, and they will help minimize distractions. Plans give everyone associated with the library the information they need to reach out to the people they serve and let them know what services and programs the library will be providing in the future. As a result, the library is more likely to attract not only grants but also other alternative funding, including gifts or donations that are appropriate for

Library Plans Checklist

The more information your library's plans provide about how the library intends to accomplish its goals by implementing projects or programs that utilize technology, the closer you will be to having a technology grant project. Use these plan checklists to help you determine elements of your library's plans that you can use to design a technology project.

Strategic Plan Checklist

_____ A community needs assessment that identifies the areas needing change or improvement or the problems to be solved in the community

_____ Goals, objectives, and activities—or solutions—to meet your community's information needs

_____ Target audiences or specific people who have specific needs

_____ Community input and the participation of stakeholders

_____ Relationships with potential partners

Technology Plan Checklist

_____ Goals and objectives that will be accomplished through the use of technology

_____ Activities for accomplishing the technology goals

_____ What technology exists to accomplish the project's goals and objectives

_____ What technology will have to be upgraded or purchased to implement the project

_____ Tentative budget for technology project costs

15

Writing Successful Technology Grant Proposals: A LITA Guide, by Pamela H. MacKellar.
© 2012 Library Information and Technology Association, a division of the American Library Association.

its goals. Potential partners or collaborators might be inspired to contribute matching or in-kind support to a grant project if they hear about an initiative you are planning that coincides with their own priorities. Libraries with plans are much more likely to find funding and support outside the library than libraries without them.

Strategic Plans Yield Proposal Components

The strategic planning process will save you time and energy when it comes to writing successful technology grant proposals. Strategic plans provide some necessary information for technology planning, designing technology projects, and writing technology grant proposals. The library's mission and vision, goals, objectives, outcomes, and activities from the strategic plan will provide the foundation for grant work and proposal writing. Strategic plans usually include a library profile and a community profile which can be customized for grant proposals. If you have already completed a strategic plan for your library, you know that a community needs assessment, performed before the planning process, informs the plan about the real needs among the people you serve. When the strategic plan is based on meeting needs, the service priorities or programs, services, and projects identified in the plan are also based on what the people you serve need in a library (see Rule #9). A community needs assessment will provide the information for another necessary component in most grant proposals, the need statement or statement of needs.

> **Rule #9**
> Your community's needs will guide you from the strategic planning phase all the way through the entire grant process.

When you understand how intertwined planning and proposal writing are, you will see that you are developing many core proposal components as you plan. You will actually be writing some components for future proposals as you execute library plans and design projects. By the time you are finished with library planning, technology planning, and project planning, your proposal components are mostly completed! Proposal writing can mean compiling these components into the format required by the funder, fine-tuning project details, and customizing the components for specific funders' requirements. With a strategic plan in place you will be better able to respond to funding opportunities whenever they arise, because you will already have much of the information you need for a grant proposal.

Before you are ready to write a technology grant proposal you will need to complete a few more steps by creating a technology plan and designing a technology project; however, the strategic plan will provide much of the information you need to do these steps.

Basics of Technology Planning

Technology planning is strategic planning for providing library services and programs that use technology. The technology planning process is an outgrowth of the library's strategic plan but focuses on how technology will help the library meet the information needs of its community in carrying out the mission of the library. Use the same process for technology planning that you used for strategic planning to streamline the process and for compatibility across plans. You must be able to work from both plans, and if they are developed similarly this will make it easier.

A technology plan aligns with the library's strategic plan, it runs parallel to the strategic plan, and it is integrated and coordinated with the library's strategic plan. It may be a component of the strategic plan or a separate but related document. A technology plan articulates clear goals, objectives, and activities for using technology to achieve the library's mission. Technology plans are not simply an inventory of current library technology and a list of what the library plans to update in the coming years.

Just as there are many ways to create a strategic plan, there are also many ways to create a technology plan. First, ground yourself in the library's mission and vision. If your library is part of a larger organization such as a university, school district, hospital, or corporation that already has a technology plan, review the technology-related roles of the library within the institution as well as the institution's technology plan. Incorporate institutional roles and plans into your library's technology plan. The library's technology plan must run parallel not only to the library's strategic plan but also to the institution's plans. An institutional library that plans independently, without regard to the institution's plans, will inevitably run into difficulties when implementing plans and seeking support from the larger institution or when its cooperation is required. This principle is also true if you are in a small public library or special library. When you are planning, always refer to the plans of your municipality, corporation, or larger organization to ensure that the library plans are compatible with the plans of your organization.

Depending on criteria such as the size and type of your library, whether your library is part of a larger organization, and your strategic planning process, decide on a technology planning process that is right for your library. One process may work better for you than another. Some approaches include the following:

- Develop the technology plan by committee.
- Develop the technology plan according to predetermined organizational criteria.
- Include outside stakeholders in technology planning.
- Technology plan is a regional collaboration with other libraries and/or institutions.

Planning is not a linear process, and it involves making purposeful and sensible choices from a wide array of needs and solutions. Involving library staff is crucial to developing a unified technology plan that is accepted and promoted by everyone working in the library. The planning process is ongoing as you receive feedback, make adjustments, and prepare for the future. There is no one single technology plan template that will work for all libraries. Beware of "cookie cutter" technology plans, created by inserting your library's name into a template. They won't work. The people who comprise every college or university, school, community, or organization are unique, and their information needs are unique; therefore, their libraries are unique, and the solutions to meeting their information needs vary from library to library. Your technology plan must be custom tailored for your situation.

In the past, when technology was new and librarians were busy figuring out what to do with it, it was not uncommon for librarians to purchase technology and put it into action without a plan. Librarians simply knew they needed computers in libraries, so they acquired them. Under the circumstances, this was often the best they could do. As time passed librarians knew they needed to upgrade the computers when they were obsolete, so they upgraded them. At that time technology plans were no more than charts showing what technology the library owned and what librarians wanted to acquire or upgrade in the future.

Today we know this is no way for libraries to plan how to excel at employing technology to meet the information needs in their communities. Technology is not an end in itself but a means to an end. Technology must be viewed as a vehicle to offer more efficient and effective delivery of current services and to add new services to help carry out the mission of the library. Librarians are no longer "making due" with technology or "doing their best" in an unfamiliar environment. Today librarians are technology leaders in their communities, colleges and universities, schools, corporations, and businesses. To maintain this position they must be informed about technology, know how to identify the appropriate technology for their libraries, and be confident that it is making a difference for the people they serve. Ask yourself what needs you are meeting by providing technology in the library.

Key Considerations for Technology Planning

Here are some things to keep in mind while you are developing a library technology plan:

- Get support from library staff and management before starting the technology planning process.
- Get input from key stakeholders, and seek their active participation. Include students and faculty; employees; leadership; government officials; school administration; business leaders; library trustees; members of the library's friends group; and other community members.
- Involve the IT department in your library or larger organization.
- If you are part of a larger organization such as a college or corporation, you must consider the technology plan of that organization.
- Find out the current information needs of the people you serve. Revisit the community needs assessment and update it if necessary. Think about how technology could help to meet identified needs.
- Determine the expected outcomes. How will the people in your community benefit from programs and services utilizing technology by gaining skills or knowledge, changing their behaviors or attitudes, or attaining an improved quality of life?
- Identify the technology you need to implement your plan. Engage staff in learning about new services and emerging technologies before you plan or as you plan.
- Assess existing hardware, software, facilities, and networks, and identify those that need to be acquired or updated to support the plan. Determine the levels of connectivity needed to support the planned services. Plan and configure new technologies for easy upgrading.
- Identify how library staff will acquire the knowledge and skills needed to use, maintain, and continuously upgrade technology, networks, and systems. The benefits of technology and its proper and effective use will be fully realized only when initial and continued training and staff development is provided.

- Identify who will do the work. Will the library contract for services or hire new staff, or will library staff be expected to learn how to use the technology? Beware of adding new job duties on top of what staff is already doing without taking away other job duties. More work requires paying staff for additional hours worked or hiring new staff or consultants. When you assign more work without extra compensation or taking away other job duties, library staff will be "turned off" to using technology.

- Develop a timeline for the technology plan. Implementing new technologies and electronic services requires careful planning and accurate, sequenced timelines. A timeline will ensure smooth transitions through each phase of implementation. Prioritize goals and objectives, and reflect their importance by their placement on the timeline.

- Evaluate progress toward the goals and objectives in your technology plan. Measuring the degree to which the people you serve are benefiting from technology projects will help you to know when you are successful and how to adjust or modify your plan if necessary.

- Create a budget for your technology plan. A technology plan must address the funds required to implement the plan. A technology plan without a budget ensures that there will not be enough money to implement it. How can you allocate funds or acquire additional funding when you don't know how much you need? Determine costs for equipment, networks, telecommunications services, staffing, training, product subscriptions, service contracts, and consulting, for example. Take into consideration that funds must be budgeted annually to maintain existing technology, to update or replace obsolete technology, to maintain contracts, and to provide necessary staff support.

- Share the library's technology plan with staff, board members, municipal officials, the college or university, business, corporation, school, administrators, business leaders, students and staff, other key stakeholders, and the community at large.

- Keep your plan current. Monitor emerging technologies, and update the plan accordingly.

Common Technology Plan Elements

As you are proceeding through the technology planning process, you will develop some of the key plan elements described briefly in this section. Depending on the planning method you use, you may have some different elements. How these topics are addressed in your plan and their actual content is up to you. These elements can be mixed, combined, or reordered to meet local needs and the circumstances of your library. Librarians who are developing technology plans for the purposes of E-Rate or other specific purposes must adhere to the guidelines of the appropriate agency. Libraries within large institutions may be required to follow a specified format.

Introduction/Overview

This section of the technology plan provides general information about the library and its programs and services that utilize technology. It includes an explanation of how the technology plan was developed, who was involved in the process, and what process will be used to review and update the plan as needed.

19

Mission and Vision

This section covers the library's vision in terms of the role technology will play in its realization. The vision should reflect your understanding that technology is not an end in itself, but a means to an end. Describe how technology contributes to carrying out the library's mission, accomplishing its goals, and delivering programs and services. Address how the library plans to use technology to help accomplish its vision, mission, and goals in the future.

Executive Summary

This section is a synopsis of the main points of the technology plan. It briefly summarizes the overall plan, highlighting major goals or initiatives that are included in the plan. The executive summary explains any projects that have been designed as part of the plan, including a general description of the scope of work, staff resources, timeline, budget, and evaluation plan. In this section the library's technology goals are prioritized along with corresponding planned technology projects or activities. Estimated overall costs for planned technology projects and initiatives are included here.

Background/History

The history or background section provides an overview of how long technology has been used in the library and the current state of the library's technology. This can be written from a chronological perspective, by service areas, or using a combination of these. This section describes any cooperative efforts involving technology with other libraries, schools, consortia, governmental departments, or local colleges and universities.

This section covers the current technology environment in terms of what specific library areas or functions use technology and how technology is integrated into daily library operations. The current state of technology in the library is outlined, including specific software/hardware, LANs/WANs and wireless networks, integrated library systems, Internet, electronic databases, e-books, and other technologies currently being used in the library. The current technology environment for library staff is also addressed here, answering the following questions:

- What are the strengths and weaknesses of the library's current technology environment?
- What problems or issues does technology help to solve?
- What problems or issues does it cause?
- What is the level of staff expertise and staff use of the technologies?
- What information resources do the patrons use via technology?
- What information resources that use technology are accessible to people with disabilities?
- How much of the library's budget is allocated to technology?

Goals, Objectives, Outcomes, and Activities

This section lists the goals for the library that will be accomplished through the use of technology and places them in priority order. Under each goal are listed the corresponding objectives or the specific implementation markers that are needed to accomplish the goals. Under each objective, list the activities that are required to accomplish the corresponding objective. Assign staff to the activities, and estimate how long each step will take a staff member to accomplish. Include the resources required for the activities, for example, staff time, training, infrastructure, hardware and software, or computer furniture. Often, outcomes are listed in the technology plan to indicate how the technology is meant to make a difference for people. Outcomes indicate a change in behavior or attitude, increased knowledge, acquired skills or abilities, or an improved quality of life for the people served.

This is the most specific part of the technology plan, and it provides the framework for the technology projects you will be developing for your grant proposals. You may also want to include in this section:

- Strengths and weaknesses concerning technology plan implementation
- Impact of technology plan on staffing, including any need for increased staff and staff training or redefining position descriptions
- What technology exists to accomplish the goals/objectives and what will have to be upgraded or purchased
- A regular review schedule for upgrades and replacement of any technology
- Any need to make building modifications including an upgrade of the electrical service

Timeline

The timeline lists all the activities required to accomplish the goals and objectives defined in the plan, showing their duration and who will do each one. For a technology plan timeline, break activities down by goal or project in priority order for easier reading. Duration usually appears in generic units such as "Month 1" rather than specific dates for planning purposes only.

Budget

All costs associated with accomplishing the goals and objectives in the technology plan are estimated as accurately as possible and presented in the budget. Remember, this is a technology plan. The budget is tentative and subject to change. Update your plan's budget as prices fluctuate.

Evaluation Plan

An evaluation plan ensures that the goals and objectives stated in the technology plan are actually implemented and progress toward accomplishing the goals and objectives is measured. Evaluation plans are developed to specifically measure the success of technology projects included in the plan. Evaluations require collecting and analyzing statistics, conducting surveys or questionnaires, or holding focus groups and interviews to measure the difference a project or technology initiative has made for community members.

Appendix

Attach any documents related to or supporting the technology plan in the appendix. For example, this may include your library's strategic plan; technology inventory;

documentation about hardware, software, or other technology appearing in the budget; training opportunities to support the plan; or cooperative agreements.

Updating the Technology Plan

Because technology changes so quickly, technology planning can be challenging. A typical three-year plan is useless in three years' time without constant updating. In smaller libraries, this is usually the job of the library director, whereas in larger libraries this may be the responsibility of a technology librarian or the library's IT department. Regardless of the library's size, librarians must make a real effort to build planning into their jobs and keep their plans up-to-date. Especially when it comes to technology, once you have fallen behind, it is very difficult to catch up. When your plan is so outdated it is irrelevant, you have lost your way. Keep your work and your library relevant by regularly updating your plans.

To update a technology plan you must stay current with both the needs of the people you serve and emerging technologies. Here are some ways to stay informed:

- Read the latest articles on library technology in periodicals such as *Library Technology Reports*, *Computers in Libraries*, *CRM Magazine*, *Database Trends and Applications*, *E-Content*, *Information Today*, *KM World*, *Internet@Schools*, *ONLINE Magazine*, *Searcher*, *Code4Lib Journal*, *Library Hi Tech News*, *D-Lib Magazine*, *Smart Libraries Newsletter*, and *Journal of Library Innovation*.
- Read nonlibrarian technology resources such as *Wired Magazine*, *First Monday*, *PC World*, *MacWorld*, and *Slashdot*.
- Attend conferences such as Computers in Libraries, Internet Librarian, Internet@Schools East and West, and the NTN Nonprofit Technology Conference. Watch for local technology conferences such as the Upstate Technology Conference (UTC) in South Carolina, iCon in Oklahoma, and the Library Technology Conference at Macalister College in Minnesota. Large national conferences such as ALA, SLA, and PLA always have multiple sessions and preconferences on library technology.
- Attend webinars on new library technologies through TechSoup (http://www.techsoup.org/) and WebJunction (http://www.webjunction.org/), for example, and watch videos on LITA's Library InfoTech's YouTube Channel (http://www.youtube.com/user/LibraryInfoTech).
- Subscribe to technology-related listservs and blogs geared toward librarians, such as the *LITA Blog* (http://litablog.org/), Library Technology Guides (http://www.librarytechnology.org/), What I Learned Today (http://www.web2learning.net/), and David Lee King's blog (http://www.davidleeking.com/).
- Communicate openly and frequently with your library's technology librarian and your library or organization's IT staff, and network with other librarians about new technologies for libraries.
- Make a habit of gathering information about new technologies and thinking critically about how they can be used to meet the information needs of the people you serve.
- Constantly seek out information about changes in your community and the information needs of the people you serve.

Key Questions for Technology Planning

As you are developing your library's technology plan, ask these key questions:

1. Which information needs can be addressed using technology?
2. How will you use technology to address these needs now and in the future?
3. What are the hardware specifications, software, locations, capabilities, peripherals, and so forth, necessary to meet the specific identified needs?
4. What is the cost?
5. Who will do the work?
6. Are you effectively using technology to maximize your delivery of services?
7. How can you improve your use of technology to improve services?
8. How are people in your community benefiting from the use of library technology?
9. What is your library's digital role within the larger institution or in your community?
10. How does your library's technology plan correlate with or support the technology plans of your larger institution, school district, university, or municipality?

Summary

With a strategic plan and a technology plan in place you will be better able to respond to funding opportunities when they arise because you will already have the basic information you need to write a grant proposal. The next chapter covers the project design process, which will yield a project description, approach or methodology, timeline, budget, and evaluation plan for each technology project. These will serve as the proposal components for grants to fund each project. Each planning step builds on the previous one. When you start at the beginning by planning strategically, proposal writing not only becomes easier but it makes more sense.

Additional Resources

Abram, Stephen. 2000. "Planning for the Next Wave of Convergence." *Computers in Libraries* 20, no. 4 (April): 46–53.

Bennett, Harvey, and Nancy Everhart. 2003. "Successful K–12 Technology Planning: Ten Essential Elements." *Teacher Librarian* 31, no. 1 (October): 22–26.

Bocher, Bob. 2008. "Library Technology Planning: An Outline of the Process." Madison: Wisconsin Department of Public Instruction, Division for Libraries and Community Learning. http://www.dpi.state.wi.us/pld/planout.html.

Bolan, Kimberly, and Robert Cullin. 2007. *Technology Made Simple: An Improvement Guide for Small and Medium Libraries*. Chicago: American Library Association.

Dugan, Robert E. 2002. "Information Technology Plans." *Journal of Academic Librarianship* 28, no. 3 (May): 152–156.

Farkas, Meredith. 2007. "The Evolving Library: Ten Timeless Tips." *American Libraries* 38, no. 6 (June): 50.

Mayo, Diane. 2005. *Technology for Results: Developing Service-Based Plans*. Chicago: American Library Association.

Morgan, Kendra, Greg Weisiger, and Donna Mattingly. 2010. "Technology Planning for Libraries Webinar." WebJunction. Presented October 12. http://www.webjunction.org/techplan/-/articles/content/106933649.

Nelson, Sandra. 2010. "The Planning Puzzle: Integrating Your Strategic and Technology Plans." WebJunction Technology Essentials 2010 Conference. Presented February 9. http://www.webjunction.org/techplan/-/articles/content/90952571.

Pace, Andrew K. 2000. "Information Technology: A Simple Plan." *Computers in Libraries* 20, no. 4 (April): 64–66.

Stephens, Michael. 2004. "Technoplans vs. Technolust: A Well-Thought-Out Technology Plan Can Help Libraries Stay on Course." *Library Journal* 129, no. 18 (November 1): 36+. http://www.libraryjournal.com/article/CA474999.html.

TechAtlas. 2011. Accessed July 5. http://www.techatlas.org/.

TechSoup for Libraries. 2011. "The Technology Planning Process." TechSoup for Libraries. Accessed July 5. http://www.techsoupforlibraries.org/Cookbooks/Planning%20for%20 Success/Planning%20and%20Decision%20Making/further-resources.

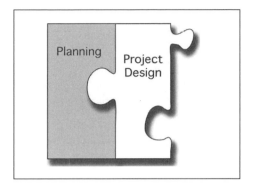

Chapter 3

Designing Library Technology Projects and Programs

The project design process involves working on a team to create viable library projects from your library's strategic plan or technology plan. The plan supplies the goals, objectives, activities, and outcomes for potential library programs or projects that utilize technology. Project design often takes place as part of strategic planning; and technology projects are sometimes defined and even developed during the technology planning process. If your library's plans provide you with technology project ideas, you are ready to develop the project design. If your library's planning process did not go so far as to identify library technology projects or programs, a team can be formed to do this after the plans are in place (see Step 1 in the later section Technology Project Design Process).

Projects and Programs

A project is a planned activity that has a defined beginning, middle, and end. If a project is ongoing it is often called a "program." When projects become programs, a different level of planning is required based on the strategic direction of the organization.

Technology Projects

Many library projects and programs today involve technology. For the purposes of this book, library projects and programs that utilize technology are called "technology projects" or "technology programs." Remember that the reason for all library projects and programs—including technology projects and programs—is to meet specific information needs in your community. Even though this book refers to "technology grants" and "technology projects," the reason for library technology projects and library technology programs is never for the purpose of technology alone. If, as you design a technology project, the purpose becomes to purchase or acquire and/or use technology for the library, stop where you are and rethink the project's focus. Step back, and redirect the project for the purpose of meeting an information need

25

among the people your library serves. If it does not make sense to use technology to meet a need, you will not end up with a technology project. This is fine. Don't allow technology to drive your project design just for the sake of acquiring technology or implementing the latest technology in the library (see Rule #10).

> **Rule #10**
> If a library project does not meet a community need, you should not be doing it.

Grant Projects

A grant project is a project of any kind for which you will be writing a proposal to seek grant funding from an outside source. A grant project can be an equipment project, a capital project, a planning or implementation project, a research project, a model demonstration project, or a project for operating expenses, to name a few. A technology project becomes a grant project when you decide to seek a grant to fund it. In this book this kind of project is referred to as a "technology grant project."

Designing Projects

Designing projects and proposal writing are closely linked. As you define your project you will be designing (and sometimes even writing) your grant proposal. By planning your project before actually writing your proposal, you are ensuring that your project comes from your desire to meet real needs. Project planning based on your library's strategic plan or technology plan not only orients you within the existing plans and mission of your organization, it will keep you focused on working to better serve your community and its specific needs. Remember Rule #2: Grants are about people, not about money or things.

If you have a strategic plan, you have by definition already completed the following preliminary steps in designing your grant project:

- Conducted a community needs assessment that identifies the areas needing change or improvement or the problems to be solved in the community
- Identified the solutions—or goals, objectives, and activities—to meet your community's needs
- Incorporated community input and the participation of stakeholders
- Developed relationships with potential partners

If you have a technology plan, you already have the following information to help you with a technology project design:

- Goals and objectives that will be accomplished through the use of technology
- Activities for accomplishing the goals
- What technology exists to accomplish the project's goals and objectives
- What technology will have to be upgraded or purchased to implement the project
- Tentative budget for the technology project

The more information your plans provide about how the library intends to accomplish its goals by implementing projects or programs that utilize technology, the closer you will be to having a technology grant project. Only after you have a technology project designed can you identify a grant to fund it.

Technology Project Design Process

When you are designing library technology projects it is important to include each of the following steps.

Step 1: Clarify the Library's Technology Goals, Objectives, and Activities

Place your library's goals, objectives, and activities from the library's technology plan into a chart (see the Technology Plan Chart Template, pp. 28–29, and a completed Library Technology Goals, Objectives, and Activities Chart Example, p. 30). This will help you see them clearly and make it easier to work with them. When you are designing projects with a team, this chart is a good tool for orienting team members and serves as a starting point for discussion. By definition, the goals, objectives, and activities in the library's technology plan relate to the utilization of technology in the library. If your library does not have a technology plan, it is essential to have one before launching into designing technology projects (see Chapter 2). The technology plan will supply you with the information you need, and it will keep you on track as you design projects. Without it you are not likely to design a technology project that addresses the needs among the people your library serves.

Step 2: Form a Technology Project Planning Team

Convene a technology project planning team of creative thinkers to develop specific technology projects using the goals, objectives, and activities in your library's technology plan. It is essential to include library technology staff as well as information technology staff from your university or municipality as well as technology experts from the community. Some members of the library's technology planning team should be included to ensure continuity and to answer questions that may arise about specific elements of the plan. There may be issues or concerns that have been discussed or resolved previously by this team, and there is no sense in reinventing the wheel. There must be someone on the team who is knowledgeable about new and emerging technologies—preferably library technology.

Consider asking library staff at all levels to join the team, including someone who is hesitant about using technology in the library. They might help you to honor this perspective and force you to consider the reasons "why not." This is potentially an opportunity to gain their support and buy-in for the technology projects your team designs. This does not mean you need to include obstructive or uncooperative team members. All team members must understand the purpose of the team and agree to contribute by helping to design library projects that utilize technology.

Others you might include are people from potential partner organizations or institutional departments who you think may be implementing a technology project in which the library could be a partner or someone from a nonprofit community agency that is currently implementing a technology project. If there is a technology business in your area, think about inviting a leader from this business to join your team. He or she could bring new and innovative ideas or have knowledge about new technologies that will help in the design phase. Your grant partners and collaborators will likely emerge during this process, and it is best if they are involved from the beginning. This is a

Technology Plan Chart Template

Use this worksheet to outline your library's technology plan. It can be helpful as you design library technology projects, and it can serve as a starting point for technology project design team discussions.

Goals from Technology Plan	Objectives from Technology Plan	Activities from Technology Plan
Goal 1	Objectives for Goal 1	Activities for Goal 1
Goal 2	Objectives for Goal 2	Activities for Goal 2

(Continued)

Technology Plan Chart Template *(Continued)*

Use this worksheet to outline your library's technology plan. It can be helpful as you design library technology projects, and it can serve as a starting point for technology project design team discussions.

Goals from Technology Plan	Objectives from Technology Plan	Activities from Technology Plan
Goal 3	Objectives for Goal 3	Activities for Goal 3
Goal 4	Objectives for Goal 4	Activities for Goal 4

Writing Successful Technology Grant Proposals: A LITA Guide, by Pamela H. MacKellar.
© 2012 Library Information and Technology Association, a division of the American Library Association.

Library Technology Goals, Objectives, and Activities Chart Example

Library's Technology Goals	Library's Technology Objectives	Library's Technology Activities
1. To promote digital literacy	• Of the community, 75 percent will think of the library as a place to learn about technology by 2013 • Five new classes on using technology will be offered to the community by 2012 • Of library staff providing pubic services, 100 percent will complete a tutorial on new technologies by July 2012	• Create a computer training lab • Offer classes for the public on using technology • Provide training for library staff on using new technology, how to educate others about how to use technology, and using technology to better serve the community • Outreach to population that underutilizes library
2. To provide access to electronic resources for those who otherwise would not have access	• Of all community members, 75 percent will say the library is their "go to" place for using current technology • Approximately 25 percent more people with disabilities will use library technology	• Purchase assistive technology for computers • Update website to include local information resources
3. To create an environment that makes technology available as a tool that can be used to access information	• Approximately 80 percent of people using library technology will say technology is readily available in the library	• Place computer kiosks in all areas of library • Create a learning commons • Create a portal where all electronic products are located in one place
4. To serve as a current and up-to-date technology resource	• Approximately 80 percent of community will say the library is a current source for using technology to access information	• Purchase new public and staff computers • Install current software on public and staff computers • Purchase iPads that will be available for checkout • Increase e-book selection • Institute mobile reference service

good opportunity to invite new people to participate in library planning, build and strengthen relationships, and gain support from the community at large. Students, faculty and staff, government officials, employees and supervisors, board members, volunteers, community members, and other stakeholders are all potential team members. Be creative when forming the team. A team that is restricted to "insiders" such as all board members, all library staff, or all IT staff is likely to result in a restrictive project design that does not stray far from what they have done in the past. New ways of thinking and new group dynamics are likely to yield some interesting and creative technology project ideas.

If you are in a large library, you may want to create more than one technology project planning team to address different technology project ideas or different aspects of using technology in the library. For instance, a technology project that involves providing mobile reference services must include reference staff, whereas a project that focuses on evaluating and updating wireless networks must include IT staff. If you are in a small library, a team of two people may be sufficient. Regardless of the team's size or make up, all team members must understand the purpose of the team and commit to fully participating by helping to design a library technology project that will meet the needs of people the library serves.

Step 3: Start the Project Planning Process

Someone must be responsible for leading the team through the process of designing the library's technology projects. It could be a member of the library staff who was instrumental in the technology planning process, or, if you have the funds, you could hire an outside consultant to facilitate. Project planning is easier, more efficient, and more effective when an objective person is responsible for keeping things on track. It is very difficult to facilitate and participate at the same time; however, if you do not have enough staff or money for a separate facilitator,

> **Rule #11**
> To be successful at grant work it is necessary to share the responsibilities with others.

this can be done. If you are a one- or two-person library, you can share facilitating responsibilities. Just make sure everyone has a chance to participate (see Rule #11).

The team's first task is to understand the library's vision, mission, and service responses to the community, as well as the goals, objectives, and activities outlined in the plan. Team members must be fully informed about the library's technology plan and any project ideas suggested or identified in the plan. It may be necessary to share some background information about the community needs assessment and how the goals, objectives, and activities were determined with those team members who were not involved in the planning process. Copies of the strategic plan and technology plan must be made available to all team members, and questions or concerns about the plans need to be addressed promptly. Make it clear to the team that their purpose is to plan one or more technology projects from the goals, objectives, and activities in the technology plan—keeping in mind the library's vision and mission as it relates to technology.

Step 4: Discover the Project Idea and Goals

Make this a fun activity for the whole team. Have flipcharts, colored index cards, markers, scissors, favors or prizes for the best ideas, or group activities, for example.

Move around. Brainstorm. Try dividing the larger group into smaller groups of three or four. Each group might have a goal, and groups are given permission to draw from any objective or activity in the technology plan to accomplish the goal. Tell team members that they can expand or alter the objectives and create new activities for the purposes of this process, as long as they address the goals and objectives stated in the technology plan. It is very important to convey this message to team members: Don't focus on technology. Focus on designing projects that meet needs utilizing technology (see the Technology Project Planning Worksheet, pp. 33–34).

It is helpful to create some ground rules for the group that encourage brainstorming and creative thinking. There are three main goals to the brainstorming process: (1) to generate new ideas, (2) to build on existing ideas, and (3) to capture all thoughts generated in the brainstorming activity. Everyone must understand that criticizing others' ideas and obstructionist thinking is not allowed during brainstorming. If a team member responds to an idea by saying the library doesn't have the money, equipment, staff, or time, they must be reminded by the facilitator about the brainstorming ground rules. A brainstorming meeting about technology projects can abruptly come to a screeching halt when negative thinkers are allowed to run amok (see sidebar).

Explain to the team that funding the projects is not their concern. You can explain that any projects they design that require supplemental funding may become grant projects; however, do not confuse the team about their role. They are responsible for designing projects only, not for finding money or writing grant proposals to fund them. This will keep quiet the person who inevitably says, "But we don't have the money" when each new idea is expressed. This team can have the fun! Finding the grants comes later.

10 Rules for Effective Brainstorming

1. Do not judge.
2. Everyone participates.
3. Strive for a high energy level.
4. Be spontaneous and quick.
5. Quantity is more important than quality.
6. Encourage wild ideas.
7. Build on others' ideas.
8. Discourage discussion except to build on an idea.
9. Capture and record all ideas.
10. Organize, filter, and discuss after brainstorming.

Step 5: Define Project Outcomes

As the team begins to discover project ideas, it is important for the members to think about outcomes. Outcomes are used to identify a change in behavior, attitude, skill, life condition, or knowledge of the people being served by the project, and they reflect the long-term impact a project is making toward solving a community problem or toward improving the lives of the people it serves. From the preliminary project planning stages and throughout the planning process, continue to ask these questions:

- How will the technology project help to solve a problem or meet a need among the people the library serves?
- How will the technology project improve the lives of the people being served?
- How will people's behavior, attitudes, skills, life condition, or knowledge change as a result of the technology project?

This will help the team focus on why a particular technology project is needed in your community, school, university, corporation, or agency and keep you grounded in the difference the grant project will make for people. When a project idea is more about

Technology Project Planning Worksheet

1. List some potential project ideas using your Technology Plan Chart as a resource.

2. Choose one idea, and write a short description of the project.

3. What are the goals of the project?

4. Identify the target audience for the project.

5. Describe the need in your community or the problem your project will address.

6. What are the specific changes in behavior, attitude, skills, life condition, or knowledge you expect to make in your community or among the beneficiaries of your project?

7. What are the objectives of the project?

8. What other projects are there like yours? What research have you done to make sure you build on the experiences of others?

(Continued)

Technology Project Planning Worksheet *(Continued)*

9. List the steps required to reach the objectives identified. Develop activities or strategies required to reach each objective.

10. List the resources you will need to accomplish the steps. What resources do you already have?

11. What is the timeframe for your project? How long will it take to accomplish the activities you have identified?

12. What is the total cost of your project?

13. Describe how you will measure your success.

14. List the keywords that describe your project.

15. Who are the potential partners in your community on a project like this?

Writing Successful Technology Grant Proposals: A LITA Guide, by Pamela H. MacKellar.
© 2012 Library Information and Technology Association, a division of the American Library Association.

the technology than meeting a community need, coming back to the outcomes and asking these questions helps to refocus the group.

Each project may have one or several outcomes. These are some examples of possible outcomes for different library technology projects:

1. As a result of the We Can! Project, unemployed community members will be able to find jobs on the Internet and fill out online employment applications.
2. The Seamy High School Virtual Learning Commons will enhance student learning by providing one central location for electronic resources that support the curriculum.
3. The Smallville History Digitization Project will increase the appreciation for and knowledge about our town's past.
4. The Wimbledon University Network Update Project will improve the attitude of students, faculty, and staff about accessing information using library technology.
5. The Ability Project will improve the lives of people with disabilities by enhancing access to information using assistive technology.

Step 6: Develop Project Objectives

The team must design SMART objectives that specifically address technology project outcomes (see sidebar). You may find that you can use objectives straight from the library's technology plan; however, it is more likely that the objectives for the team's technology project ideas will be a subset or adaptation of the objectives in your library's technology plan.

Ask how you will demonstrate that your project was a success. It might help to think of objectives as what is left when the project is over. Do not skip this important step. Eventually the grant team will use these objectives to design an evaluation plan for the grant proposal. Below are some sample objectives for technology projects:

SMART Objectives Are:
• Specific
• Measurable
• Achievable
• Realistic
• Time-bound

1. By the end of the project, 50 percent of participants in the We Can! Project will identify and apply for jobs using technology.
2. In June 2012, 75 percent of Seamy High School students will say that the Virtual Learning Commons enhanced their educational experience.
3. Of Smallville residents, 60 percent will say that they learned about our town's history from the Digitization Project in 2013.
4. By the end of the project, 50 percent of Wimbledon University staff will indicate that increased network speed and ease of use resulting from the Network Update Project has enhanced their ability to do their jobs.
5. In one year 65 percent more people with disabilities will use library technology to access information that has the potential to improve their lives.

Step 7: Do the Research

As the team develops technology project ideas, it is important to research other similar projects. If you are designing a model project, you will want to make sure you are not duplicating work that has already been done. Contact managers of other projects like the one you are considering, and ask them about their experiences and what they have

35

learned. Incorporate this knowledge into your project design. It makes good sense to build past experiences and research into your project design. This makes for a more viable, successful, and sustainable project design.

Investigate other technology projects that are already being implemented or are under consideration in your institution, university, municipality, school system, or state. This often means making phone calls and introducing yourself to new people. This is essential (see Rule #12). In these economic times, funders want to know that you are not duplicating another similar project. While you are doing this you may discover a partner or collaborator who is interested in participating or contributing to your project.

Rule #12
It doesn't make sense to duplicate efforts—especially when it comes to technology projects.

Research the latest technology and trends concerning the specific technology you plan to use in your project. Technology changes rapidly, and it is essential for your technology project to incorporate leading-edge ideas and information. Keep up this technology research throughout the project design and proposal writing process.

Step 8: Define Project Activities

The next step is to develop the activities that are going to accomplish the project's goals and objectives and produce the desired outcomes. These activities can be taken directly from the activities in your library's technology plan or adapted from them. You can create new activities to accomplish a project design, but make sure that they relate back to the goals and objectives in the technology plan. This step can be challenging, because the team is striving to be creative and innovative, allowing you to incorporate new activities suited to the project design, yet at the same time adhering to the spirit of the technology plan. Make sure to include all aspects of a project as you determine the activities that will be required. It is easy to forget about the administrative, outreach, or marketing aspects of a project when you are focused on technology and making a difference in people's lives. Include every activity associated with a project even if it is not mentioned in the technology plan.

Think about which personnel will do the activities. If it is determined that grant funding is required to implement the project, the activities and who will do them becomes the methodology, strategy, or approach in the proposal. This information will also provide the basis for the timeline, budget, and evaluation plan. As you can begin to see, each element of the project plan builds on the previous one, and most steps will eventually lead to a grant proposal component.

Step 9: Make a Project Timeline

Timelines are project-planning tools that are used to represent the timing of tasks required to complete a project. They are easy to understand and construct, and most project managers use them to track the progress of a project. There are many ways to construct timelines. Simple timelines list each activity in one column of a simple table with dates heading each column in the top row. The expected time for each task is represented by check marks or shaded bars marking the expected beginning and end of the task. A timeline is most useful when it also shows who is responsible for doing each activity.

Step 10: Develop a Project Budget

Project budgets are usually composed of a personnel budget and a non-personnel budget. Personnel budgets show the personnel required to complete the project and the FTE (full-time equivalent or the percentage of a full-time position required for that position to accomplish the project activities), salary, and benefits for each position. From Step 8, select one position and determine the activities the person in that position will perform. Then determine the amount of time required to complete these activities over the life of the project, and calculate the cost of the salary to cover that amount of time. Calculate the cost of benefits for each position, and show this amount in a separate column. Consultant costs are included in the personnel budget; they are usually calculated by number of hours required times the hourly charge. Consultants usually don't receive benefits; however, if the consultant charges tax it must be included in the personnel budget. Then total the personnel costs for the personnel budget. You will add that amount to the non-personnel budget for the project budget.

Non-personnel budgets include the cost for items other than personnel, such as hardware, software, equipment, electronic product costs, space rental, marketing, and supplies. Itemize these costs, because this will make it easier when you will inevitably need to adjust the budget later. If the non-personnel budget is one large number, then there is no way you will be able to adjust a specific hardware cost, for instance, when the cost has fluctuated in the future. Especially when it comes to technology, the costs can be a moving target. Obtain several estimates for items with higher costs to ensure you are in the right ballpark. Do not look for sales or cut-rate deals. Estimate the actual current cost of the technology your project requires. You can expect some changes by the time your project is funded; however, if you have broken down the non-personnel budget by line items, you can easily make cost adjustments. Add all costs in the non-personnel budget, and then create a project budget by combining the personnel budget and the non-personnel budget together, adding the total costs of each to determine the total project cost.

Step 11: Create an Evaluation Plan

Evaluations are conducted to show the success of a project's impact, and they can also point out improvements you can make in the project design during implementation. In general there are these basic kinds of evaluations: formative, summative, quantitative, and qualitative. Formative evaluations are conducted throughout the life of a project. This enables project staff to measure the success of the project while it is being carried out and make needed adjustments as the project is in progress. One evaluation at the very end of a project that reports all accomplishments and stresses the outcome of the project is a summative evaluation. A quantitative evaluation measures how much was accomplished, such as how many people attended a class, what skills did students learn, or what was the cost to the project per student? Quantitative evaluations require obtaining and analyzing data via pretests and posttests, questionnaires, and surveys, for example. Qualitative evaluations tell the project's story by communicating participants' experiences using interviews, case studies, observation, and documentation reviews. Decide on an evaluation approach that serves the needs of your customers and that will best measure the success of your particular project. You may use more than one kind of evaluation in a single evaluation plan.

Outcome-based evaluation (OBE) is an evaluation methodology that many government agencies and larger organizations have increasingly adopted for their programs and focuses on measuring the effect of a project on the people it serves (outcomes) rather than on services (outputs). OBE methods can be used at many points in a project to provide indicators of a project's effectiveness, and they provide a greater degree of accountability. OBE measures results by making observations that demonstrate change, and it systematically collects information about specific indicators to show the extent to which a project achieves its goals.

When the team has worked through the project design process to this point, it already has the information needed to easily develop an evaluation plan. The key to creating an evaluation plan is to first have SMART objectives. Then the evaluation plan will become a natural extension of the objectives, and it will be relatively easy to compose. By devising evaluation plans for your technology projects in the design stages you can incorporate OBE into your grant proposals, define the project in measurable terms of its impact on the community, and have the evaluation section of your grant application already prepared. This method ultimately leads to more focused and successful programs and services.

Ask the team to consider the following key questions when it is designing a project evaluation plan:

1. What is the purpose of the evaluation, that is, what do you want to measure as a result of the evaluation?
2. Who are the audiences for the evaluation results, for example, funders, government, board, staff, partners, other libraries, potential partners?
3. What kinds of information do you need to measure your progress, the strengths and weaknesses of the project, the impact on customers, or how and why the project failed?
4. What sources will you use to collect the information, for example, staff, customers, program documentation?
5. How can the information be collected, for example, questionnaires, interviews, observation, conducting focus groups?
6. When do you need the information?
7. What resources are available to collect the information?

Step 12: Outline the Project Design

When you have completed all 11 steps in the technology project design phase, you will have a project design. Outline the plan for ease of use and to use as a clarifying tool as you explain the project to others (see the Library Technology Project Outline Example, pp. 39–41).

When a Technology Project Becomes a Grant Project

During the project design phase, the team will most likely be able to design several technology projects. Now it is up to the library director, library finance officer, technology

Library Technology Project Outline Example

Goal: To meet the information needs of the growing unemployed adult population.

Outcomes:

1. Unemployed adults will gain confidence in their ability to find employment using technology.
2. Unemployed adults will know how to use technology to find work.
3. Unemployed adults will acquire new technology skills that will help them in gaining employment.
4. The attitude of unemployed adults about using technology to become employed will improve.
5. The quality of life for unemployed people will improve because of their confidence, new skills, improved attitude, gained knowledge, and potential employability because they can use technology.
6. Unemployed adults will view the library as a place where they can use technology to find information about employment.

Objectives:

- By July 2012, 50 percent of unemployed adults who took a class on completing online employment applications will fill out an online application and submit it.
- Over the course of this project, 45 percent of unemployed adults who participated in any aspect of this project will say the service improved their quality of life.
- In 2012, 25 percent more unemployed adults will say they used computers in their job search as a result of the project.
- In 2012, 45 percent of unemployed adults who took a class in creating a résumé on a computer will say this has improved their chances of becoming employed.

Activities:

1. Plan and provide six classes on completing online employment applications. (Technology Librarian, Library Technician)
2. Plan and provide six classes on using computers to prepare résumés. (Technology Librarian, Library Technician)
3. Create a library webpage with links to current employment opportunities and local employment resources. (Web Librarian, Reference Librarian)
4. Establish "Employment Center" in Library where computers and printed materials are available, classes are held, and librarians are available to assist the unemployed becoming employed. (Reference Librarian, Maintenance Worker)
5. Market classes, webpage, and Employment Center. (Technology Librarian, Web Librarian, Reference Librarian)
6. Outreach to unemployment office, recreation centers, senior centers, and homeless shelters. (Technology Librarian, Web Librarian, Reference Librarian)

(Continued)

Library Technology Project Outline Example *(Continued)*

Timeline:

Activities	Staff	Month 1	Month 2	Month 3	Month 4	Month 5	Month 6
Develop online application classes	TL, LT	X	X				
Teach online application classes	TL, LT			X			
Develop computer résumé classes	TL, LT		X	X			
Teach computer résumé classes	TL, LT				X		
Prepare class materials	TL, LT		X	X			
Create employment webpage	WL, RL	X					
Purchase Employment Center computers	RL	X					
Set up Employment Center	RL, MW	X					
Market classes, webpage, and Employment Center	TL, WL, RL	X	X	X	X	X	X
Outreach to unemployment office, recreation centers, senior centers, and homeless shelters	TL, WL, RL	X	X	X	X	X	X
Conduct evaluation	TL, LT, RL		X	X	X	X	X

LT = library technician; MW = maintenance worker; RL = reference librarian; TL = technology librarian; WL = web librarian.

Budget:

Personnel Budget	
.25 Technology Librarian	$10,000
.25 Reference Librarian	$10,000
.25 Library Technician	$7,500
.10 Maintenance Worker	$2,500
Total personnel costs	$30,000

(Continued)

Library Technology Project Outline Example *(Continued)*

Budget *(Continued)*:

Non-Personnel Budget	
Two computers	$5,000
Résumé software	$100
Copying costs	$2,000
Computer furniture	$1,000
Total non-personnel costs	$8,100
Project Budget	
Total personnel costs	$30,000
Total non-personnel costs	$8,100
Total project cost	$38,100

Evaluation Plan:

Objective/Outcome	Evaluation Method
By July 2012, 50 percent of unemployed adults who took a class on completing online employment applications will fill out an online application and submit it.	Surveys will be conducted among class participants at the conclusion of the project.
Over the course of this project, 45 percent of unemployed adults who participated in any aspect of this project will say the service improved their quality of life.	Surveys and interviews will be conducted among class participants at the conclusion of the project.
In 2011, 25 percent more unemployed adults will say they used computers in their job search as a result of the project.	Surveys will be conducted among class participants at the conclusion of the project.
Of unemployed adults who took a class in creating a résumé on a computer, 45 percent will say this has improved their chances of becoming employed.	Questionnaires will be conducted among class participants at the conclusion of the project.
Of unemployed adult participants who use the webpage and printed materials, 50 percent will know more about how to find work using technology.	Exit surveys will be conducted on the webpage.
Unemployed adults will view the library as a place where they can use technology to find information about employment.	Surveys, questionnaires, and exit interviews will be conducted for classes, webpage, and Employment Center.

department head, or other members of library leadership to prioritize the technology projects and to determine how to fund them.

The prioritized projects will become part of the library's technology plan, and the technology plan budget will address funding these projects. Some projects may be funded with the existing budget, and some may be only partially funded with current funds. There may be no funding for some technology projects designed by the team. Of the unfunded and partially funded projects, some will be recommended for grant funding. Once it is clear which projects or parts of projects are appropriate for grant funding and there is commitment and support from administration and leadership for continuing the grant process, the next phase is to form grant teams to work on securing grants for the identified technology projects.

Summary

The project design process involves creating technology projects from your library's strategic plan or technology plan. Be clear about the projects your library has identified to meet community needs if any were created during the library's technology planning process. If your library has no technology plan, identify projects in the library's strategic plan that utilize technology. Alternatively, locate the goals, objectives, outcomes, and activities in the strategic plan that could be accomplished using technology, and design one or more technology projects to accomplish the library's goals incorporating these elements. If your library has no strategic plan, you must do this planning before seeking grants. At the conclusion of this phase, you will have identified or designed one or more library technology projects that require grant funding.

Additional Resources

Bauer, David G. 2001. *How to Evaluate and Improve Your Grants Effort*. American Council on Education/Oryx Press Series on Higher Education. Westport, CT: American Council on Education/Oryx Press.

Burke, J. 2000. *I'll Grant You That: A Step-by-Step Guide to Finding Funds, Designing Winning Projects, and Writing Powerful Grant Proposals*. Portsmouth, NH: Heinmann.

Carlson, Mim. 2002. *Winning Grants Step by Step: The Complete Workbook for Planning, Developing, Writing Successful Proposals*. Jossey-Bass Nonprofit and Public Management Series. San Francisco: Jossey-Bass.

Harris, Dianne. 2007. *The Complete Guide to Writing Effective & Award Winning Grants: Step-by-Step Instructions*. Ocala, FL: Atlantic Publishers.

Hayes, L.C., ed. 1999. *Winning Strategies for Developing Grant Proposals*. Washington, DC: Government Information Services.

Koch, Deborah. 2009. *How to Say It—Grantwriting: Write Proposals That Grantmakers Want to Fund*. New York: Prentice Hall Press.

MacKellar, Pamela H., and Stephanie K. Gerding. 2010. *Winning Grants: A How-To-Do-It Manual for Librarians with Multimedia Tutorials and Grant Development Tools*. New York: Neal-Schuman.

Margolin, Judith B. 2008. *Grantseeker's Guide to Winning Proposals*. Fundraising Guide. New York: Foundation Center.

Miner, Jeremy T., and Lynn E. Miner. 2005. *Models of Proposal Planning & Writing*. Westport, CT: Praeger.

———. 2008. *Proposal Planning and Writing*. Westport, CT: Greenwood Press.

Smith, Nancy Burke, and Judy Tremore. 2008. *The Everything Grant Writing Book: Create the Perfect Proposal to Raise the Funds You Need*. Avon, MA: Adams Media.

Smith, Nancy Burke, and E. Gabriel Works. 2006. *The Complete Book of Grant Writing: Learn to Write Grants Like a Professional*. Naperville, IL: Sourcebooks.

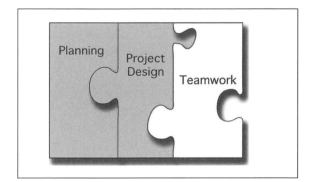

Chapter 4

The Grant Team

Making the Commitment

In the project design phase, your team identified or designed one or more library technology projects to meet the information needs of the people your library serves. Some projects will require alternative or outside funding, and of those some will be appropriate for grant funding.

If you are a director in a small library, it may be up to you to prioritize these technology projects and select which ones are worth the time and effort required to seek grant funding. If you work in a large academic library, public library system, or school library within a school district, chances are good that this will be an administrative or departmental decision. If this is the case, it may be your responsibility to recommend a technology project for grant funding.

When deciding which projects are appropriate for grant funding it is important for you to consider the ROI (return on investment) for the library, particularly where staff time is concerned. How much staff time and resources you can commit to the grant process will be determined in part by the value or outcome of the project to the library and the people you serve. Another important consideration is the dollar amount you are comfortable investing in the process.

For instance, if 100 hours of staff time worth $5,000 are required to work on a stand-alone grant that returns $2,000, this is probably not a good ROI for the library dollar-wise. However, if the $2,000 grant will provide seed money for a $250,000 project that is likely to be funded by another funder and will also attract valuable partners, it may provide a good ROI for the library value-wise. If a $2,000 grant will implement a pilot project to provide information that is vitally important to improve the lives of the people you serve, but it will require a commitment of $2,500 in staff time, this may also be a good ROI outcome-wise. There are no hard and fast rules when it comes to determining ROI from grants. Use your common sense about what projects are worth the time and cost it takes to seek a grant.

Once library leaders, municipal officials, school district administrators, or organizational leadership have recommended that you seek grant funding for a specific library technology project, they must commit to providing the resources and support required to do grant work (see Rule #13). The grant team will do the work to secure a grant for the recommended technology project. Staff must be allowed the time they need to work on a grant team and to do the work required to be successful with grants. Resources and support required in grant work may include:

> **Rule #13**
> Library leadership and the organization must commit to providing the resources and support required to do grant work.

- Space for the team to meet, organize materials, concentrate on writing, make phone calls, and do research (could range from a tabletop to a separate grants office)
- Print and online resources for easy access to grant resources in all formats
- Computers for organizing research, performing searches, sending e-mail, and writing grant proposals
- Office equipment such as copiers, printers, postage meters, phones, and faxes
- Ongoing professional development
- Administrative support staff to assist with grant work
- Professional consulting in specialized subject areas
- Time for team meetings, research, proposal writing, and other grant work

Library staff must understand that the grant process and what is involved in grant work is time-consuming. People who don't fully understand grant work may think the team is spending too much time on grant work, or they may resent the fact that grant team members are away from their regular duties while they are working on a grant proposal. Library leadership must inform library staff about the technology project for which the library is seeking grant funding, who is on the grant team, the timeframe or application deadline, and the end result should the library receive grant funding for the technology project. Answer these questions: What will a successful grant mean for the people served by the library? What will a successful grant mean for library staff? Often when staff members don't fully understand what is going on and the purpose, misunderstandings arise and it becomes difficult to gain their support. In the end, the grant team's work will be much easier when everyone not only understands what they are doing but also are committed to supporting them in their efforts.

The Importance of Teams in Grant Work

Next you need to form a team to do the work of researching and finding an appropriate grant for funding the technology project, writing and compiling the proposal, and all that is involved in preparing and submitting the proposal. Grant work is a team activity (see Rule #5, p. 7). Not even experienced proposal writers can do everything involved in seeking a grant on their own. There's still a lot to do before you are ready to submit a proposal, and sharing this work with a team helps enormously.

One common pitfall is for an individual to attempt to write a grant proposal alone, without seeking help from others. This approach is unrealistic. Working on a grant proposal alone can be stressful, daunting, and even overwhelming. People who write grant proposals alone usually end up frustrated and conclude that grants are too much work. Grant work requires many different skill sets, and it can be time-consuming. You don't want to be drained from going through the grant process only once on your own. You will need energy and motivation to continue the process.

Even if you are successful working alone, it is no way to approach grant work in the long run. Grant teams share the rewards of working together to fulfill the library's mission by helping to accomplish a project's goal. A shared vision and sense of belonging to a meaningful and valued group can boost morale, especially when things get tough. Teams usually produce better proposals than individuals because they provide:

- A broad range of vision
- Multiple viewpoints
- A larger skill set and pooled talents
- A variety of experiences and more ideas
- More energy and greater momentum
- More available time
- Buy-in from partners and collaborators, library staff, and the people you serve
- Shared resources

Forming a Grant Team

Writing grant proposals takes diligence and plenty of time. Forming a grant team to share the burden of grant work is a sensible approach that is likely to result in a better success rate. It is advantageous to work on a team when it comes to the conceptual work of aligning project goals and objectives with a funder's priorities, fine-tuning the project timeline and activities, and designing an evaluation plan, for instance. Responsibilities of grant team members may include:

- Reviewing the library profile, organizational profile, and capacity
- Reviewing the community needs assessment to substantiate need
- Collecting, updating, and analyzing data to update needs
- Researching demographics of the people your library serves
- Researching other technology projects
- Researching grant opportunities
- Creating a timeline and proposal planning
- Coordinating the work of the team
- Writing, editing, and revising the proposal
- Working on a budget, including pricing technology
- Establishing memoranda of understanding with partners
- Obtaining authorized signatures
- Working on a sustainability plan
- Collecting the components and compiling them into the finished proposal

When you form a grant team you will learn a process that can be implemented more easily the next time around. With enough practice at forming teams and working together this will become a familiar activity in your library, and grant work won't seem so intimidating. In the long run, when you work on teams your library will be able to sustain grant work, and your chances of success with grants will increase.

Grant Team Skills

First think about the skills it will take to complete a grant proposal, and make a point of inviting people with those skills to join the team. It is important to include library staff members at all levels, including library technology staff. Consider people at other agencies or in other departments in your organization, including IT personnel, town council members, or school personnel who are involved with technology or who have a good understanding of the focus of your project. In addition to valuable team members, you are likely to discover some partners for this project or future library projects. Below are some skills you might need on the grant team:

- Technology expertise
- Subject matter expertise
- Knowledge about the need being addressed
- Knowledge of the larger organization or community
- Planning skills
- Research skills
- Accounting or mathematical skills
- Writing and editing skills
- Partnering and collaborative skills
- Leadership skills
- Coordinating and organizational skills
- Administrative support skills
- Detail oriented

Look for self-starters and people with initiative, people who work well with others, those with excellent communication skills, and good time managers. Creative people who can think outside the box and have fun are an asset to grant teams, as well as those who are aware of details and can keep the team on track. Good problem solvers and positive thinkers, people who can work under pressure and meet deadlines, and those who are able to follow directions make good team members.

Keep the team as small as possible while still bringing in all the necessary skills. A smaller group is easier to manage and keep focused on specific tasks. In small libraries or libraries with very few staff members, or for solo librarians, it is still recommended to form a team of at least two to three people. A small library can create a team of volunteers, community leaders, and library board members. Enlisting someone from leadership on your grant team will only strengthen the buy-in and support of your larger organization or government entity. Continue to involve community members from the strategic planning or technology planning committees. Involve board members, business leaders from the community, faculty and staff, students, employees, and volunteers. People with expertise in technology, such as library staff, library technology staff, organizational IT staff, and people from outside the library, will be a great asset to your team as you work on technology grant proposals.

You have a ready-made team in your staff members, stakeholders, and partnering agencies. The best teams are diverse in gender, age, background, expertise, and ethnicity. Although one person may fill several roles, remember that the benefit of teamwork is to make less work for those involved. Selecting the right number of people to work on the grant team is crucial. Keep the team small enough to easily manage and keep focused. Preparing a grant proposal means doing extra work above and beyond team members' regular jobs, but, when the work is shared evenly, grant work can be an exciting and productive undertaking.

Don't leave out library staff or board members who are hesitant about using technology in the library or who are not technology experts, especially if they have skills your team needs. This is a good opportunity to invite them to see firsthand how technology can help meet community needs. These people can be valuable in helping other team members see a project from their perspective. They may point out the obvious when other team members who are more tech-savvy might assume participants' knowledge about technology and overlook key concerns.

Grant Team Positions and Responsibilities

Once you have identified the skills you need on the grant team, the next step is to determine team positions. Every grant team is different depending on your library, your organization, the people you serve, the technology project you want to fund, and the grant proposal you are writing. Take time to customize your team to your situation. As you select people to fill the team positions, consider those with the skills you previously identified. Here are some basic grant team positions and their overall responsibilities.

Team Leader

The team leader oversees the team and coordinates activities. In small to medium-sized libraries of all types, this person is most commonly the library director or branch manager. In large libraries team leaders are division or department heads or managers. This person is involved in developing the team's schedule or timeline and tracks the overall progress and is available to help team members who need guidance or clarification of duties. The team leader checks in with all team members periodically to monitor their progress and helps to remove barriers or solve problems they may encounter along the way.

Team leaders schedule team meetings and establish meeting agendas. They lead team meetings or delegate meeting leadership duties to others, assigning meeting responsibilities to appropriate team members. Team leaders may also serve as team coordinators on small teams. On larger teams they work closely with team coordinators. If possible a library leader or administrator leads the team, as they usually have the best overview of the library's role in the organization and community. When there is a question or a fork in the road they are best able to steer the team in the right direction, and if the team needs assistance or support from another agency, department, or community leader, they are the best people to make that connection. The team leader is the main point of contact for partners or collaborators and funders, and they keep city, university, or school administrators and leaders, board members, and trustees informed about the team's progress. They act as the liaison with partners and collaborators, and they are the appropriate person to communicate with the grants office in a large organization about other similar projects on campus or within the organization.

49

Especially in large organizations and academic institutions, there may be an established process for submitting grants. If a grants office or pre-awards office requires following rules and procedures or special training or there are supporting publications with guidelines to follow, the team leader ensures that all team members have the information or training they need to do grant work.

Team Coordinator

Team coordinators are responsible for the "nuts and bolts" or the smooth operation of the team and steady progress of the grant proposal. They develop the team's schedule and make sure the proposal is progressing according to the timeline. They usually begin with the grant deadline and work backward to determine what must be done by when and who is responsible for doing the work. The coordinator promotes communication among team members and makes sure that team members are aware of their responsibilities and deadlines. Coordinators may be responsible for obtaining memoranda of understanding (MOUs), letters of support, and required signatures. In larger organizations such as universities, the coordinator will communicate with the pre-award office, track progress of the proposal through the system, and promptly supply other university offices with the information they need. This person understands the budget cycle and any stipulations about applying for grants in your organization.

Researcher

The researcher identifies appropriate grant opportunities and potential funders and compiles and updates the library profile, community profile, and organizational profile. This person analyzes and synthesizes community data that applies to a specific grant and gathers demographic information relating to the target population. This may involve interpreting data from a community needs assessment or extrapolating census data. A researcher investigates the literature for trends or other similar projects that have been implemented and compiles results or lessons learned in the past by others. This person is often responsible for presenting data and information in a format that demonstrates a specific need within a target population. The researcher may seek supporting information from other departments, agencies, or school and community leaders.

Subject Matter Expert

Subject matter experts supply specialized expertise in various stages of the team's work. They may be called on to help with writing a project description, working on a budget, or communicating with partners. They are considered "floating" team members who support others in accomplishing their duties and meeting deadlines. Flexibility is required. These people could be systems librarians or someone from the information technology office in a larger organization. In a small library, this is the person who knows the most about technology whether he or she is a staff member, board member, or volunteer. You may want to enlist someone from the community or larger organization with expertise in technology or the specific technology your project will employ. A technology grant team must include someone with technology expertise and knowledge of emerging technologies. Additional subject matter experts as team members include people who have knowledge of the project's focus or the specific need being met, such as literacy, employment services, or health information.

Writer/Editor

The writer/editor is responsible for writing and compiling the proposal, from the cover letter to the appendix. Some proposal components may be written by other team members, for instance, the researcher may write the library profile and need statement using the data he or she has gathered; or a subject matter expert may write the narrative explaining why a certain technology will be utilized or explaining the details about the importance of, for example, the health information or employment or literacy services and programs the project will provide. In this case, the editor ensures that the proposal flows and reads as one consistent document coming from a single source, making sure that each part fits together sequentially and that the proposal makes a logical case for funding the project.

The writer/editor ensures that the proposal guidelines are followed precisely, that is, that each component requested appears in the correct order, the margins and spacing adhere to standards, and only those items requested appear in the appendix. The writer/editor lines up outside readers, reviewers, and proofreaders during final editing.

Some libraries prefer to hire professional grant writers for this position. This approach could help if you don't know anyone with writing expertise or if you have the funds to pay a writer; however, most libraries seeking grant funding do not have extra dollars to spend on this service. If you decide to take this route, it is important for the coordinator to closely oversee the writer's work. When writers are from outside the organization, they have less knowledge of the library's strategic plan and technology plan, the library's resources and organizational capacity, and the community the library serves. It is easy for an outside writer to get "off track" without this basic knowledge. Time is money, so you want to keep the writer on target to avoid wasting money.

Administrative Support

No grant team is complete without administrative support staff. This person's responsibilities primarily include assistance with research, proofreading, and final proposal preparation. Duties include taking minutes at team meetings, word processing, photocopying, collating, binding, making follow-up phone calls, and sending e-mails. The workload is usually concentrated closer to the proposal deadline.

Recruiting Team Members

The team leader should schedule initial conversations with potential team members individually to discuss the technology project that needs funding, potential funders (if known), extent of grant work and projection of time commitment, desired skills, their interest in working on the grant team, how they will be supported by freeing up time or providing training, and expectations. To do this job effectively the team leader must be organized and have already thought this through. Any questions or concerns must be addressed at this time to avoid future misunderstandings. Team members must have a clear understanding of what lies ahead, and they must confirm that they want to be a part of this effort.

Grant Team Meetings

Although much of their work is done individually, grant team members are interdependent, and it is essential for them to meet regularly throughout the process to share what they are doing and how things are going and to get input from others. Once grant team members have committed to the team, it is time to bring them together for their first meeting. The team leader or coordinator usually leads grant team meetings.

Ground Rules

The first activity for any healthy team is to establish ground rules. Ground rules are statements of values and guidelines that a group establishes to help members know how to act. They address how people treat each other, communicate, participate, cooperate, support each other, and coordinate joint activities. Ground rules must be clear, consistent, agreed to, and followed. When ground rules are missing, natural behavior patterns emerge and entire meetings can be driven off into a ditch. These are some examples of team ground rules:

1. We treat each other with respect.
2. We address conflict by dealing with the issue, not the person.
3. We value constructive feedback.
4. We strive to recognize and celebrate individual and team accomplishments.
5. We will pitch in to help where necessary to help solve problems and catch up on behind schedule work.
6. Meetings will start and end promptly on time.
7. Meetings are uninterrupted.
8. One person talks at a time; there are no side discussions.

Establish the Team's Goal

In the first meeting, the team establishes the team goal. A grant team's goal is likely to be something like, "To fulfill the mission of the University Library by preparing and submitting a grant proposal for the purpose of securing funding for the Important Papers Digitization Project."

Clarify the Technology Project Design

The team must be fully informed about the technology project that needs funding. For this activity it is helpful to invite someone who was involved in the technology planning or, preferably, the technology project design phases. They can clarify the project design and answer questions team members may have about the technology project. Although the team can work further on developing the project design, the original intent of the project design must be maintained. The project design needs to be understood thoroughly by all grant team members for them to effectively seek funding by preparing a grant proposal for the project.

One important concern when explaining the technology project to team members who have not been involved in library planning is to stress that the project is about people, it's not about technology. This can be a challenging concept for some who are unfamiliar with it. Keep explaining this until everyone on the team is viewing the technology project in this way. If team members are working from different paradigms, there are likely to be disagreements along the way that arise from this basic misconception. It's akin to a belief system, and it can be very difficult for some to let techno-lust go.

Create a Timeline

At this stage, you can propose an initial schedule or timeline for doing the work of the grant team. If you have not already identified a grant opportunity, the initial timeline will cover the time period between the first team meeting and when you do identify a grant for which you will write a proposal. Until the grant research has been done and a grant that is a good match for your technology project has been identified, you cannot develop a timeline for the remainder of the grant process that involves proposal writing.

For example, you might propose an initial timeline that takes into consideration some preliminaries, such as gathering library profile, organizational profile, and community profile information; performing community needs assessments; establishing the technology project design and library technology plan; and researching similar technology projects and possible grants. You might include a date by which the team prefers to have a grant identified; however, there is no predicting when the "right" grant opportunity will come along for your technology project. The team may want to take a recess after the preliminary work has been completed until a grant has been targeted.

Once the researcher has found a grant that is a good match for your technology project and the team and leadership are in agreement, a proposal writing timeline may be created to keep the team on track and within the application deadline. Begin with the application deadline and work backward. Build in extra time for unexpected events and obstacles. If you are in a large organization or academic institution find out when the grants or pre-award office needs your proposal for review and how long this will take. Make sure to allow enough time for authorized signatures if they are required.

If a grant opportunity has already been identified, you can begin with the proposal writing timeline. This is a difficult way to work because things are on the "fast track" for the team right from the start. There will be limited time to select team members, establish ground rules, clarify the team's goal, understand the technology project, and conduct research. If your library has been through the grant process before, you undoubtedly already have in place some core proposal components such as a library profile, organizational profile, and a community needs assessment. This will be helpful if you need to get to work quickly to meet a tight deadline; however, even if you have these components on hand, they must be customized to suit each grant and funder.

Other Things to Do Right Away

- Clarify team members' roles and responsibilities. All team members must understand their roles and responsibilities. Team members must be encouraged to work together. Everyone must know how to contact each other and when are the best times to contact them.
- Send team members away from the first meeting with something to do. Agendas that have time estimates and outcomes listed for each action item are very effective. At the end of each meeting summarize the action items, what team members will do them, deadlines, and follow-ups for the next meeting.

- Tell team members about their role in the institution and community to pitch the technology grant project idea. Partners and collaborators, buy-in, and even unexpected funding can be attracted this way. Especially in the initial stages before a grant opportunity has been identified, spreading the word about the library's plans and the need for funding can be a powerful way to attract funding.
- Someone must take meeting notes or minutes and distribute them in a timely manner, ideally within 24 hours.

Recap Before Beginning the Research

This is a good time to take stock and make sure everything is in alignment: the organization, leadership, library plans, project design, and team. Use the Recap Checklist (see p. 55) to make sure you are ready to go forward with the grant process.

Summary

Before you begin the next phase of researching grants to fund the technology project, it is important to understand the technology project for which the grant team will seek funding. To effectively conduct focused research, a researcher must be very clear about the goal and scope of a project, including the need it will meet, the target audience, and a projected cost. Librarians know all too well how much time can be wasted trying to find an answer to the "wrong question." By now the team has done the work to clearly formulate the parameters of the project for the research phase, which is next in the grant process. The clearer you are about every aspect of the project you want to fund, the more quickly you will be able to identify a matching grant for it and the more persuasive your grant proposal will be.

Additional Resources

Landau, Herbert. 2010. "Winning Grants: A Game Plan." *American Libraries* (September): 34–36. http://americanlibrariesmagazine.org/features/08242010/winning-grants-game-plan.

Perry, Emma Bradford. 2000. "Winning Money: A Team Approach to Grant Writing." *Computers in Libraries* 20, no. 5 (May): 32–36.

Recap Checklist

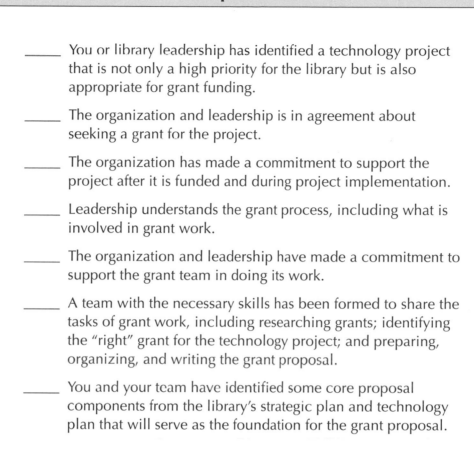

_____ You or library leadership has identified a technology project that is not only a high priority for the library but is also appropriate for grant funding.

_____ The organization and leadership is in agreement about seeking a grant for the project.

_____ The organization has made a commitment to support the project after it is funded and during project implementation.

_____ Leadership understands the grant process, including what is involved in grant work.

_____ The organization and leadership have made a commitment to support the grant team in doing its work.

_____ A team with the necessary skills has been formed to share the tasks of grant work, including researching grants; identifying the "right" grant for the technology project; and preparing, organizing, and writing the grant proposal.

_____ You and your team have identified some core proposal components from the library's strategic plan and technology plan that will serve as the foundation for the grant proposal.

Writing Successful Technology Grant Proposals: A LITA Guide, by Pamela H. MacKellar.
© 2012 Library Information and Technology Association, a division of the American Library Association.

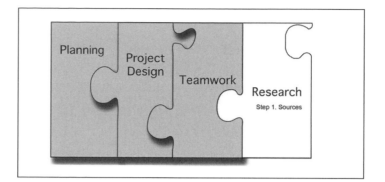

Chapter 5

Sources for Funding Technology Projects

Once you or the grant team and library leadership have settled on a technology project that needs grant funding to be implemented, you are ready to search for grants and be on the lookout for any alternative funding opportunities that match your project design. To do this work effectively and efficiently, it is helpful to first know about the basic sources for grant funding and, more specifically, where funding for projects that utilize technology is likely to originate. Most important, remember to stay focused on the purpose of the project and the community need it will meet as you do your grant research. A good approach is to search for funding sources that support the goals, objectives, and outcomes of the project and a funder whose priorities support solving the problem being solved by the project. As mentioned earlier, the goal of a library project is never to buy technology, but it is about improving people's lives (see Rule #3, p. 4).

Although funding sources do exist that fund primarily technology and technology projects, it is conceivable that any funder could fund a library project that employs technology. For this reason, keep your vision broad while researching grants. It is limiting to look at sources whose primary interest is funding technology alone. For instance, if your library is seeking funding for a literacy project that employs technology, it is essential to research funders whose priority is to fund literacy projects rather than looking only at funders that fund technology. The fact that the library plans to use technology to implement the literacy project is not of primary interest to some funders. They will be attracted by the idea that the project goal is to promote literacy, not the technology you plan to buy. If the literacy project meets a need in the community and literacy is a priority for the funders,

> **Rule #14**
> Identify a funding source that is interested in supporting the goals and purpose of your project and improving the lives of your target population.

they are likely to seriously consider your project, technology or not. In most cases, the technology itself will not be the focus of your research (see Rule #14).

This chapter focuses on sources that are likely to fund library projects that utilize technology. This is not an exhaustive list of all funding sources for library technology projects; however, it is a good starting point for understanding funding sources, and it will familiarize you with the general landscape of funders. New funding sources continuously come and others go. For this reason it is essential to stay updated about who is funding projects like yours, especially when you are doing the research.

To help you conduct and organize your grant research, it is useful to understand that there are two basic grant types: government and private. Within each type there are several categories (see Funding Source Types below).

Funding Source Types	
Government	**Private**
• Federal government • State government • Local government (municipality, town, city, village, county, regional)	• Foundation and nonprofit • Corporations and corporate foundations • Clubs and organizations • Professional and trade associations

Government Funding Sources

Federal

The federal government awards billions of dollars annually for research and development, facilities improvement, demonstration and model projects, and a broad range of educational and social reforms and initiatives designed to carry out the purposes established by federal legislation. The federal government issues two kinds of grants: (1) discretionary and (2) formula (or block) grants. Discretionary grants are awarded directly to grantees by a federal agency, whereas formula (or block) grants put federal money into the hands of states, cities, or counties for them to distribute. Libraries can apply for either kind; however, it is important to keep in mind that the federal government awards discretionary grants and state or local governments award formula and block grants.

The federal government is the largest source of grant funding in the United States, and each governmental department, bureau, or office has its own unique and separate priority list and grant guidelines. There are hundreds of federal government grant programs managed by a wide variety of departmental bureaucracies. Grant programs end, and new ones emerge constantly; and funding priorities are always changing. If you know of a government agency or office that has funded projects similar to your project, it is well worthwhile to stay informed about any new initiatives, programs, or grant-funding opportunities coming from that agency or office.

In the years since the 2008 economic crisis, funding has become available and distributed relatively quickly without much time between the notices of availability and application deadlines. Most notably, the American Recovery and Reinvestment Act of 2009 (Recovery Act) created some new federal grant opportunities of interest to libraries, information clearinghouses, archives, technical information services, and their partners and collaborators. Federal programs and available grants are constantly changing; therefore, some specific programs listed below may no longer be available. However, it is likely that new federal grant opportunities could be offered by these same sources in the coming years until the United States is out of the current economic situation. Check these federal agency and office websites frequently or subscribe to their RSS feeds to stay up-to-date on their new priorities and programs. In these changing times, librarians who are well informed and ready to apply for emerging funds quickly will have the best success.

U.S. Department of Agriculture Rural Utilities Service Telecommunications Programs

The Department of Agriculture Rural Utilities Service (RUS) funds a variety of grant programs. Grants of most interest to libraries looking for technology-related grants can be found in the Telecommunications Programs (http://www.rurdev.usda.gov/RUSTelecomPrograms.html):

- **Broadband Initiatives Program (BIP)**

  http://www.broadbandusa.gov/BIPportal/index.htm

  The BIP administers $3 billion of a $7 billion Recovery Act program to expand broadband access and adoption in communities across the United States, which will increase jobs, spur investments in technology and infrastructure, and provide long-term economic benefits. BIP provided loans, grants, and loan/grant combinations to assist with addressing the challenge of rapidly expanding the access and quality of broadband services across rural America and to meet the objectives of the Recovery Act. By September 30, 2010, there were 320 awards obligated totaling $3.529 billion in 45 states and one territory for last-mile projects, middle-mile projects, satellite awards, and technical assistance awards (see the library success stories in Chapter 11 for examples).

- **Community Connect Grant Program**

  http://www.rurdev.usda.gov/utp_commconnect.html

  The Community Connect Grant Program serves rural communities where broadband service is least likely to be available but where it can make a tremendous difference in the quality of life for citizens. The projects funded by these grants help rural residents tap into the enormous potential of the Internet. Funds may be used to build broadband infrastructure and establish a community center that offers free public access to broadband for two years.

- **Distance Learning and Telemedicine Program (DLT)**

  http://www.rurdev.usda.gov/UTP_DLT.html

  The DLT is designed specifically to meet the educational and health care needs of rural America. Through loans, grants, and loan/grant combinations, advanced telecommunications technologies provide enhanced learning and health care opportunities for rural residents.

- **Farm Bill Broadband Loan Program**
  http://www.rurdev.usda.gov/utp_farmbill.html

  The Farm Bill Broadband Loan Program is designed to provide loans for funding, on a technology neutral basis, for the costs of construction, improvement, and acquisition of facilities and equipment to provide broadband service to eligible rural communities.

- **Telecommunications Infrastructure Loan Program**
  http://www.rurdev.usda.gov/utp_infrastructure.html

  The Telecommunications Infrastructure Loan Program makes long-term direct and guaranteed loans to qualified organizations for the purpose of financing the improvement, expansion, construction, acquisition, and operation of telephone lines, facilities, or systems to furnish and improve telecommunications service in rural areas.

U.S. Department of Commerce National Telecommunications and Information Administration (NTIA)

The Department of Commerce offers a variety of technology grant programs through the National Telecommunications and Information Administration (NTIA) (http://www.ntia.doc.gov/).

- **Broadband Technology Opportunities Program (BTOP)**
  http://www2.ntia.doc.gov/

  The BTOP has administered $4 billion of a $7 billion Recovery Act program to support the deployment of broadband infrastructure, enhance and expand public computer centers, encourage sustainable adoption of broadband service, and develop and maintain a nationwide public map of broadband service capability and availability. By September 30, 2010, NTIA awarded grants in three project areas: Comprehensive Community Infrastructure, Public Computer Centers, and Sustainable Broadband Adoption (see Chapter 11 success stories for examples).

U.S. Department of Education

The Department of Education (ED) administered a budget of $63.7 billion in regular FY 2010 discretionary appropriations and $96.8 billion in discretionary funding provided under the Recovery Act and operated programs that touched on every area and level of education. The ED's elementary and secondary programs annually serve nearly 14,000 school districts and approximately 56 million students attending some 99,000 public schools and 34,000 private schools. Department programs (http://www2.ed.gov/programs/gtep/gtep.pdf) also provide grant, loan, and work-study assistance to more than 14 million postsecondary students.

The 2010 Guide to U.S. Department of Education programs provides an overview of ED grant programs. The following ED offices administer grants of potential interest to libraries looking to fund projects that utilize technology:

- **Office of Elementary and Secondary Education (OESE)**
  http://www2.ed.gov/about/offices/list/oese/programs.html

  OESE provides financial assistance to state and local education agencies for both public and private preschool, elementary, and secondary education. Working together with these and other education partners, the OESE promotes and supports equal educational opportunities and educational excellence for all students. **Improving Literacy through School Libraries Program** helps local education agencies (LEAs) improve reading achievement by providing students with increased access to up-to-date school library materials; well-equipped, technologically advanced school library media centers; and professionally certified school library media specialists. **School Support and Technology Programs (SSTP)** provide funds for education technology, school facilities, parent information assistance centers, and comprehensive education assistance centers. The primary goal of this program is to improve student achievement through the use of technology in elementary and secondary schools. Additional goals include helping all students become technologically literate by the end of the eighth grade and, through the integration of technology with both teacher training and curriculum development, establishing innovative, research-based instructional methods that can be widely implemented. Under the **Enhancing Education through Technology (Ed-Tech) Program**, the U.S. Department of Education provides grants to state educational agencies (SEAs) on the basis of their proportionate share of funding under Part A of Title I. In 2010, $100,000,000 was appropriated to SEAs across the United States for the Ed-Tech Program.

- **Office of English Language Acquisition, Language Enhancement, and Academic Achievement for Limited English Proficient Students (OELA)**
  http://www.ed.gov/about/offices/list/oela/index.html

  OELA administers programs designed to enable students with limited English proficiency to become proficient in English and meet challenging state academic content and student achievement standards.

- **Office of Innovation and Improvement (OII)**
  http://www.ed.gov/about/offices/list/oii/index.html

  OII makes strategic investments in innovative educational practices through 24 discretionary grant programs to states, schools, and community and nonprofit organizations. It also leads the movement for greater parental options and information on education. The **Ready to Teach Program** supports projects that promote online professional development for teachers in core curricular areas and projects that develop, distribute, and produce educational video programming. **Star Schools Program Grants** are used to obtain telecommunications facilities and equipment; develop and acquire instructional programming for students; provide pre-service and in-service staff development for teachers; provide educational programming for parents and community members; obtain technical assistance for teachers, school personnel, and other educators in the use of the facilities and programming; and improve instruction in the areas of reading and math by utilizing emerging mobile technologies and the use of games and simulations.

- **Office of Postsecondary Education (OPE)**
  http://www.ed.gov/about/offices/list/ope/index.html

  OPE directs, coordinates, and recommends policies for programs that are designed to provide financial assistance to eligible students; improve postsecondary educational facilities and programs; recruit and prepare disadvantaged students for post-secondary programs; and promote the domestic study of foreign languages and international affairs, research, and exchange activities. **Technological Innovation and Cooperation for Foreign Information Access** provides grants to develop innovative techniques or programs that address national teaching and research needs in international education and foreign languages by using technologies to access, collect, organize, preserve, and widely disseminate information on world regions and countries other than the United States.

- **Office of Special Education and Rehabilitative Services (OSERS)**
  http://www.ed.gov/about/offices/list/osers/index.html

  OSERS assists in the education of children with disabilities and the rehabilitation of adults with disabilities and conducts research to improve the lives of individuals with disabilities regardless of age. **Assistive Technology Program** supports state efforts to improve the provision of assistive technology to individuals with disabilities of all ages through comprehensive, statewide programs that are consumer responsive. The State Grant for Assistive Technology Program makes assistive technology devices and services more available and accessible to individuals with disabilities and their families. The program provides one grant to each of the states, the District of Columbia, Puerto Rico, and the outlying areas. **Technology and Media Services Program** (1) improves results for children with disabilities by promoting the development, demonstration, and use of technology; (2) supports educational media services activities designed to be of value in the classroom setting to children with disabilities; and (3) provides support for captioning and video description that is appropriate for use in the classroom setting.

- **Office of Vocational and Adult Education (OVAE)**
  http://www.ed.gov/about/offices/list/ovae/index.html

  OVAE works to ensure that all Americans have the knowledge and technical skills necessary to succeed in postsecondary education, the workforce, and life. Through the **Preparing America's Future** initiative's comprehensive policies, programs, and activities, OVAE is helping reform America's high schools, supporting America's community colleges, and expanding America's adult education programs. These efforts will transform the federal role, sparking state and local reform efforts.

U.S. General Services Administration

The U.S. General Services Administration, located online at http://www.gsa.gov/, offers the Computers for Learning Program.

- **Computers for Learning Program**
  http://computersforlearning.gov/htm/hp_programDesc.htm

  The Computers for Learning Program allows schools and educational nonprofit organizations to view and select the computer equipment that federal agencies have reported as excess.

U.S. Department of Health and Human Services (HHS)

The U.S. Department of Health and Human Services (HHS) (http://www.hhs.gov/) offers many grant programs that support technology. Key programs for libraries originate with the National Library of Medicine.

- **National Library of Medicine (NLM)**
  http://www.nlm.nih.gov/grants.html

  NLM provides the following grants and fellowships to organizations and individuals:
  - Research grants, awards supporting career development and training, fellowship programs at NLM
  - Support for outreach initiatives to improve access and eliminate health disparities
  - Trans-NIH programs and initiatives supported by NLM

  NLM has a vital interest in information management and in the enormous utility of computers and telecommunication for improving storage, retrieval, access, and use of biomedical information. NLM provides extramural support through grants-in-aid and, less commonly, contracts. **Information Resource Grants to Reduce Health Disparities** (http://www.nlm.nih.gov/ep/GrantInfoSys.html) is an NLM grant that funds projects that will bring useful, usable health information to health disparity populations and the health care providers who care for those populations. Access to useful, usable, understandable health information is an important factor during health decisions. Proposed projects should exploit the capabilities of computer and information technology and health sciences libraries to bring health-related information to consumers and their health care providers.

- **National Network of Libraries of Medicine (NN/LM)**
  http://nnlm.gov/funding/

  NN/LM advances the progress of medicine and improves the public health by providing all U.S. health professionals with equal access to biomedical information and improving the public's access to information to enable them to make informed decisions about their health. NN/LM is coordinated by the National Library of Medicine and carried out through a nationwide network of health science libraries and information centers. Grants are offered by each region in the network and focus on access to health information through outreach, professional development, technology, and training, for example. For instance, the **Technology Improvement Award** (http://nnlm.gov/gmr/funding/technology/techrfp.html) is an NN/LM grant that funds the purchase, installation, and/or upgrading of information technologies that enhance access to health information.

Institute of Museum and Library Services (IMLS)

The IMLS (http://www.imls.gov/) is the primary source of federal support for the nation's 123,000 libraries and 17,500 museums. The Institute's role is to provide leadership and funding for the nation's museums and libraries, resources these institutions need to fulfill their mission of becoming centers of learning for life crucial to achieving personal fulfillment, a productive workforce, and an engaged citizenry.

63

IMLS grants are available for archives, federally recognized Native American tribes, historical societies, libraries, museums, nonprofits that serve Native Hawaiians, professional associations, regional organizations, state library administrative agencies, state or local governments, and public or private nonprofit institutions of higher education.

- **Library Services and Technology Act (LSTA) Grants to States Program**

  http://www.imls.gov/programs/use_of_funds_by_state.aspx

  LSTA grants represent the only federal funding exclusively for libraries. These grants are allocated annually by the IMLS to state library agencies using a population-based formula. LSTA priorities specify that all states develop the goals and objectives for their five-year plan to strengthen the efficiency, reach, and effectiveness of library services in their state. Applicants for this grant program must be one of the 59 State Library Administrative Agencies that may use the appropriation to support statewide initiatives and services by conducting competitive subgrant competitions or cooperative agreements for public, academic, research, school, and special libraries in their states (see also State Library Agencies under the later section State and Local, pp. 66–67).

- **Learning Labs in Libraries and Museums**

  http://www.imls.gov/about/macarthur.shtm

  Learning Labs in Libraries and Museums supports the planning and designing of up to 30 Learning Labs in libraries and museums throughout the country. The Labs are intended to engage middle- and high-school youth in mentor-led, interest-based, youth-centered, collaborative learning using digital and traditional media. Grantees will be required to participate, in person and online, in a community of practice that will provide technical assistance, networking, and cross-project learning. Projects are expected to provide prototypes for the field and be based on current research about digital media and youth learning.

- **National Leadership Grants**

  http://www.imls.gov/applicants/grants/nationalLeadership.shtm

  National Leadership Grants support projects that have the potential to elevate museum, archival, and library practice within the context of national strategic initiatives. The IMLS seeks to advance the ability of museums, archives, and libraries to preserve culture, heritage, and knowledge; contribute to building technology infrastructures and information technology services; and provide twenty-first-century knowledge and skills to current and future generations in support of a world-class workforce.

- **Native American Library Services Enhancement Grants**

  http://www.imls.gov/applicants/grants/nativeEnhance.shtm

  Native American Library Services Enhancement Grants support projects to enhance existing library services or implement new library services as they relate to LSTA priorities, including providing electronic and other linkages between and among all types of libraries.

- **Sparks! Ignition Grants for Libraries and Museums**

  http://www.imls.gov/applicants/grants/SparksIgnition.shtm

  Sparks! Ignition Grants for Libraries and Museums address problems, challenges, or needs of broad relevance to museums, libraries, or archives, including projects that rapidly prototype and test new types of software tools or create useful new ways to link separate software applications used in libraries, archives, or museums.

National Endowment for the Arts

National Endowment for the Arts (NEA) (http://www.nea.gov/) is a public agency dedicated to supporting excellence in the arts, bringing the arts to all Americans, and providing leadership in arts education. The NEA is the nation's largest annual funder of the arts, bringing great art to all 50 states, including rural areas, inner cities, and military bases.

- **Access to Artistic Excellence**

  http://www.arts.gov/grants/apply/index.htm

  Access to Artistic Excellence encourages and supports artistic creativity, preserves our diverse cultural heritage, and makes the arts more widely available in communities throughout the country. This grant supports technology projects that provide online access to collections, exhibitions, organizational history, and other programming information.

National Endowment for the Humanities

The National Endowment for the Humanities (NEH) (http://www.neh.gov/grants/) is an independent grant-making agency of the U.S. government dedicated to supporting research, education, preservation, and public programs in the humanities.

- **Digital Humanities Start-Up Grants**

  http://www.neh.gov/grants/guidelines/digitalhumanitiesstartup.html

  Digital Humanities Start-Up Grants encourage innovations in the digital humanities and may involve research that brings new approaches or documents best practices in the study of the digital humanities; planning and developing prototypes of new digital tools for preserving, analyzing, and making accessible digital resources, including libraries' and museums' digital assets; and innovative uses of technology for public programming and education utilizing both traditional and new media, for example.

- **Humanities Collections and Reference Resources Grants**

  http://www.neh.gov/grants/guidelines/HCRR.html

  Humanities Collections and Reference Resources Grants support projects that provide an essential foundation for scholarship, education, and public programming in the humanities. Projects may address digitizing collections; preserving and improving access to born-digital sources; developing databases, virtual collections, or other electronic resources to codify information on a subject or to provide integrated access to selected humanities materials; or designing digital tools to facilitate use of humanities resources, for example.

- **National Digital Newspaper Program**

  http://www.neh.gov/grants/guidelines/ndnp.html

  The National Digital Newspaper Program funds projects that digitize newspapers published in the applicant's state between 1836 and 1922.

National Historical Publications and Records Commission (NHPRC)

The National Historical Publications and Records Commission (NHPRC) (http://www.archives.gov/nhprc/announcement/) is the grant-making affiliate of the National Archives and Records Administration (NARA). The NHPRC promotes the preservation and use of America's documentary heritage essential to understanding our democracy, history, and culture. Each year Congress appropriates up to $10 million for grants to support the nation's archives and for projects to edit and publish historical records of national importance.

- **Digitizing Historical Records Program**

  http://www.archives.gov/nhprc/announcement/digitizing.html

  The Digitizing Historical Records Program funds projects that utilize cost-effective methods to digitize nationally significant historical record collections and make the digital versions freely available online.

- **Electronic Records Projects Program**

  http://www.archives.gov/nhprc/announcement/electronic.html

  The Electronic Records Projects Program funds projects that increase the capacity of archival repositories to create electronic records archives that preserve records of enduring historical value.

State and Local

Some federal funding is passed directly to states, counties, or local governments for their use or for redistribution through formula (or block) grants. A state or local government entity may acquire a grant of its own that requires others to perform part of a project's scope of work. In this case, the local government will issue a Request for Proposals (RFP) for services or products. Libraries may be eligible for a formula or block grant or may respond to an RFP to perform work on a state formula or block grant.

State Library Agencies

- **Library Services and Technology Act (LSTA) Funding**

  http://www.imls.gov/programs/libraries.shtm

  LSTA funding is appropriated to state library agencies by the federal government (IMLS). Each state may use its LSTA appropriation to support statewide initiatives and services. Funding priorities are determined by each state based on its state library agency's five-year plan. Some state libraries conduct competitive subgrant or minigrant competitions or cooperative agreements for public, academic, research, school, and/or special libraries in their states. LSTA funding has increased over the past several years and continues to be a good source of funding for most libraries. In 2010, $172,561,000 was allocated to state libraries for the Grants to State Library Agencies program.

State Humanities Councils, Arts Councils, Cultural Services Agencies, and Departments of Education

In many states there are grant opportunities available through other state, county, or city agencies and departments, such as humanities councils, arts councils, cultural services agencies, and departments of education.

Private Funding Sources

Private funding sources include foundations and nonprofit organizations, corporations and corporate foundations, clubs and organizations, individuals, and professional associations. Private funding sources are all funding sources other than government sources.

Foundations

Foundations exist to support specific ideals that inspired the creation of the foundation. Billions of dollars are granted annually by foundations to help schools, communities, libraries, and other nonprofit organizations reach their goals. Following are a few examples:

- **Barbara Bush Foundation for Family Literacy**
  http://www.barbarabushfoundation.com/

  This foundation supports the development and expansion of family literacy programs in all 50 states.

- **Cisco Foundation**
  http://www.cisco.com/web/about/ac48/about_cisco_cisco_foundation.html

  This foundation supports Cisco's efforts to team with NPO/NGO organizations around the world to develop public investment programs focused on critical human needs, access to education, and economic empowerment. This work is focused on underserved communities. The funder looks for solutions that harness the power of the Internet and communications technology.

- **MetLife Foundation**
  http://www.metlife.com/about/corporate-profile/citizenship/metlife-foundation/index.html

  The goal of the MetLife Foundation is to empower people to lead healthy, productive lives and strengthen communities. Underlying the Foundation's programs is a focus on education at all ages and a commitment to increasing access and opportunity.

- **Motorola Mobility Foundation**
  http://responsibility.motorola.com/index.php/society/comminvest/empowerment grants

  The Motorola Mobility Foundation, the philanthropic arm of Motorola Mobility, Inc., offers Empowerment Grants, an opportunity for U.S. nonprofit organizations

67

to apply for funding to empower their communities through technology. Grants are provided for programs in the foundation's three areas of focus: education, health and wellness, and community. The program is designed to support and celebrate everyday, real-life efforts to leverage technology to build stronger communities. Successful programs may include providing technology, and tutoring in the skills needed to use it, for teachers, mentors, and community leaders.

Library Foundations

Library foundations are independent nonprofit organizations established according to relevant state and federal regulations. Many communities, regions, and states have created library foundations to solicit donations to support the libraries in their areas. Frequently, library foundations are created for a single purpose, such as to raise funds for a new library building or to purchase new library computers; however, some library foundations offer ongoing grant opportunities for changing priorities. Your state library is the resource for locating library foundations in your area that may support projects like yours.

Community Foundations

Community foundations are foundations in communities that act as central access points for local funding. They are responsible for managing the application process and distributing funding for many different funders in their communities, such as small foundations, businesses, corporations, organizations, or individuals. Projects funded through community foundations vary widely as to purpose, depending on the priorities of individual local funders.

Corporations

Corporations offer many opportunities in the form of partnerships, material resources, mentors, expertise, and funds to schools, communities, libraries, and other nonprofits. Corporations are usually interested in establishing their names and are driven primarily by their desire for public recognition. Often they provide funding and seek relationships within the communities in which they operate. Here are some examples of corporations that are receptive to funding technology projects:

- **Acclinet**

  http://www.acclinet.com/tech_grant.asp

  Acclinet regularly presents qualifying college students, teachers, and nonprofit organizations with free industry-best Sun server and workstation equipment they need to do what they do best. Acclinet's technology grant program focuses on two groups: college students and teachers learning or teaching UNIX and open-source technologies and nonprofit organizations dedicated to bettering the lives of children.

- **AT&T Aspire Grants**

  http://www.att.com/gen/corporate-citizenship?pid=17884

  AT&T Aspire Grants provide funds to schools and local community agencies to support student success and workforce readiness.

- **Best Buy**

  http://www.bestbuy.com/

  Best Buy teams across the United States select nonprofit organizations that provide positive experiences to help teens to excel in school, engage in their communities, and develop leadership skills. Special consideration is given to programs that provide youth with access to opportunity through technology.

- **Cisco Community Impact Cash Grants**

  http://www.cisco.com/web/about/ac48/cash_grants_community.html

  Cisco Community Impact Cash Grants support the unmet needs of underserved communities in the areas of Education and Critical Human Needs. The Community Impact Cash Grant process is designed to meet the unique needs of the local community while aligning and extending the impact of Cisco's broader philanthropic goals.

- **Dell**

  http://content.dell.com/us/en/corp/cr-dell-giving-us-giving.aspx

  Dell's strategy focuses on closing the technology gap and unleashing student potential for children worldwide. **Dell YouthConnect** is Dell's signature initiative to promote technology-supported education for youth through 22 years of age. It works with partner agencies in nine countries to directly benefit underserved students with this innovative program. Dell is currently piloting the program in the United States with 25 partner agencies.

- **Dollar General**

  http://www.dollargeneral.com/dgliteracy/pages/grant_programs.aspx

  Dollar General grant programs help improve the lives of people of all ages in many different communities.

- **HP Ed-Tech Innovators Awards**

  http://www.hp.com/hpinfo/socialinnovation/edtech.html

  HP Ed-Tech Innovators Awards showcase and support educators who are using technology in groundbreaking ways inside and outside of the classroom.

Clubs and Organizations

Local clubs and organizations such as the Rotary Club, Kiwanis, Civitan, Elks, and the Junior League provide support for local projects and programs. Motivated to help local communities through service, materials, and financial investments, these local funding opportunities are usually not widely advertised or promoted. It may require some networking on your part to discover them and some "pitching" to promote your project idea.

Professional Associations

Professional associations often make grant funds available to members of their association or organization that carry out missions that are compatible with the interests of the professional organization. Local chapters and divisions may offer grants for local technology projects, and specialized library associations may offer grants in their subject area of specialization. Here are some examples:

- **American Library Association Awards, Grants, and Scholarships**
  http://www.ala.org/ala/awardsgrants/index.cfm

- **Public Library Association Awards and Grants**
  http://www.ala.org/ala/mgrps/divs/pla/awards/index.cfm

- **Special Library Association Grants and Scholarships**
  http://www.sla.org/content/resources/scholargrant/index.cfm

Summary

With a clear understanding of the funding sources that make grants available for projects employing technology, you will have a better idea about where to start your search for grant opportunities. The next chapter will cover the second step in the research phase, "Resources for Finding Technology Grants," where you will be introduced to the resources, or tools, you will use to find the right grant for your technology project.

Additional Resources

Falkenstein, Jeffrey, A., ed. 2001. *National Guide to Funding for Libraries and Information Services*. 6th ed. New York: Foundation Center.

Grants for Information Technology. 2011. New York: Foundation Center.

Grants for Libraries and Information Services. 2011. New York: Foundation Center.

Grantsmanship Center. 2011. Accessed September 21. http://www.tgci.com/.

GuideStar. 2011. Accessed September 21. http://www2.guidestar.org/.

Hall-Ellis, Sylvia D., and Ann Jerabek. 2003. *Grants for School Libraries*. Westport, CT: Libraries Unlimited.

MacKellar, Pamela H., and Stephanie K. Gerding. 2011. *Library Grants Blog*. Accessed September 21. http://librarygrants.blogspot.com/.

Michigan State University Libraries. 2011. "Grants and Related Resources." Last revised September 20. http://staff.lib.msu.edu/harris23/grants/index.htm.

Peterson, Susan Lee. 2001. *The Grantwriter's Internet Companion: A Resource for Educators and Others Seeking Grants and Funding*. San Francisco: Jossey-Bass.

Taft Group. 2007. *Big Book of Library Grant Money: Profiles of Private and Corporate Foundations and Direct Corporate Givers Receptive to Library Grant Proposals*. Chicago: American Library Association.

See also this book's Appendix B.2. Federal Government Funding Sources At-A-Glance, p. 219.

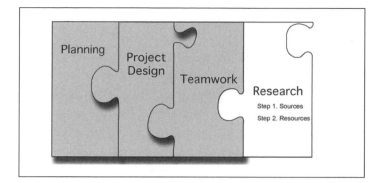

Chapter 6

Resources for Finding Technology Grants

This chapter focuses on resources you will use to identify grants that could fund your technology project. For our purposes, "resources" are the tools you will use to find grants that match your technology project idea (see Rule #15). Grant resources are available in a variety of formats. Grant opportunities are compiled and listed in print directories, electronic directories, online databases, websites, print and electronic newsletters, and e-mail discussion groups. The resources you will use for locating grants to fund library technology projects will vary depending on the source—whether government or private, the purpose of your technology project, and the need the project will meet for the people you serve. It is beneficial to understand the scope of sources and resources available to you prior to starting the research, as this will help you plan a course of action, select appropriate resources to research, and organize

> **Rule #15**
> Use grant resources that focus on the goal or purpose of your project or on your target population. Do not limit your research to resources that include only grants for technology.

your findings. Purposeful and methodical research conducted with a solid foundation of knowledge and confidence in the process will result in a more thorough investigation of grant opportunities for your project in less time.

You will use many resources in the course of your grant research. There is not one directory or database that will contain all the grants available to fund your project. Some resources are more readily available than others, and some are expensive; however, you should be able to find most of them in your state library, a college or university library, the reference collection in a large public library, the web, or your local community foundation.

What follows is a general overview of resources you may want to use in your search for grants to fund a project that utilizes technology. It is not an exhaustive list of all resources that include grants for library projects that utilize technology; however, it is a good place to start learning about the kinds of resources you might want to use and to find out what to look for in a resource. Remember that there are going to be resources specific to the topic of your project or your geographical region that are beyond the scope of this overview. This means you must take your research to the next level by uncovering the unmentioned resources on your own.

Starting Points

The *Library Grants Blog* (http://librarygrants.blogspot.com/; Figure 6.1) is a resource that lists national and large regional grants for libraries. This will give you an idea about what kinds of grants are available for library projects of all kinds and about what funders are looking for in projects to fund.

You also might want to start by looking over the resources that list the largest government funders and those that fund primarily libraries. Grants.gov (http://www.grants .gov/; Figure 6.2) is the single largest access point for federal grant opportunities; and the Available Grants page of the Institute of Museum and Library Services' website (http://http://www.imls.gov/applicants/available_grants .aspx; Figure 6.3) lists the grants currently available from the largest federal funder of libraries.

Another place to look as you get started on your research is the Library Services Technology Act (LSTA) funding page on your state library agency's website. Most state libraries have devoted space to their LSTA allocations where they list available grant opportunities for libraries in their state (Figures 6.4, 6.5, and 6.6).

Government Resources

Federal Government Resources

The resources you will use for finding federal government grants exist primarily in electronic formats, with print options sometimes available. Use electronic resources

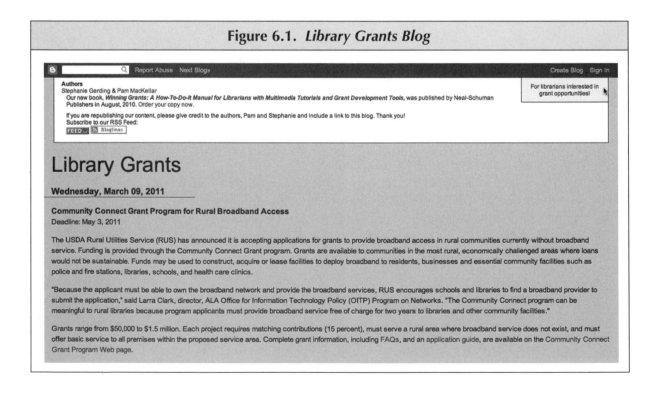

Figure 6.1. *Library Grants Blog*

Figure 6.2. Grants.gov Main Page

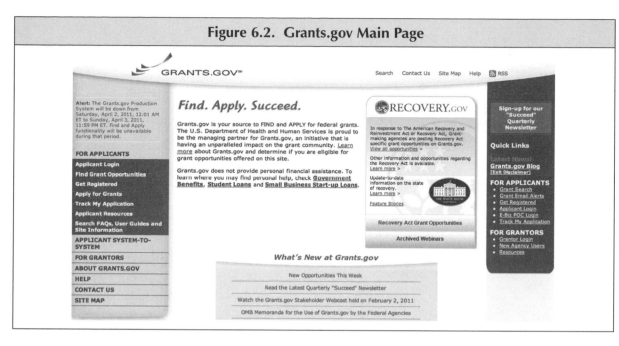

Figure 6.3. IMLS Available Grants Page

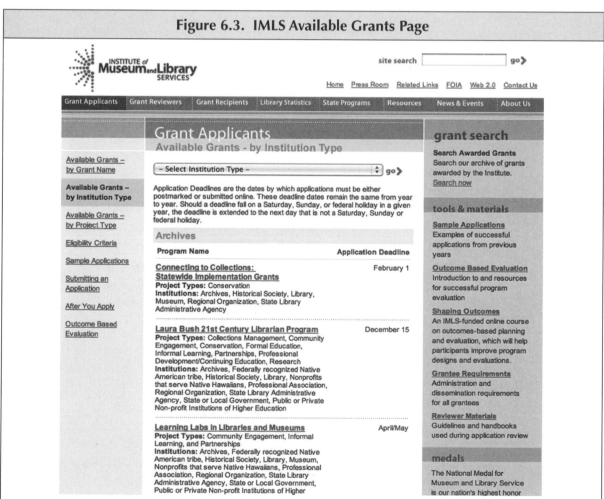

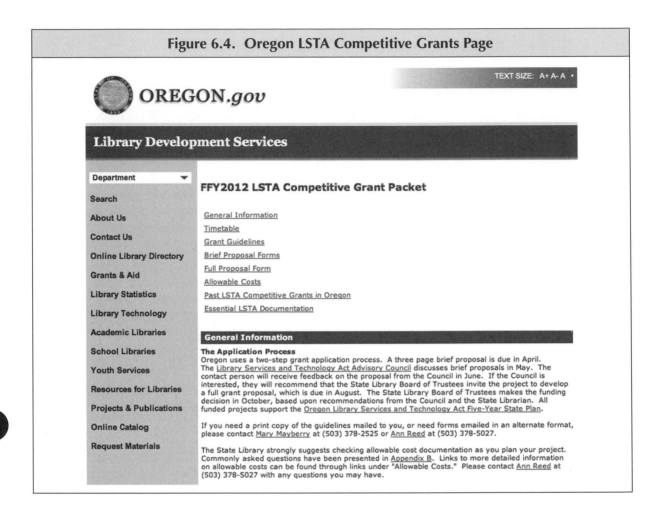

Figure 6.4. Oregon LSTA Competitive Grants Page

74

whenever possible for the most current and up-to-date information about federal funding availability. Federal grant deadlines can be very short, and the sooner you are aware of a grant opportunity, the more time you will have to prepare your application package.

Most federal agency websites list grants currently available from that agency, including guidelines and application materials. In many cases, federal agencies devote a section on their websites for announcing currently available grants. Look for a link or tab near the top of the agency's homepage labeled "Grants" or "Grant Applicants," or perform a search for "Grants" using the site's search box (Figure 6.7).

- ***Catalog of Federal Domestic Assistance (CFDA)***
  http://www.cfda.gov/

  The *Catalog of Federal Domestic Assistance* (*CFDA*) provides a full listing of all federal programs available to state and local governments; federally recognized Indian tribal governments; territories and possessions of the United States; domestic public, quasi-public, and private profit and nonprofit organizations and institutions; specialized groups; and individuals. All federal programs, including grant programs, are listed whether or not funding is currently available for a program. The *CFDA* is disseminated electronically via its website (Figure 6.8) where a printable version is also available for downloading. Print and electronic.

Figure 6.5. Texas LSTA Cooperation Grant Programs Page

TEXAS STATE LIBRARY & ARCHIVES COMMISSION WEB SITE

Agency Info | General Interest | Librarians | Govt Agencies | Catalogs & Searches | Publications | News | TRAIL

Funding
Texas State Library and Archives Commission

Services to Librarians > Funding

Library Services and Technology Act (LSTA) Special Projects and Cooperation Grant Programs for State Fiscal Year 2012

Program Descriptions | Grant Management System | Scoring Rubrics | Past Grant Recipients | Contact Information

The Texas State Library and Archives Commission (TSLAC) is now accepting applications for projects covering the period September 1, 2011 to August 31, 2012 (FY2012). To learn more about the Special Projects and Cooperation grants, download the guidelines below.

A webinar offering tips and guidances on successful applications was held in November 2010. Click here to access the recording of the "Special Projects and Cooperation Grants Available from TSLAC" webinar.

Program Descriptions

Cooperation Grants

This grant program provides funds for programs that promote cooperative services for learning and access to information. Programs involving collaboration are encouraged. Programs must emphasize improved services by the library to its customers. Programs may be in the following categories:

1. Expand services for learning and access to information & educational resources in a variety of formats;
2. Develop library services that provide all users access to information through local, state, regional, national, & international electronic networks;
3. Provide electronic and other linkages between and among all types of libraries; or
4. Develop public & private partnerships with other agencies & community-based organizations.

These programs must meet the following LSTA goal as identified in the **Texas LSTA 5 Year Plan**:
Need
Texans need technology based library services to help them achieve economic, educational, & other personal goals.
Goal
Assist libraries with technology to serve the information needs of Texans.

75

- **Grants.gov**
  http://www.grants.gov/

Grants.gov (Figure 6.2) is the single central location for accessing grant funds available through 1,000 federal grant programs, providing access to approximately $500 billion in annual awards. Here you can electronically find competitive grant opportunities from all 26 federal grant-making agencies. Grants.gov also supports electronic applications that can be downloaded and provides online user support tools and personalized assistance. Grants.gov offers e-mail subscriptions notifying subscribers about new grant opportunity postings and updates. Notices can be customized based on advanced criteria. RSS feeds are also available.

The American Recovery and Reinvestment Act of 2009 (Recovery Act) created some new federal grant opportunities of interest to libraries, information clearinghouses, archives, technical information services, and their partners and collaborators. All Recovery Act grant opportunities are searchable at Grants.gov.

Figure 6.6. Indiana State Library LSTA Grants Page

Library > Services for Libraries > Library Services and Technology Act Grants

Library Services and Technology Act Grants

The Library Services and Technology Act (LSTA)

The Library Services and Technology Act (LSTA) was signed into law September 30, 1996 as part of the Museum and Library Services Act. As a result, federal LSTA funds are distributed from the Institute of Museum and Library Services to states for the purposes of increasing the use of technology in libraries, fostering better resource sharing among libraries, and targeting library services to special populations. For more information about the current IMLS five-year plan, please visit the IMLS website.

The Indiana State Library manages distribution of LSTA funds according to an IMLS-approved five-year plan  for the funds (also read the formal evaluation of the 2003-2007 five-year plan).

Information for Applicants: LSTA Sub-Grant Opportunities

The Indiana State Library annually awards sub-grants to Indiana libraries for programs that contribute toward five-year plan goals and objectives.

- **Current Grant Guidelines**
- **Open Deadline Grant Guidelines**
- **Sub-Grant Frequently Asked Questions**
- **Past Grant Recipients**

- **Grant Application**
- **Application Recommendations**
- **Grantee Responsibilities**

Figure 6.7. National Historical Publications & Records Commission Main Page

NATIONAL ARCHIVES

Blogs | Bookmark/Share | Contact Us

Search Archives.gov   GO

Research Our Records | Veterans Service Records | Teachers' Resources | Our Locations | Shop Online

National Historical Publications & Records Commission

Home > NHPRC > Grant Opportunities

Grant Program

Grant Opportunities
Application Instructions
FAQs
What We Do/Do Not Fund

NHPRC
DOCUMENTING DEMOCRACY
NHPRC grant recipients are asked to download and use our logo in public materials to acknowledge Federal support for documenting democracy.
Download our Logo

Learn why Democracy Starts Here

Grant Opportunities

Listed are our current grant categories. If the deadline has passed, the announcement is being revised and will appear at least 90 days before the new deadline.

- Archives Leadership Institute
  The National Historical Publications and Records Commission seeks proposals from organizations to continue the Archives Leadership Institute.
  - Final Deadline: October 6, 2011

- Documenting Democracy: Access to Historical Records
  The National Historical Publications and Records Commission seeks proposals that promote the preservation and use of the nation's most valuable archival resources. Projects should expand our understanding of the American past by facilitating and enhancing access to primary source materials.
  - Final Deadline: October 6, 2011

Questions?
- Contact the NHPRC
- **E-mail:** nhprc@nara.gov*
- **Telephone:** 202-357-5010
- **Fax:** 202-357-5914
* Please see our Privacy Statement

Consult the Help Section
- Frequently Asked Questions
- Sample Projects
- DUNS Number Requirement

Select an Instruction:
- First Time Using Grants.gov?

Figure 6.8. *Catalog of Federal Domestic Assistance* Main Page

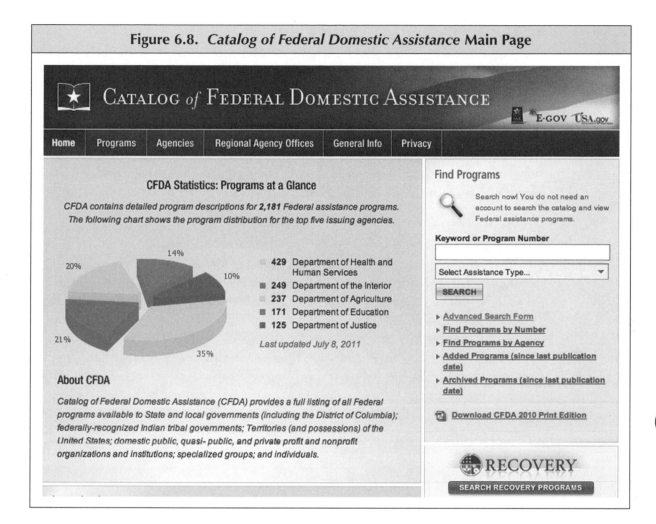

Because federal programs and available grants are constantly changing and deadlines for some programs are short, it is important to check Grants.gov and individual federal agency websites frequently or subscribe to their RSS feeds for updates as they happen. Electronic.

- ***Federal Register***

  http://www.gpo.gov/fdsys/browse/collection.action?collectionCode=FR

  Published by the Office of the Federal Register, National Archives and Records Administration (NARA), the *Federal Register* is the official daily publication of U.S. federal agency information for rules, proposed rules, and notices of federal agencies and organizations, as well as executive orders and other presidential documents. This includes notifications and announcements of grant opportunities by federal agencies and may be in the form of Notices of Funds Availability (NOFAs) and Solicitations for Grant Applications (SGAs). Notices and solicitations typically include funding priorities, eligibility requirements, application deadlines, and contact information for inquiries or help with applying for funds. The *Federal Register* is available in print at Federal Depository Libraries and electronically through FDsys, the Government Printing Office's Federal Digital System. Federal Register 2.0

(http://www.federalregister.gov/; Figure 6.9), launched in July 2010, another means for accessing the *Federal Register*, organizes and displays the *Federal Register* in an easy-to-read format designed to make it accessible for citizens and communities. Print and electronic.

- *Primary Source*
  http://www.imls.gov/news/source.shtm

  This newsletter from the IMLS (Figure 6.10) contains brief articles that alert readers to new information pertinent to libraries, including new grant opportunities from IMLS. Available by e-mail subscription.

- **TGCI *Federal Register* Grant Announcements**
  http://www.tgci.com/Filter/index.asp

  An alert service provided by The Grantsmanship Center (TGCI) draws announcements from TGCI's daily search of the *Federal Register* (Figure 6.11). Electronic format. Free registration.

State and Local Government Resources

Most state and local governments don't have centralized websites for finding grant opportunities. This means you must check individual state and local government agency and department websites regularly for grants, subgrants, and RFPs. Make contact with key officials in departments that are likely to fund library technology projects like yours. If no funding is currently available, ask to be notified should funding become

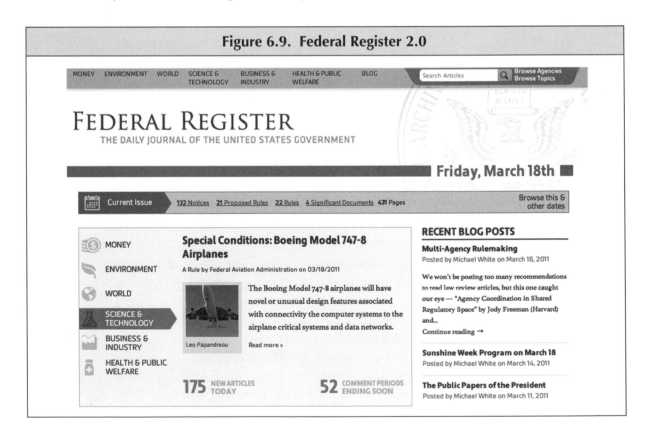

Figure 6.9. Federal Register 2.0

Figure 6.10. *Primary Source* Main Page

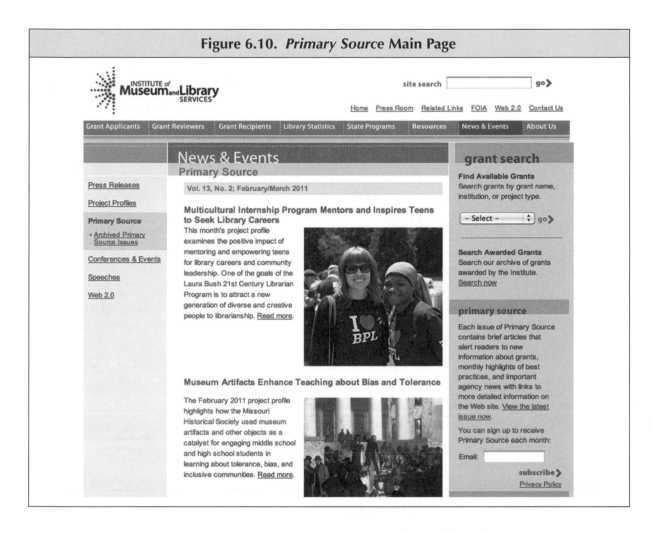

Figure 6.11. TGCI *Federal Register* Grant Announcements Page

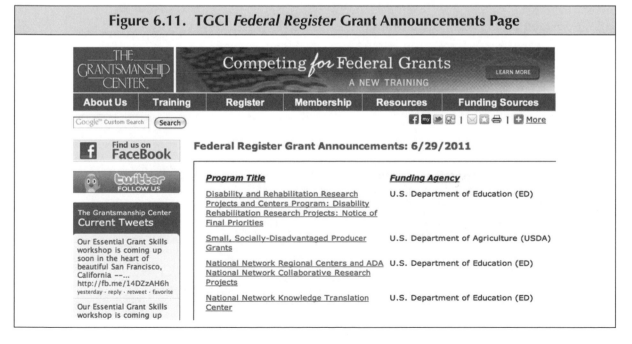

available. Most Recovery Act funding funnels through states, and subgrants for this money often have short deadlines. Stay current by making contact and checking often.

State Library Agencies

Your state library's website and the grants coordinator at your state library are the resources for LSTA funding distributed by the federal government as well as resources for other grants available to libraries in your state. You can find your state library's website address at http://www.publiclibraries.com/state_library.htm. Look for a link to "Grants" or "Funding" on your state library's website and check often. Many state libraries have comprehensive Grants webpages that compile all kinds of grant opportunities available for libraries in their state (Figure 6.12). The grants coordinator at your state library is an important resource, so call or visit this person for more information on grants for libraries in your state. Ask to be notified if a grant that matches your technology project idea becomes available.

State Humanities Councils, Arts Councils, Cultural Services Agencies, and Departments of Education

Investigate grant opportunities available through state, county, or city agencies and departments by checking their websites. Grants coordinators at local government departments, councils, and agencies are important resources. You can find grant information and contacts in your state using the following links:

Figure 6.12. Grants for Alaska Libraries Page

Home Division EED State SLED Catalog Ask a Librarian   Search ASL Website [   ] find ▸

Grants for Alaska Libraries

Alaska State Library > For Librarians > Grants

Alaska State LIBRARY ★

Public Library Assistance Grants

Alaska public libraries and combined school public libraries may apply for the Public Library Assistance grant each year. In order to receive this grant, the library must continue to meet a variety of ongoing eligibility requirements. Grant funds may be used to pay staff, purchase library materials, or pay for any other daily operating cost of the library.

- Public Library Assistance Grant Application Packet: FY2012 (DOC)
- Public Library Assistance Grant Budget Revision Form: FY2012 (DOC)
- Public Library Assistance Grant Final Report Form: FY2011 (DOC)
- Public Library Annual Report: FY2011 (DOC)
- Public Library Technology Report Form: FY2011 (DOC)
- Grant Timeline (PDF)

Interlibrary Cooperation Grants

Each year, the State Library funds a limited number of grants which have statewide significance or direct impact on library users. Libraries of all types are encouraged to submit applications for interlibrary cooperation grants. Grants have been awarded for a wide variety of projects, such as reading incentive programs, automation projects, computers and printers for public use, and the development of special programs for patrons. To see the broad range of grants awarded in recent years, please look at the summaries of interlibrary cooperation, regional services, and netlender reimbursement grants below on this page.

- Interlibrary Cooperation Grant (ILC) Application Packet: FY2012 (DOC)
- Interlibrary Cooperation (ILC) Grant Budget Revision Form: FY2012 (DOC)
- Interlibrary Cooperation Grant Final Report Form: FY2011 (DOC)
- Grant Timeline

Quick Links

- ▸ Services for Librarians
- ▸ Services for the Public
- ▸ Services for State Government
- ▸ Alaska Historical Collections
- ▸ Digital Pipeline
- ▸ Articles and Databases
- ▸ Summer Reading Program
- ▸ Library Grants
- ▸ Alaska Library Directory
- ▸ Online Image Collection
- ▸ Alaska State Publications
- ▸ ASL Publications

Spotlight

- ▸ Alaska FAQ blog
- ▸ E-rate for Libraries & Schools

- **Your State Humanities Council**
  http://www.neh.gov/whoweare/statecouncils.html
- **Your State Arts Council**
  http://www.nasaa-arts.org/About/State-Arts-Agency-Directory.php
- **Your State Department of Education**
  http://wdcrobcolp01.ed.gov/Programs/EROD/org_list.cfm?category_ID=SEA

Private Resources

Resources for finding funding opportunities among private foundations are varied. They include entire collections, dedicated databases, websites, electronic directories, print directories, and newsletters and periodicals.

Private Foundation Resources

The Foundation Center (http://fdncenter.org/) is the largest producer of directories and databases of private grant-giving foundations. The Center publishes print and electronic resources by subject, foundation name, geographic region, and grants previously funded. Their database allows for effective searching by multiple fields. The Foundation Center's website is a rich resource itself, offering free basic information about grantmakers, funding trends in the United States, and access to Form 990s filed by private foundations, for example.

Foundation Center Cooperating Collections

The Foundation Center's Cooperating Collections (http://foundationcenter.org/collections/) are free funding information centers in libraries, community foundations, and other nonprofit resource centers that provide a core collection of Foundation Center publications and a variety of supplementary materials and services useful to grant seekers. There are more than 400 Cooperating Collections across the United States and in other locations around the world. Figure 6.13 lists the materials in a 2011 Cooperating Collection core collection.

Foundation Center Digital Grant Guides

The Foundation Center's digital grant guides (http://foundationcenter.org/market-place/catalog/subcategory_gg.jhtml;jsessionid=XVM0GIOKWEPYZLAQBQ4CGW 15AAAACI2F?id=cat620002) provide descriptions of recent foundation grants of $10,000 or more awarded in 25 different subject fields. They cover topics such as grants for the aging, arts and culture, children and youth, education, employment, environmental protection and animal welfare, public health, housing, libraries and information services, information technology, minorities, women and girls, religion, religious welfare, and religious education. Of course you will want to access the guides on libraries and information services and information technology, but remember that grant projects that utilize technology will address a broad range of needs in widely varying subjects or topical areas. Don't make the mistake of limiting your research to resources on technology grants only or grants for libraries only. Focus on the purpose of your project, not on the technology you will use to accomplish the purpose.

Figure 6.13. Foundation Center 2011 Cooperating Collection Core Collection

2011 Core Collection
Foundation Center Cooperating Collections

ELECTRONIC RESOURCES

Foundation Directory Online Professional
Foundation Grants to Individuals Online
Philanthropy In/Sight

PRINT RESOURCES

21st Century Nonprofit: Managing in the Age of Governance (2009)
After the Grant: The Nonprofit's Guide to Good Stewardship (2010)
Board Member's Book (2003)
Foundation Center's Guide to Proposal Writing, 5th edition (2007)
Foundation Directory (2011)
Foundation Directory, Part 2 (2011)
Foundation Directory Supplement (2011)
Foundation Fundamentals (2008)
Foundation Grants to Individuals (2011)
Foundation Growth and Giving Estimates (2011)
Foundations and Public Policy (2009)
Grantseeker's Guide to Winning Proposals (2008)
Guia para Escribir Propuestas (2008)
Guide to Funding for International and Foreign Programs (2010)
International Grantmaking IV (2008)
National Directory of Corporate Giving (2011)
Securing Your Organization's Future (2001)
Social Justice Grantmaking (2009)

Here are some 2011 Digital Editions that might be useful technology grant resources:

- *Grants for the Aging* covers the 717 foundations that awarded 3,647 grants last year worth close to $344 million.
- *Grants for Arts, Culture, and the Humanities* covers the 1,195 foundations that awarded 24,708 grants last year worth almost $3 billion.
- *Grants for Children and Youth* covers 1,245 foundations that awarded 37,063 grants worth close to $4.5 billion.
- *Grants for Elementary and Secondary Education* covers 1,146 foundations that awarded 18,410 grants last year worth close to $2.4 billion.
- *Grants for Employment* covers 654 foundations that awarded 4,037 grants last year worth more than $417 million.
- *Grants for Higher Education* covers 1,241 foundations that awarded 21,204 grants last year worth more than $5.5 billion.
- *Grants for Information Technology* covers 512 foundations that awarded 3,099 grants last year worth $592 million.
- *Grants for Libraries and Information Services* covers 701 foundations that awarded 2,697 grants last year worth more than $565 million.
- *Grants for Minorities* covers 1,003 foundations that awarded 17,491 grants last year worth more than $2 billion.
- *Grants for Women and Girls* covers 1,016 foundations that awarded 10,757 grants last year worth more than $1.7 billion.

These digital guides lead you to essential funder information through hyperlinks. Downloadable from the Foundation Center.

Newsletters and Periodicals

- *Arts Funding Watch*

  http://foundationcenter.org/afw/

  This Foundation Center newsletter is devoted entirely to the arts. It includes funding opportunities for organizations and resources. Published by the Foundation Center. Subscription available. Registration required. Free.

- *Education Funding Watch*

  http://foundationcenter.org/efw/

  This Foundation Center newsletter is devoted to education-related topics. It includes funding opportunities for organizations and resources. Published by the Foundation Center. Subscription available. Registration required. Free.

- *Philanthropy News Digest (PND)*

  http://foundationcenter.org/pnd/

  This is a daily news service that collects philanthropy-related articles and features culled from print and electronic media outlets nationwide. Published by the Foundation Center. Subscription and RSS feed available. Free.

- *RFP Alert*

  http://foundationcenter.org/pnd/rfp

  This PND e-newsletter is a roundup of recently announced RFPs from private, corporate, and government funding sources. Each listing provides a brief overview of a current funding opportunity offered by a foundation or other grant-making organization, along with the date the RFP was posted and the deadline. Published by the Foundation Center. Published weekly. Subscription available. Free.

Directories

- *Celebrity Foundation Directory* includes detailed descriptions of more than 1,700 foundations started by VIPs in the fields of business, entertainment, politics, and sports. Published by the Foundation Center. Downloadable only.

- *Foundation Directory* includes key facts on the 10,000 largest U.S. foundations, including their fields of interest, contact information, financials, names of decision makers, and nearly 60,000 sample grants. Foundation Center. Print and as DIALOG File 26. *Foundation Directory Part 2* features the next 10,000 largest U.S. foundations to broaden your fundraising base. Foundation Center. Print. *Foundation Directory Supplement* provides revised entries for hundreds of foundations in the *Foundation Directory* and the *Foundation Directory Part 2*. Published by the Foundation Center. Print.

- *Foundation Directory Online* (http://fconline.foundationcenter.org/), available from the Foundation Center, includes over 100,000 U.S. foundations and corporate donors, over 2.2 million recent grants, and over half a million key decision makers. Up to nine comprehensive databases are available, including grant makers, companies, grants, and Form 990s; plus five unique databases covering RFPs, philanthropy news, foundation-sponsored publications, nonprofit literature, and foundation jobs. Offers up to 54 search fields including keyword searching. At every plan level subscribers can:

- Search by county, metro area, ZIP code, and congressional district as well as by city and state
- Save searches and store them in a password-protected "My FDO" e-folder
- Tag records with any reminder word or phrase
- E-mail, print, and save records
- Export lists of up to 100 search results at a time into Excel with a single click
- Exclude grant makers that don't accept applications

Published by the Foundation Center. Five subscription plan levels. Monthly, annual, and two-year subscription options. Updated weekly. Available at Cooperating Collections.

- *Foundation Grants Index* contains descriptions of grants that have been awarded to nonprofit organizations by U.S. independent, operating, company-sponsored, and community foundations as well as by corporate giving programs and grant-making public charities. It compiles grant records found in the Foundation Center's online publication the *Foundation Directory Online Professional*, adding an average of 10,000 new grants per month. DIALOG File 27.

Other Private Foundation Resources

- *Annual Register of Grant Support* is a comprehensive directory that provides details on more than 3,200 major grant programs offered by traditional corporate, private, and public funding programs as well as lesser-known nontraditional grant sources such as educational associations and unions. Published by Information Today. Print.

- *Big Book of Library Grant Money 2007: Profiles of Private and Corporate Foundations and Direct Corporate Givers Receptive to Library Grant Proposals* profiles foundations and corporate grant makers that have made grants to libraries or have listed libraries as typical recipients. Published by the Taft Group. Print.

- *Everything Technology: Directory of Technology Grants* provides funding sources for technology projects for nonprofits, libraries and museums, K–12 schools and districts, and colleges and universities. Each entry includes current deadline, brief program description, eligibility, and website address for a complete description of program and application, as well as contact person and telephone number. Published by Technology Grant News. Print and electronic.

- *Foundation Grants for Preservation in Libraries, Archives, and Museums* (http://www.loc.gov/preservation/about/foundtn-grants.pdf) lists 2,270 grants of $5,000 or more awarded by 505 grant makers from 2005 through 2010. It covers grants to public, academic, research, school, and special libraries and to archives and museums for activities related to conservation and preservation. Published by the Foundation Center and the Library of Congress. Downloadable.

- *Foundation Reporter* (http://books.infotoday.com/directories/FoundationReporter.shtml) provides important foundation contact, financial, and grants information. It covers the top 1,000 private foundations in the United States that have at least $10 million in assets or have made $500,000 in charitable giving. Published by Information Today. Print.

- *Grants for Libraries E-News Alerts* (http://west.thomson.com/signup/newsletters/209.aspx) is a free weekly e-mail newsletter from Thomson Reuters that provides timely information on new grant opportunities and funding programs for libraries.

- *Private Grants Alert* (http://www.cdpublications.com/pga/) offers 12 issues per year that provide grant opportunities from foundations, corporations, and individuals; details about preparing letters of intent and applications; grant seeking and proposal writing advice; and more. Published by CD Publications. Print and online by subscription.

- *Technology Grant News* (http://technologygrantnews.com/network-funding-subscribe.html) offers detailed coverage of the latest funding made available by professional trade groups, corporate funders, and all levels of government. It includes articles, news briefs, coverage of past grant recipients, plus timely information on upcoming grants and corporate support for nonprofit/educational/community technology. Published by Technology Grant News. Quarterly. Electronic or electronic with print.

Corporate Resources

Corporations often create corporate foundations for the purpose of granting money for specific projects. Corporations also give directly to projects. Check the foundation resources listed above for corporate foundations as well as the following resources for additional corporate foundations and corporate direct-giving programs.

- *Corporate Giving Directory*
  http://www.infotoday.com/books/directories/CorporateGivingDirectory.shtml
  This directory provides complete profiles of the 1,000 largest corporate foundations and corporate direct-giving programs in the United States, representing nearly $6 billion in cash and nonmonetary support annually. Published by Information Today. Print.

- *Corporate Giving Online*
  http://foundationcenter.org/marketplace/catalog/product_cgo.jhtml?id=prod9200 01&navCount=1&navAction=push
  Corporate Giving Online provides online access to information about corporate donors that support nonprofit organizations and programs through grants as well as in-kind donations of equipment, products, professional services, and volunteers. It includes over 3,600 detailed company programs, over 1,300 direct corporate giving programs, more than 2,500 company-sponsored foundations, and more than 250,000 recently awarded grants. It is searchable by companies, grant makers, and grants with access to data portfolios. Published by the Foundation Center. Monthly, annual, and two-year subscriptions available.

- *Corporate Philanthropy Report*
  http://onlinelibrary.wiley.com/journal/10.1002/(ISSN)1949-3207/homepage/ProductInformation.html

This is a monthly newsletter for corporate giving officers and nonprofit development officers that covers important corporate philanthropy news, provides an insider's guide to charitable giving, and publishes the latest foundation and corporate grants alerts. Published by Wiley. Print.

- *National Directory of Corporate Giving*
  http://foundationcenter.org/marketplace/catalog/product_directory.jhtml?id=prod10009&navCount=1&navAction=push

  This directory includes comprehensive profiles of close to 3,300 company-sponsored foundations and over 1,400 direct-giving programs. It includes nearly 3,900 company profiles, including giving priorities, essential contact information, website links, and more. Published by the Foundation Center. Print.

Club and Organization Resources

Funding opportunities available through local clubs and organizations are usually not widely advertised. This is where your networking and people skills will come in handy. Resources for these funding opportunities are often found by talking to people and by word of mouth. Ask friends, neighbors, and family members who are involved in local organizations and clubs what their organizations support. Mention your idea or project to them, and inquire about the possibility of presenting it to the organization. Ask if they know any other local organizations that might support ideas or projects like yours.

- **Michigan State University Service Clubs and Civic Organizations That Provide Funding**
  http://staff.lib.msu.edu/harris23/grants/servicec.htm

  This Michigan State University website (Figure 6.14) provides links to clubs and organizations that provide local community support. Look for these clubs and organizations in your town, county, region, or state.

Professional Association Resources

- **American Association of School Librarians Awards & Grants**
  http://www.ala.org/ala/mgrps/divs/aasl/aaslawards/aaslawards.cfm

  This website offers information on research grants, leadership grants, a school library disaster relief grant, and innovative reading grants (Figure 6.15).

- **American Library Association Awards, Grants & Scholarships**
  http://www.ala.org/template.cfm?template=/CFApps/awards_info/browse.cfm&FilePublishTitle=Awards,%20Grants%20and%20Scholarships&rtype=ALL

  This database is searchable by grants available from specific ALA units, divisions, offices, and round tables. Also make direct visits to ALA's Pubic Programs Office (http://www.ala.org/ala/aboutala/offices/ppo/index.cfm) and individual websites of ALA units, divisions, offices, and round tables to ensure current and updated information.

- **Association for Library Service to Children**
  http://www.ala.org/ala/mgrps/divs/alsc/awardsgrants/profawards/index.cfm

Figure 6.14. Michigan State University Service Clubs and Civic Organizations That Provide Funding

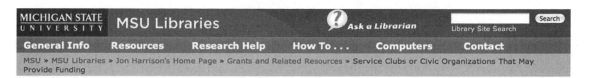

Service Clubs or Civic Organizations That Provide Funding

This page provides links to a number of service clubs or civic organizations which provide local community support and include philanthropy among their activities.

Civitan International
http://www.civitan.org
Local Civitan groups support a wide range of community service activities. The Civitan International Foundation also supports programs which assist children and persons with developmental disabilities. Check out the Local Clubs section for links to local Civitan groups. (Last checked 10/20/10)

Elks of the United States
http://www.elks.org
Provide scholarships for youth attending college among other service projects. The Elks National Foundation also provides grants to the first 250 Lodges who pledge to hold a drug-, alcohol-, and violence-free party for the youth of their communities each year. The Michigan Elks Association assists handicapped children under the age of 18. The Major Project provides facilitating services essential to treatment such as special examinations, therapy and special prescriptions. The Major Project also sponsors attendance at Speech Camps, Diabetic Camps, and Special Therapy Camps. The overall aim of the Michigan Elks Major Project is to help handicapped children become self-sufficient, healthy, contributing citizens of our communities.. For more information contact the James J. Campbell, Executive Director, P.O. Box 620, Lawton, MI, 49065-0620, (616)624-6618. (Last checked 10/20/10)

Figure 6.15. American Association of School Librarians Awards & Grants

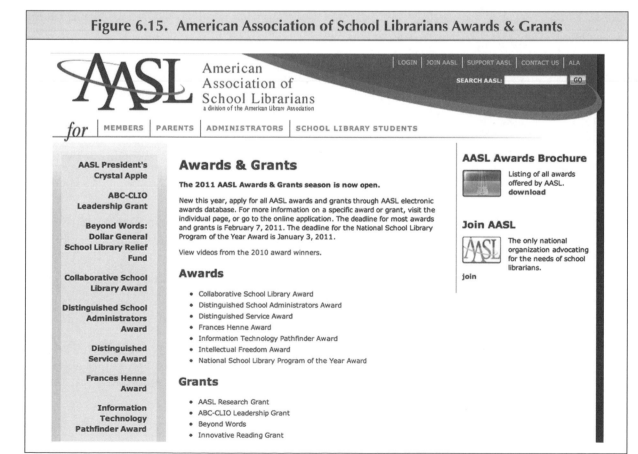

87

This website covers grants for new library materials, summer reading programs, author/illustrator visits, outreach to the underserved, and reading programs.

- **Public Library Association**
  http://www.ala.org/ala/mgrps/divs/pla/awards/index.cfm

  This association provides information on grants to build collections and for professional development.

- **Young Adult Library Services Association**
  http://www.ala.org/ala/mgrps/divs/yalsa/awardsandgrants/yalsaawardsgrants.cfm

  Grants for collection development and for new library materials and research are identified.

To find professional association funding opportunities at the local level, investigate your ALA, ACRL, and SLA chapters:

- Find state library associations or ALA chapters at http://www.ala.org/ala/mgrps/ affiliates/chapters/state/stateregional.cfm.
- Find ACRL chapters at http://www.ala.org/ala/mgrps/divs/acrl/about/chapters/ roster.cfm.
- Find SLA chapters at http://www.sla.org/content/community/units/chapters/ index.cfm.

Multitype Resources

Blogs, Databases, Websites, and Social Media

If you are at an academic institution, investigate databases available through your grants or research office. Academic grants databases include IRIS, InfoEd SPIN, GrantSelect, GrantWire, ResearchResearch, and GrantAdvisor Plus. Subscribe to grants alert services available through your institution. Some specific resources follow:

- **Grantsmanship Center Funding Sources**
  http://www.tgci.com/funding.shtml

  The Grantsmanship Center provides a resource for researching local funding sources by state, including top grant-making foundations, community foundations, corporate giving programs, and state government homepages. There are also links to federal funding sources at the Grantsmanship Center Funding Sources webpage.

- **GrantStation**
  http://www.grantstation.com/

  This is an online funding resource for organizations seeking grants throughout the world. It provides access to a comprehensive online database of grant makers via the Internet linking nonprofits and public libraries to current grants. By subscription. Includes weekly e-newsletter and web-based teaching tools.

- *Library Grants Blog*
  http://librarygrants.blogspot.com/

This free blog posts national and large regional grants appropriate for libraries (see Figure 6.1, p. 72). The hard work of sifting through the multitude of grants available and selecting those of interest to libraries has already been done for you. Follow the links in each posting to the actual grant announcements, application guidelines, and eligibility requirements. Visit the *Library Grants Blog* regularly or subscribe to the RSS feed, and you will be notified about grants as soon as they are posted.

Community Foundations

Community foundations often have solid collections or libraries of materials about writing proposals; print, electronic, and local directories of funding sources; and information about local corporations and foundations including annual reports. Some community foundations offer classes for community members about their funding, other grant resources, and how to apply for grants. Visit your community foundation and talk to the staff there about your technology project. Ask if there are any grants appropriate for your project, and subscribe to their alert service. Find your local community foundations at http://www.cof.org/whoweserve/community/resources/index.cfm?navItemNumber=15626#locator (see Figure 6.16 for an example).

Figure 6.16. The Community Foundation of Sarasota County

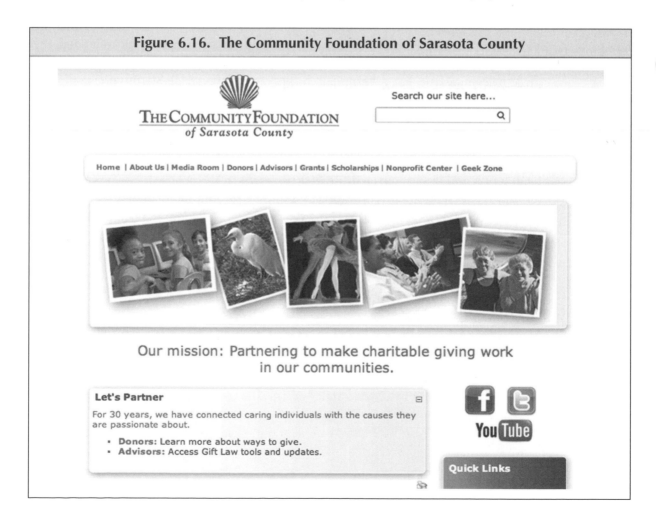

Grants and Contracts or Research Offices

You may be fortunate to work for an academic institution, municipality, or school district that has a centralized administrative office charged with overseeing the grants process and providing support for grants work and grant seeking for your entire organization, academic institution, municipality, or school district. This office may provide ongoing information regarding funding opportunities, and this is where you go to find out about institutional policies regarding grants and contracts. This office assists with all aspects of the grants process, including pre-award activities such as budget resolution, assistance with indirect costs, and acquiring the proper signatures. You may find that they offer training on researching their grants databases or instruction on the grants process in your organization. They are usually responsible for grants administration following the grant award. Often, this office offers grants alert services and grants databases tailored specifically for your organization. It is important to note that if you work in an organization with such an office, all your grants activities must be directed through them. Contact them well before you begin your research for their regulations and parameters. They are an essential resource if such an office is available to you, and they may be able to assist with finding partners and collaborators within your organization.

State and Local Funding Directories

State and local funding directories are invaluable resources for finding foundations and corporations that limit their giving to a specific geographic area. Search your local or state grant directory for clubs and organizations in your area that offer grants. Local directories may also list government and private grants available in your area. Find your local state or local funding directory at http://fdncenter.org/getstarted/topical/sl_dir.html.

Summary

Chapters 5 and 6 have covered the first two steps in the research phase: (1) sources for funding technology projects and (2) resources for finding technology grants. Now you have a solid understanding of the possible funding sources available for library technology projects and the basic resources you might use to locate grants that are a good match for your technology project. The next chapter will show you the third step in the research phase, how to use this knowledge in conducting your grant research.

Additional Resources

See this book's Appendix B.3. Technology Grant Resources At-A-Glance, p. 220.

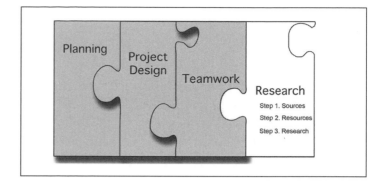

Chapter 7

Researching Technology Grants

The purpose of grant research is to identify grants that support the goals, objectives, and outcomes of your technology project. This means finding one or more grants (1) with a purpose that coincides with your project's purpose and (2) whose funders' priorities mesh with your library's mission and vision.

Librarians are trained to do research, and they have the skills necessary to effectively and efficiently find the grant opportunities that are appropriate for funding library technology projects. Librarians make themselves aware of the information resources that are available to them, they learn how to use them, and they have the necessary skills to find information in even the most remote places. Librarians develop their research skills every day in their jobs, and they pursue continuing education to stay up-to-date with current resources and how to access them. No matter what kind of librarian you are or the type of library where you work, you can be confident with conducting grant research because this is what librarians do. Librarians have a clear advantage over all others who are seeking grants when it comes to research.

Grant research can be a daunting task when you don't know where to start. Random and haphazard grant research will likely take more time and cause you to overlook some prime opportunities along the way. When you understand the sources of grant funding and the tools used to find funding opportunities—which you learned in Chapters 5 and 6—and you conduct thorough and methodical research—covered in this chapter—you will save time and avoid some common pitfalls in grant work.

This chapter will take you through the research process, from showing you how to identify keywords in your technology project design, first doing broad research and then narrowing it down, to recording your research results and keeping your research organized.

Kinds of Grants

Prior to starting the research, familiarize yourself with the different kinds of grants. This will save you time, because you can limit your research to only the kinds of grants that are appropriate for your technology project and your library.

- **Block Grant:** A federal grant awarded to state or local governments for a specific need or issue. Local and state governments then set specific grant guidelines within their own jurisdictions and make smaller grants to local agencies and nonprofits.
- **Capacity-Building Grant:** Grants that help agencies and nonprofits strengthen their internal operations so that they can be more effective/efficient in fulfilling their missions.
- **Capital/Building Grant:** "Bricks and mortar" funding used to purchase land and construct, renovate, or rehabilitate buildings and facilities. These grants may also fund major equipment purchases or endowments.
- **Challenge Grant:** A grant promised to awardees on the condition that they raise additional funds from other sources to reach a specific fundraising goal.
- **Discretionary Grant:** Federal or state grants that are awarded directly to community organizations, schools, and/or local governments.
- **Emergency Grant:** Grants made to help an agency through an extraordinary short-term or unexpected financial crisis.
- **Formula Grant:** Noncompetitive grants awarded by federal or state governments to lower levels of government based on a predetermined formula to address specific needs.
- **General Operating Support:** Funding for the general purpose or work of an organization such as personnel, administration, and other expenses for an existing program.
- **Matching Grant:** A grant that requires awardees to provide a certain amount and funders to provide the rest. For example, a 1:1 match means that the funder and the library each provide half of the cost of the project.
- **Planning Grant:** Funds projects that need further development before applying for implementation. This may include development and refinement of a project, consultation with experts, preliminary needs assessments, or additional research.
- **Project/Program Grant:** Funding for a specific initiative or new endeavor, not for general purposes.
- **Research Grant:** A grant that supports a specific research project or issue.
- **Seed Grant:** Funding designed to help start a new project or charitable activity or to help a new organization in its start-up phase.
- **Technology Grant:** A grant that provides funding for a project that utilizes technology.

The Research Process

Grant research is similar to other kinds of research you are already familiar doing as a librarian. Before you begin your research, clarify the question by understanding your project idea, review the grant sources and resources covered in Chapters 5 and 6, and then follow these basic steps in the research process:

1. Identify keywords that describe your project.
2. Decide which resources to search based on your understanding of the sources.

3. Translate your project keywords to the language of the funder.
4. Work from the general to the specific.
5. Record what you find.
6. Organize your research findings.

Identify Keywords That Describe Your Project

When identifying keywords describing your project, be open-minded about choosing terms, and broaden your thinking. Avoid narrowly defining your project, and eliminate any preconceived ideas or stereotypes you may have about libraries and what libraries traditionally do.

Bring together your grant team to develop a comprehensive list of keywords that describe your project. Think of broad, narrow, and related terms. Start with general words like "library," "libraries," "information," "technology," "computers," "network," "digitize," or "information." Then think of broad terms that describe the purpose of you project, like "unemployed," "students," "instruction," "seniors," "financial literacy," or "mobile lab." Give team members a few minutes to write down keywords on their own, to start. Then do a brainstorming activity or work in small groups to share their lists and generate more terms.

Incorporate keywords taken directly from the goals, objectives, outcomes, and activities of your project plan. It is helpful for each team member to have a copy of the project plan or project outline (see Chapter 3, p. 39, for a Technology Project Outline Example) for reference. Continue until you have compiled a thorough list of broad to narrow terms describing your project. Record all the keywords taken from your plan and identified by your team. Include all synonyms, alternate spellings, and multiple terms with similar meanings.

Decide Which Resources to Search

By now you should have a good idea about what resources you will use to find grants for your technology project or know how to find them. Don't limit yourself to resources that focus on libraries and technology. Remember, your project is about meeting a community need, not about acquiring library technology. As you identify resources, keep your vision broad while at the same time focusing on the purpose of your project. Include the large, general resources like Grants.gov, the *Foundation Directory*, and the *National Directory of Corporate Giving*, but also include library-specific and technology-specific resources like *Grants for Libraries and Information Services, Grants for Information Technology*, the *Big Book of Library Grant Money, Technology Grant News, Everything Technology: Directory of Technology Grants*, and the *Library Grants Blog*. Don't overlook other subject guides such as the *Grants for Arts, Culture & the Humanities* if your project involves art, a humanities program, or cultural performance; *Grants for People with Disabilities* or *Grants for the Aging* if your project will benefit people with disabilities or older community members; and your state or local grants directory. Remember to look for local or lesser-known specific subject-oriented funding resources that may help you in your search for a grant. Make a list of all the resources you know about where you might find grants to fund your project.

Translate Your Project Keywords

Find the resources you have listed, and spend some time examining each one to understand the unique terms used in that resource and how the resource defines the terms it uses. Definitions are usually included in a glossary, appendix, or user's guide. Online resources usually have "Help" or "FAQ" tabs where definitions and use of terms are covered. Be clear on how a resource defines different kinds of grants, and use their terms to narrow your search in that particular resource. Because there is no common thesaurus that is used across all grant directories and databases, you will need to translate your terms for each resource to do your research effectively.

When funders issue a call for proposals or resources index directories or databases, or describe their entries, they do not use a subject heading system or controlled vocabulary. For example, the terms "jobless" and "laid off workers" may not be descriptors in one resource, but the terms "unemployed" and "displaced workers" are used instead. In another resource, the reverse might be true. "Computer training" could be used in one resource and "online classes" used in another to mean the same thing. In another resource both terms could be used, having entirely different meanings.

Start with a Broad Search

Using the keywords and descriptors unique to each resource, first do your broad research in all the general resources appropriate for your project, such as national directories and grants databases for government, foundation, corporate, and local funders. The idea is to begin by casting a wide net to see the scope of funding opportunities that are available for projects like yours. Your broad search results will help you know where to go next with your research (see Rule #16).

> **Rule #16**
> Begin by searching broadly. Your broad search results will guide you in narrowing your search to eventually pinpoint the right grant for your project.

Start with the broad terms identified in the previous step. Be careful about using terms like "library," "libraries," "computers," and "technology" in your broad search. Instead, first try terms that broadly describe the purpose of your project.

Grant directory and database entries are extracted from information provided by the funders. Funders are focused on attracting grant applicants who will address their priorities or meet community needs that are of greatest interest to them. They are usually not focused on the organizations that might apply (for example, libraries) or how applicants might address their priorities (for example, using computers or technology). For instance, an RFP for projects that assist unemployed people may not include the term "libraries" if the funder has not considered libraries as potential applicants. This does not mean that the funder is not interested in proposals from libraries. A funder that is open to a wide range of creative ideas may make a conscious decision not to limit applications to proposals for technology projects. In a case like this, the term "technology" will not appear in the directory or database entry for this grant opportunity, and you will not find it using the keyword "technology." Narrowing your search to library technology grants right away could limit your search, eliminating all kinds of grant opportunities.

Remember, the fact that you plan to use technology to implement your library project may be of little interest to the funder. Funders are more interested in how your project will meet a need among the people you serve than they are about how you are going to meet it. Exceptions are funders that are interested only in funding library technology projects or funders that just want to buy or donate technology to an organization.

Narrow Your Search

To narrow your search, you will use more specific resources such as databases, local directories, and subject directories. Databases allow you to combine multiple fields in one search, and they often will provide more in-depth information about targeted funding sources. Make yourself aware of what is available in the various resources you are using, and take full advantage of the information provided.

Local funding directories list funders that limit their grant giving to your geographic area, as well as local corporate giving programs and small corporate grants that may not appear in the national directories. Likewise, subject directories may include funding sources just right for your project that because of their size may not be included in the national directories. As you narrow your search, you will begin to see some real funding possibilities. This part of your research can be time-consuming; however, this is an important part where you will find the right funder for your project.

As you examine the funder entries in the research resources, compare your project keywords with a potential funder's purpose, field of interest or focus, and the type of support it gives. Make a decision about whether or not a funder is a good match based on how relevant the information in the entries is to your project.

Record What You Find

When you find a funder that looks like a good match for your project, record the information about the funder on a worksheet. The Foundation Center's Prospect Worksheet (http://foundationcenter.org/findfunders/wrksheet/prospect_worksheet.pdf) is an example of a worksheet for institutional funders (see also the Funder Worksheet, p. 96). Don't scrutinize too much at this point. You simply want to record what you find about funders that look like good prospects so that you don't lose track of a funder or forget where you found it. If you record information about funders consistently while you do your research, when you finish, you will have a stack of worksheets full of information about a number of likely funders. The worksheets are your research notes, providing the information you need to move ahead.

Organize Your Research

Now look through your funder worksheets and prioritize them. If you determine that some are definitely not good matches, file them away. They were close enough for you to start a worksheet, and they may be right for a future project. If you have questions on some, or need further clarification on whether or not a funder may be interested in a project like yours, contact the funder. By now you are very familiar with the foundation, agency, or corporation; therefore, you will be asking intelligent, informed questions. Use this initial contact to develop a rapport with the contact person. Contacts are usually happy to answer your questions and work with you, and they will be pleasantly surprised at how much you already know from the research you have done. After this contact, you will know more about whether or not the funder is a likely match.

Funder Worksheet

Funder Name:	
Funder Address:	
Contact Name:	Contact's e-mail address:
Contact's Phone #:	Website address:

Funding Record

Amount funder gave last year/average amount:

Number of grants given last year:

Organizations/projects funded last year:

Interests and Priorities

Purpose/mission:

Funder's interests/priorities:

Who/what is eligible for funding?

Who/what is ineligible?

Geographic limitations:

Application

Application Format: ____ Form Proposal ____ Online Proposal ____ Full Proposal ____ Letter Proposal

Deadline:	Application URL:

Resources

Directories/indexes/guides used (include page #):

Databases used (include search strategies):

Newsletter/alert services/discussion group (include date):

Website addresses:

990 Forms (include years):

Annual reports (include years):

Keep additional notes on the back of this page.

Writing Successful Technology Grant Proposals: A LITA Guide, by Pamela H. MacKellar.
© 2012 Library Information and Technology Association, a division of the American Library Association.

96

Separate the highest priority worksheets into a "yes" pile. These are the funders you will approach for a grant. Then start a separate file for each funder. Here you will keep the worksheet, a record of contacts, phone notes, correspondence, more information about the funder, and grant announcements.

The kind of library and the nature of the community need your project addresses will determine the course of your research. Here is an overview of how to search several resources to get you started. You must decide which ones are appropriate for finding a grant to fund your technology project.

Searching Federal Government Websites

Searching Grants.gov

Grants.gov (http://www.grants.gov/) includes all discretionary grants offered by the 26 federal grant-making agencies, and it is the best place to start your search for federal grants awarded directly to community agencies and organizations, schools, and libraries. Go to the main Grants.gov page and click on "Find Grant Opportunities" in the left margin to see the search options (see Figure 7.1). Here you can select:

- Basic Search
- Browse by Category
- Browse by Agency

- Advanced Search
- Find Recovery Act Opportunities

To do a basic search, click on "Basic Search." From the Basic Search page, you may do a Basic Keyword Search or find a grant using its Funding Opportunity Number (FON) or *Catalog of Federal Domestic Assistance* (*CFDA*) number. The Basic Search option searches grant titles only and returns grants that are open and closed and those for which the deadline has passed. In the search box, spaces default to OR,

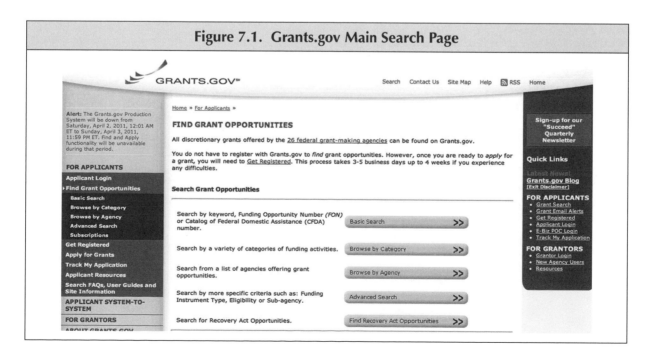

Figure 7.1. Grants.gov Main Search Page

and there is no Boolean searching option. Use the Grants.gov Basic Search if you know the title of a grant or the FON or *CFDA* number.

For better results, try the other Grants.gov search options, Browse by Category (see Figure 7.2), Browse by Agency (see Figure 7.3), Advanced Search (see Figure 7.4),

Figure 7.2. Grants.gov Browse by Category Page

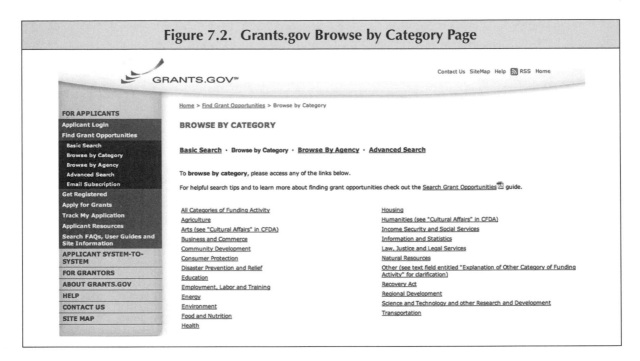

Figure 7.3. Grants.gov Browse by Agency Page

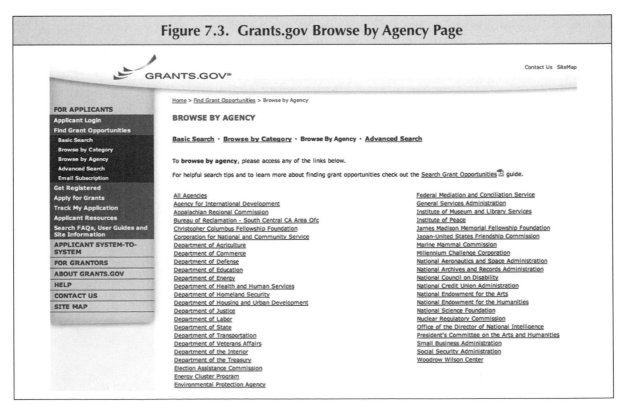

and Recovery Act Opportunities. When you browse by agency, look at all appropriate federal government agencies that fund libraries, clearinghouses, archives, and technical information services mentioned in Chapter 5. When you browse by category, think about the community need your project will address.

To narrow your search on Grants.gov, use the "Advanced Search" option (see Figure 7.4). Here you can combine multiple fields such as title keywords, dates, funding activity categories, funding instrument types, eligibility, agencies, and subagencies. Using the advanced search, you can limit your search to "Open Opportunities," which is a big advantage when you are narrowing your results to current grant opportunities. This will eliminate all closed programs and grants for which the deadline has passed. The Keyword Search box will search only words in the title.

Figure 7.4. Grants.gov Advanced Search Page

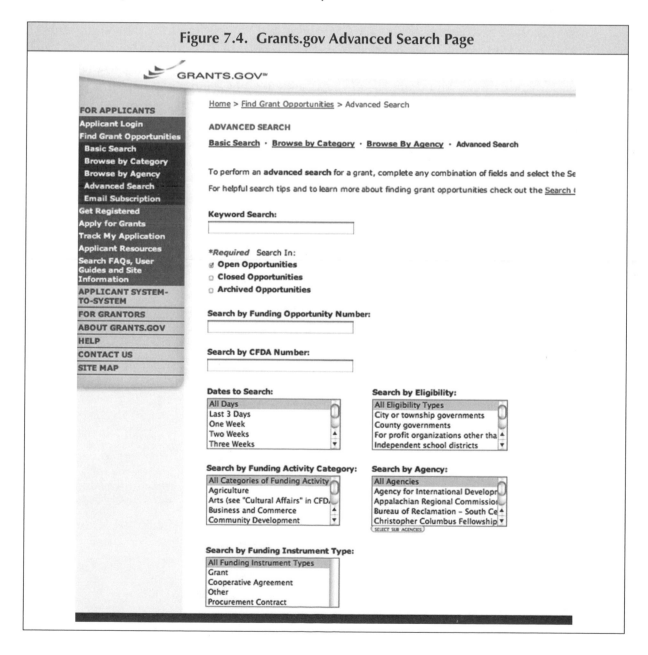

For help with searching Grants.gov, click on "Search Grant Opportunities" for a guide downloadable from the Basic Search page and the Advanced Search page.

Searching the *Federal Register*

To search the *Federal Register* (http://www.gpo.gov/fdsys/), go to the FDsys (Federal Digital System) homepage (see Figure 7.5) and click on "Advanced Search" next to the "Search Government Publications" box.

From the Advanced Search page (see Figure 7.6) select the dates you want to search; select *Federal Register* from the "Available Collections" dropdown menu and add it to the "Selected Collections" box; and select "Full-Text of Publications and Metadata" in the "Search In" box. You can add up to five additional search criteria when narrowing your search. Boolean searching is supported. Remember to limit your results to "Notices of Funding Availability and Solicitations for Grant Applications." Click on "Help" for more details about searching the *Federal Register*.

Remember that you are starting with a broad search, so your results may require major sifting. You don't want to miss something by conducting a narrow search too soon. The extra work up front is sometimes worth it in the long run. If your broad search yields an overwhelming amount of results, slowly begin to narrow your search with additional keywords until your results list is manageable (see Figure 7.7).

When you click on an entry in the *Federal Register* search results, you will go straight to the corresponding announcement in the *Federal Register*. Notices include complete information about a grant, including eligibility information, priorities, application and submission information, application review information, definitions, and who to contact if you have questions.

Figure 7.5. FDsys Homepage

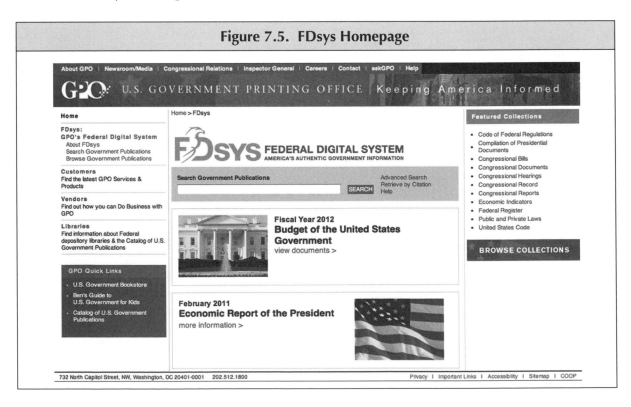

Figure 7.6. FDsys Government Publications Advanced Search Page

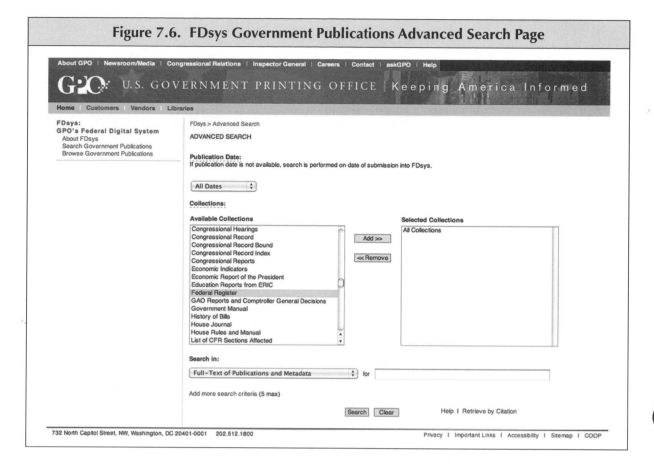

Figure 7.7. *Federal Register* Results Page

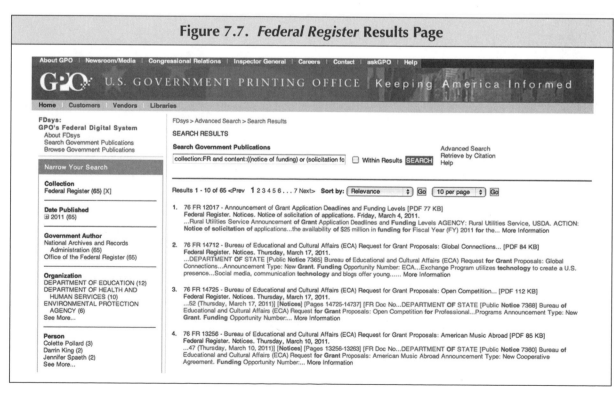

Figure 7.8. *CFDA* Main Page

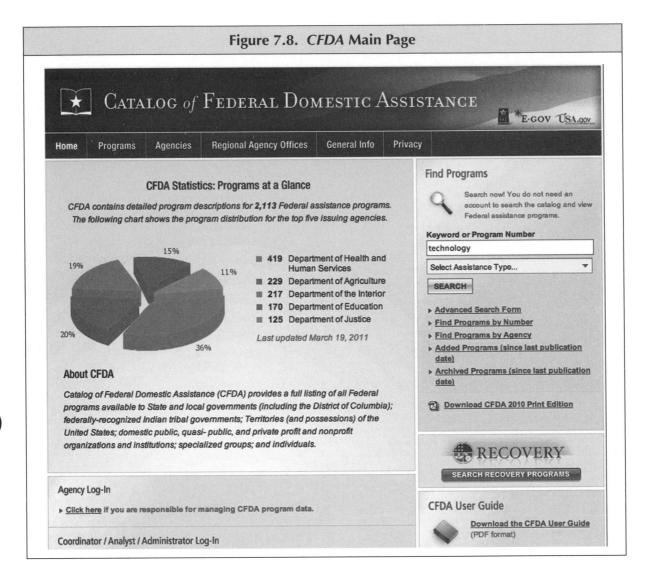

Searching the *Catalog of Federal Domestic Assistance*

There are many ways to navigate the *CFDA* website (http://www.cfda.gov/). One way is from the "Find Programs" box in the upper right of the main page (see Figure 7.8) where you can enter keywords and combine them with "Assistance Type," find programs by number, or find programs by agency.

The *CFDA*'s Advanced Search (see Figure 7.9) is an especially powerful tool, providing numerous search fields with many options to help you narrow your search. Full-text keyword searching supported by Boolean operators is available. See the "Keyword Search Tips" for detailed assistance.

Remember that the *CFDA* contains all federal grant programs whether or not they are active. You will be able to research federal programs and what agencies fund projects like yours on the *CFDA* site; however, to find out if a grant is currently available you must go directly to an agency's website.

The *CFDA* site is an excellent place to get an overall "big picture" view of federally funded grant programs in your area of interest. If you see a potential match that is not

Figure 7.9. *CFDA* Advanced Search Page

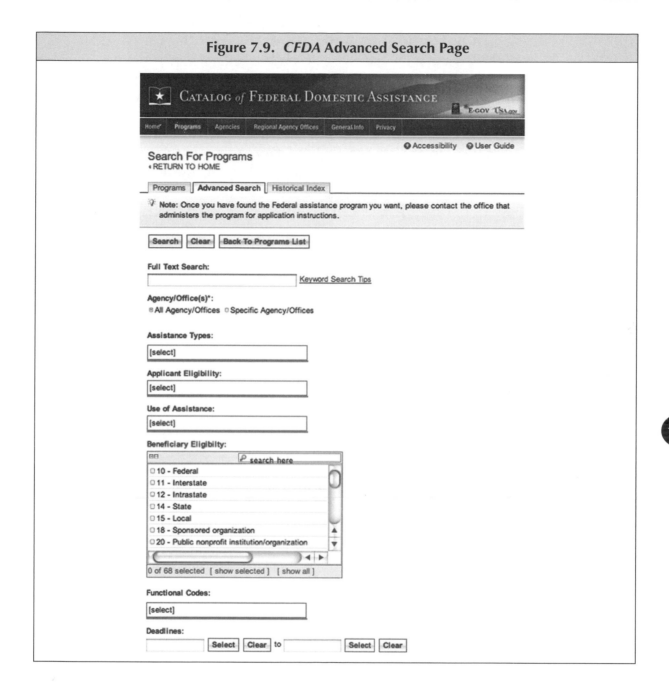

an active grant program, you can watch for an announcement in the *Federal Register* or periodically revisit the agency's website for new grant announcements. If you find a grant match that is active, complete a worksheet with information about the agency and grant.

At the *CFDA* website you can search for formula grants, which are grants that funnel funds through state agencies. If you see a potential formula grant opportunity, follow up by contacting your state agency to inquire about applying for these funds. Using the Advanced Search form you can narrow your search by functional area, agency, subagency, applicant eligibility, beneficiary eligibility, deadlines, type of assistance, and more.

Researching Foundation and Corporate Grants

Any of the large general foundation or corporate grant directories mentioned in Chapter 6 is a good place to start your broad search for foundation and corporate grants: *Annual Register of Grant Support*, *Foundation Grants Index*, and the *National Directory of Corporate Giving*, for example. Narrow your search by referring to more specialized directories like *Foundation Grants for Preservation in Libraries, Archives, and Museums*; *Grants for Libraries and Information Services*; *The Big Book of Grant Money*; and *Everything Technology* or to specialized subject directories.

Once you identify possible funders, you can find more in-depth information about particular foundations by referring to the *Foundation Directory* and the *Foundation 1000*. For even more detailed information about a foundation's finances, the grants it gives, and who serves as board members, Form 990s are a great source.

A nonprofit legally established in any state must obtain recognition as a charitable organization from the IRS so that contributions can be tax deductible. Most foundations apply for this 501(c)(3) status. The IRS requires foundations to make their information available by filing a Form 990. Form 990s for foundations and community foundations can be searched at the Foundation Center's 990 Finder (http://tfcny.fdncenter.org/990s/990search/esearch.php). GuideStar (http://www .guidestar.org/) also provides Form 990s for many tax-exempt organizations.

Foundation websites are excellent sources of current information about a foundation, including its mission, what it is interested in funding, upcoming deadlines, application guidelines, recently funded projects, and contact information. You can find links to foundations by searching for a foundation at The Foundation Center's main page (http://foundationcenter.org/).

Many major corporations have created their own foundations and corporate giving programs. This is a good starting place for researching corporate grants as well as the corporations' websites. In general, corporations give to organizations in communities in which they operate. Go to the corporation's main webpage, and look for a link containing the word "Community," such as Community Involvement, Community Giving, or Community Outreach. Click on this link to find information about grants the corporation awards to community organizations. One example of a corporation that gives to communities is Best Buy (see Figure 7.10). For more information on a local corporation, contact the corporation directly or visit your community foundation.

Each corporate site is arranged a little differently, so you may need to explore a little to get to the information you need. If you have questions, contact the corporation's community outreach office. They are usually happy to talk to you about what they fund and where to find additional information.

Visit your local community foundation and ask to see the information it has about corporations in your area that fund local projects. You may find annual reports or other compilations that include descriptions of the corporation's granting interests and grant-making history. Check local funding directories for your state or geographical region for more corporate funding opportunities.

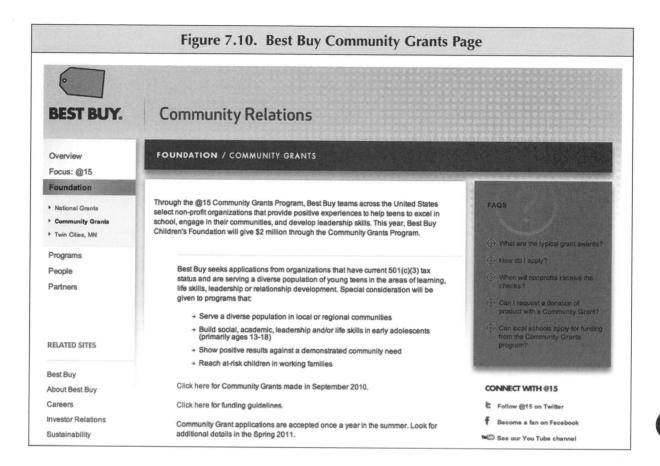

Figure 7.10. Best Buy Community Grants Page

Researching Local Grants

It is very possible that there are many local grant opportunities that you will not find while you are researching the national directories, websites, periodicals, and newsletters. Local research requires legwork, phone calls, networking, relationship building, and marketing your project idea. Here are some places for you to start your local research.

State Agencies and Departments

Check regularly with state agencies and departments for current grant opportunities.

- State Library Agency: To find out if your state library offers LSTA subgrants, state grants-in-aid, or other funding or state resources, check on their websites (http://www.publiclibraries.com/state_library.htm); many provide applications online, and some also offer free grant workshops.
- State Humanities Councils: http://www.neh.gov/whoweare/statecouncils.html.
- State Arts Councils: http://www.nasaa-arts.org/aoa/saaweb.shtml.
- State Departments of Education: http://wdcrobcolp01.ed.gov/Programs/EROD/org_list.cfm?category_ID=SEA.

State and Local Funding Directories

Find your local or state funding directory at http://fdncenter.org/getstarted/topical/sl_dir.html. State libraries and college and university libraries generally provide these types of funding directories and research tools.

Community Foundations

Visit your local community foundation to use its library or collection of information on local corporations and foundations. Talk to the people at your community foundation about appropriate funding sources for your project idea. Their business is to match funders with organizations like yours. You can locate your local community foundations at http://www.cof.org/whoweserve/community/resources/index.cfm?navItemNumber =15626#locator. Visit your community foundation's website for grant opportunity announcements and application guidelines. Subscribe to their RSS feed.

Local Clubs, Agencies, and Organizations

Talk to friends and contacts who are associated with local agencies and organizations that may fund projects like yours. Visit with your Chamber of Commerce and local clubs to tell them about your project. Look at a local corporation or foundation's website for detailed information about its community involvement. Talk to local banks and stores to find out if they have giving programs. Ask your board for help in connecting with potential funders in your community. Watch the local newspaper for articles about grants (see Figure 7.11) given to other nonprofits in your community, and follow up with the funders. Join your local chapter of the Association of Fundraising Professionals (http://www.afpnet.org/international.cfm?folder_id=873).

Research your local community directory, and refer to Michigan State University's list of service clubs and civic organizations that provide funding (http://www.lib.msu.edu/harris23/grants/servicec.htm). Your yellow pages, library board or friends, and staff may also help identify local clubs and organizations that provide funding. The best way to find out about these opportunities is through local websites or by contacting the associations directly.

Professional Associations

Regularly check your professional associations' websites for grant funding that is available for members. Join their electronic discussion groups.

Talking with Funders

Throughout your research, you will be contacting funders to clarify your questions and to discuss their possible interest in your project (see Rule #17). Remember that funders are people, too, and grant work involves building relationships with them. At this point in your research, you should feel comfortable calling any of the contacts on your "match" list should questions or concerns arise.

> **Rule #17**
> Developing working relationships with potential funders is part of the grant process.

Keeping Your Research Current

An important part of your research is staying up-to-date with new grant opportunities. You can do this by reading blogs, subscribing to RSS feeds, e-mail notification services and electronic newsletters, reading periodicals, and participating in electronic discussion groups.

Figure 7.11. Advertisement in Local Newspaper

Kiwanis Club of Corrales has Grant Funds Available for local Charities and Non-Profits

Your Kiwanis Club through its Charitable Foundation supports local charities and non-profit organizations.

All type of registered organizations are eligible, but our emphasis is to continue work with groups that support children and youth in our community.

Funds are available as a result of Kiwanis' ongoing fund raising projects including the Harvest Festival.

Recent organizations that have benefitted from our grants include: Music In Schools and various special programs at Corrales Elementary, Corrales Senior Center, D.A.R.E. (Drug Abuse Resistance Education), CARMA and other community, animal and environmental groups.

For full details and Grant Applications email: info@kiwanis-corrales.org

The Kiwanis Club of Corrales Charitable Foundation

from the *Corrales Comment*, vol. XXX, no. 3, March 19, 2011. p.8.

E-mail Notification Services and RSS Feeds

Grants.gov

At Grants.gov you can receive notifications of new grant opportunity postings and updates by subscribing to various RSS feeds (http://www.grants.gov/help/rss.jsp) or e-mail notification services (http://www.grants.gov/applicants/email_subscription.jsp). You can subscribe to Grants.gov RSS feeds for:

- New Opportunities by Agency
- New Opportunities by Category
- Modified Opportunities by Agency
- Modified Opportunities by Category

Grants.gov e-mail notification services (http://www.grants.gov/applicants/email_ subscription.jsp) include the following:

- All Grants Notices sends you e-mail notifications of all new grant opportunities.
- Grants.gov Updates sends you updated information about critical issues, new tips, and other updates.
- Notices Based on Advanced Criteria sends you e-mail notifications based on specific criteria such as funding instrument type, eligibility, or subagency.
- Notices Based on Funding Opportunity Number sends you notifications based on Funding Opportunity Numbers (FON). A FON is a number that a federal agency assigns to its grant announcement.

Library Grants Blog
See Chapter 6 for more information about this resource.

Your Organization's Grants and Contracts or Research Office
If you work for a municipality, school district, academic institution, or large organization, investigate grants alert opportunities through your grants and contracts or research office. Subscription databases that offer RSS feeds may include IRIS, InfoEd SPIN, ResearchResearch, GrantSelect, GrantWire, or GrantAdvisor Plus.

RFP Bulletin
See Chapter 6 for information about this resource.

Newsletters and Periodicals
Read newsletters and periodicals from local nonprofit agencies, your state library, state library association, local public library association, or special library association chapter for announcements of recently funded library projects in your area. Contact your colleagues at these libraries, and ask how they found their success, about their project, about the grant process, and whom they worked with at the funding source. See Chapter 6 for detailed information about the following resources:

- *Arts Funding Watch*
- *Centered*
- *Chronicle of Philanthropy*
- *Education Funding Watch*
- *Grants for Libraries E-news Alerts*
- *Philanthropy News Digest (PND)*
- *Primary Source*
- *Private Grants Alert*
- *RFP Alert*
- *TGCI Federal Register Grant Announcements*
- *Technology Grant News*

Electronic Discussion Groups
Charity Channel Forums (http://www.charitychannel.com/) are online discussion groups where nonprofit professionals join discussions on topics related to funding and other nonprofit issues. There is an annual subscription fee.

Summary
You have completed your grant research when you have identified grants that support the goals, objectives, and outcomes of your technology project. You are on the right

track if you have found one or more grant opportunities with a purpose that coincides with your project's purpose and whose funders' priorities match your library's mission and vision (see Research Tips).

Keep your research findings close at hand and stay up-to-date with funding trends and the priorities of funders that typically fund projects like those your library is planning. You have done the hard work of building a solid foundation of grant research that you can use in the future to continue your search for library funding opportunities. The next time around you will have a better understanding of the sources, resources, and research process. Use these skills to help your library fund and implement projects that will make a difference for the people you serve.

> **Research Tips**
> - Let everyone know that you are seeking funding, and tell them about your project idea. Tell library staff, board members, the city council, other department heads, corporate employees, colleagues, family and friends, and local business leaders. You never know who might be on a foundation's board or know someone who is a board member for a foundation that has just the right funding for your project.
> - Read publications like newsletters, journals, and local newspapers for funding opportunities.
> - Subscribe to the *Library Grants Blog* (http://librarygrants.blogspot.com/) RSS feed.
> - Subscribe to other grant-related RSS feeds and electronic discussion groups.
> - Contact other libraries in your area that have received grants for technology and other kinds of projects.
> - Talk with potential funders about their interests and priorities. Let them know about your project idea.

Additional Resources

New, Cheryl Carter. 1998. *Grantseeker's Toolkit: A Comprehensive Guide to Finding Funding.* New York: John Wiley.

Peterson, Susan Lee. 2001. *The Grantwriter's Internet Companion: A Resource for Educators and Others Seeking Grants and Funding.* San Francisco: Jossey-Bass.

Schladweiler, Kier, ed. 2001. *The Foundation Center's Guide to Grantseeking on the Web.* New York: The Foundation Center.

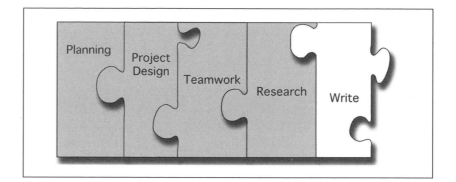

Chapter 8

Writing and Submitting Your Proposal

You're probably saying to yourself, "Finally, we're going to learn about writing grants." As you can see by now, proposal writing is not the first step in the grant process. One of the main points of this book is to help you understand that first you must make the commitment, then plan and design technology projects, form a team, understand the sources and resources for technology grants, do the research, and select a grant that is appropriate for the technology project you want to fund. Only when you have completed these steps are you ready to begin writing the grant proposal.

If there is one thing you learn from this book, I hope it is that grant work does not start with writing a proposal. This is a common error, and it is the reason why many proposals are rejected. When you begin by writing a proposal you are focused primarily on getting the money, not on meeting the needs of the people you serve. Funders can see this a mile away. If funders perceive that you are interested in the money or technology more than helping the people you serve, this tells them that your priorities don't match theirs. Funders want to meet needs first. This is their main concern. If the needs your project will meet match their interests, then they will consider granting you the funds for that purpose. If your main purpose is to get the money or buy technology, they will lose interest in your proposal as soon as they figure this out. If you approach grant work from the perspective of meeting needs you will have more success.

Common Core Proposal Components

A funder wants to find out about your library, the people you serve, and your project; how the project will help people in your community; and whether or not your priorities are a good match for theirs. Not all proposals will have the same components, nor will the components have identical criteria; however, it is important to be aware of some common core proposal components that you will need to write and know what a funder expects to see in each one. A funder may call the components by different names, they may list specific information for you to include in each one, or they may combine two or three components into one. You must read the grant application guidelines very carefully to determine how to name each section, what to include in each one, and how to organize your proposal components according to a funder's specific application requirements for a particular grant. Following are brief descriptions of some common core proposal components you can expect to write or prepare:

Executive Summary

This condensed version of your proposal is usually about one page long. It comprises a synopsis of each major proposal component and should address the project's goal, its objectives and outcomes, the need the project fills and how it matches with the funder's priorities, the scope of work and who will do the work, how success will be measured, what is the project budget and how much you are requesting, what type of grant you are seeking, and how your organization is qualified to implement the project. This is where you sell your idea and make your points succinctly. The executive summary stands alone and makes every aspect of your proposal immediately clear to the funder. Often funders decide whether or not to continue reading your proposal depending on the executive summary.

Abstract

Sometimes a funder requests an abstract rather than an executive summary. Abstracts are usually shorter than one page and serve as an overview of the proposal to give the reviewers an idea of what they will find in the full proposal. Abstracts can be challenging to write, because you are trying to convince the reader of the project's importance in a small amount of space. This can also be called a "summary." Executive summaries and abstracts should be written after the proposal has been entirely written. By that time you have thoroughly thought through the project design and worked out any unexpected wrinkles. Only after you have written about every detail of the project will you be able to effectively write a "short version" or summary of the proposal.

Library Profile

This component usually appears at the beginning of a proposal and introduces the funding agency to the grant applicant. This is where you describe your library, focusing on the mission and strengths of your organization. Detail your library's history, mission, vision, who you serve, your achievements and qualifications, your leadership, key library staff and their talents, your primary programs and services, supportive statistical information, current budget, and board members. Pay special attention to the current state of your library's technology, and specifically address any aspects of technology that play a role in your project design. Outline your library's technology plan, stressing the part of your plan that is addressed by the project you are proposing. If your library is part of a larger organization, relate your library's technology plan and how it supports the larger organization's technology plan. Mention any partnerships or collaborations with local, regional, and statewide partners. The library profile can usually be used in multiple grant applications with only minor adjustments and updates. It must be customized to each funder so that it speaks to their interests and priorities. This is one of the easiest parts of a proposal to write, because the information already exists in brochures, plans, marketing materials, and other places, including the institutional memory of administrators and staff.

Organizational Overview

This section describes the larger organization if your library operates as part of a municipality, college or university, school, hospital, or corporation, for instance. Address your organization's mission, vision, and technology plans, including the role of the library within the organization. It is important to address the organization's capacity to support you in carrying out the proposed project and that the organization is a capable and credible one. Describe any technology projects the organization has implemented recently, and specify how the organization will support the proposed project. There is not always an organizational overview section. It may be part of the library profile, or a grant application could require an organizational capacity component instead. This section, combined with the library profile, introduces your organization to the funder and demonstrates your ability to implement a successful project.

Community Profile

A community profile describes the "community" or people the library serves. Paint a picture of these people using data about students, faculty, and staff in your school or academic institution; employees or researchers in your corporation; your geographic location; census information; current population trends; and current events or trends affecting the people you serve. Pay special attention to the target population your proposed project will serve. The community profile is sometimes part of the statement of need.

Statement of Need

The statement of need identifies the specific needs in your community that your library project will address. It includes facts, data, and information from the community needs assessment and community profile that justify these needs. Focus on the specific need your project will address, and explain why the library has decided to meet that need by referring to the library's mission, vision, goals, and objectives, as well as to relevant information from the community profile. This is also called a "need statement."

Project Description

A project description describes the nuts and bolts of the project, explaining how you are going to meet the goals and objectives. Explain your approach or methodology by relating community needs to project goals and objectives and to how project activities will achieve specific outcomes for the people you serve. Identify staff who will do project activities, when they will do them, and required materials, equipment, and supplies. Explain how the project will be supervised and managed and the roles and responsibilities of project partners. Include a sustainability plan. Sometimes this component is called an "approach" or "methodology."

Timeline

The timeline explains when each activity you have proposed will be conducted and by whom. Often the timeline is presented in a chart or table format, presenting the project at-a-glance. The timeline helps keep track of the project's progress and reflects who is responsible for accomplishing each task within a timeframe.

Budget

A budget shows the cost of your project by including the sum of all expenses in a line-item format, including personnel, consultants, materials and supplies, rent, equipment, administrative costs, communication costs, and travel costs, for instance. Often budgets are in two parts: personnel and non-personnel. Budgets reflect match and in-kind contributions and indirect costs required of large organizations and most academic institutions.

Evaluation Plan

Evaluation plans explain how you will measure the success of your project and what tools you will use to determine the project's success. Often the evaluation plan articulates how the project may be adjusted or amended if anticipated results aren't transpiring.

Appendix

The appendix includes supporting documentation such as letters of support, memoranda of understanding, letters of agreement, a list of board members, résumés for key project staff, the library's plans, or the library's budget, for instance.

Different Kinds of Grant Proposals or Applications

Although most grant applications include some combination of the basic proposal components above, no two applications, proposal formats, or proposals are the same. The requirements of the funder and the specific grant opportunity are what determine the form your proposal will take. This means you must customize every proposal for the specific grant you are applying for and for the funder awarding the grant. It is essential to carefully read the application package or proposal guidelines before you begin writing and organizing your proposal. Skimming over instructions or ignoring details and the small print will only get you in trouble. The four basic kinds of proposals are described next.

Letter Proposals

A letter proposal is short, usually two to five pages long. Written in a letter format, it is primarily targeted to smaller private foundations and corporations—although some larger entities such as state or federal agencies may request a preproposal letter, inquiry letter, or letter of intent before you are invited to submit a full proposal. Writing pre-proposal letters, inquiry letters, letters of intent, and letter proposals is similar in the sense that you are writing a condensed version of your entire proposal in a letter format.

With many private funders, the letter proposal is all that is required. This means that they will make their funding decisions based on the letter alone. Some funders use the letter proposal as a screening tool and request a full proposal only if your idea interests them. It can be a real challenge to describe your community, organization, need, project, approach, timeline, budget, and evaluation plan all in a few pages. On the other hand, writing a letter proposal can be an exercise that helps you synthesize your thinking about your project into a clear, succinct, and manageable document. After going through this process you should be able to tell anyone all the important points about your project and convince them to fund it in a short amount of time. Reducing your proposal to a few pages will familiarize you with every detail of your project; so, if you need to write a full proposal for this project later, or you are invited to submit a full proposal based on your letter, it will be a much easier task after you have written a successful letter proposal.

Many small foundations, associations, clubs, and organizations requesting letter proposals have little or no professional staff to assist them in selecting projects to fund. Letter proposals in this case are a practical means by which they can reduce the volume of what they must evaluate while at the same time increasing their ability to consider more proposals. It is essential that you stay under the maximum page guidelines and refrain from including any attachments that have not been requested.

One advantage of the letter proposal is that it allows you to make a more personal connection with the reader, because the format encourages a one-on-one approach. Although writing a letter proposal takes discipline and persistence, it can be more enjoyable because it is more like letter writing—something that is generally more familiar, relaxed, and comfortable than proposal writing.

A successful letter proposal presents a strong case for your grant project and incorporates the essential information from all basic proposal components: library profile, organizational profile, community profile, statement of need, project description, timeline, budget, and evaluation plan. Don't leave anything out.

One way to organize a letter proposal is to break it down into seven basic sections of one to two sentences each:

1. **Summary:** Summarize the entire proposal by identifying your library, citing a brief mission statement or explaining your reason for existing, explaining what you want the funder to do, how much money you are requesting, and the major project outcomes.
2. **Funder Match:** Explain why you are approaching this particular funder based on your knowledge of its funding patterns and values and how its interests match the goals for your project.
3. **Need:** Summarize the current community need, identifying the gap between what is and what should be and how funding your project will bridge the gap or meet the needs of the people you serve.
4. **Solution:** Describe your project and how you plan to approach the problem by articulating your methodology; summarizing the project goals, objectives, outcomes, and activities; and detailing why your library is the one to do this project.
5. **Capabilities:** Establish your credentials by demonstrating your library's credibility, the viability of your project idea, the capability of the staff who will implement the project, the ability of your organization to support the project, and any partners or collaborators and resources you have.
6. **Budget:** Request a specific dollar amount, relating it to project outcomes so that the funder knows how people will benefit. Mention any match or in-kind funds and other grants you have applied for to fund this project.

7. **Conclusion:** Summarize what the requested funding will mean to your community, and provide a contact name and phone number.

(See Appendix A.1 for a Letter Proposal Example.)

Form Proposals

Form proposals are forms into which you insert all your proposal information. Often you will be able to find a required form online. Some proposal forms must be downloaded and completed offline, whereas others can be completed and submitted online. There are many ways that funders require forms in proposals. For instance, sometimes funders want you to use a form for the cover sheet to show the basic information about your project, such as your organization name, contact information, project name, and amount requested. The federal government requires you to use separate forms in your proposal for budgets and authorized signatures (see Appendix A.2 for a Form Application Example and Appendix A.5 for a Full Proposal Application Example).

Funders use forms as a means to ensure that they receive information from all applicants in a uniform way. This can make evaluating proposals easier, because funders know where they will find each proposal component. Also, they can compare a single component submitted by different applicants. This method can be fairer, because form proposals submitted by larger organizations cannot be easily distinguished from those submitted by smaller organizations. This tends to flatten the playing field.

As with letter proposals, your skill as a writer and the quality of your writing are put to the test with form proposals where space and formatting are restricted. You must do an impeccable writing job to make all your points while at the same time conforming to the restrictions of a form.

Many regional grant-maker associations provide standard or common application forms that sometimes consist of no more than a cover sheet, an outline for developing your proposal, and a budget form. The idea behind the Common Grant Application is to make it simpler for applicants to write a proposal as well as to make it easier for grant makers to review them.

Even though several funders may use the same Common Grant Application, you still must take care to customize your proposal for each funder. Individual funders will provide their own guidelines for completing the form proposal. Remember, you must carefully read the specific funder's guidelines to which you are applying before writing a proposal of any kind (see Appendix A.3 for a Common Grant Application Form).

Online Proposals

More and more funders are making it mandatory to submit grant applications online. For our purposes, online proposals are (1) forms that are submitted online and (2) proposals that are e-mailed to the funder. One advantage to online proposals is that you can submit them on the deadline date, thus eliminating the exciting part of grant work when you rush to the post office at the last minute (or to the airport to catch the last plane out in one of my experiences). With online proposals, there are no worries about paper, binding your proposal, stamps, certified mail, delivery confirmation, or overnight express delivery costs.

One disadvantage to online proposals is that it is much more difficult to make a personal appeal that stands out when presentation ceases to be a factor. Most online forms yield plain, unformatted text so that all the proposals look the same to a reviewer. Another disadvantage is that there are still bugs to work out in many online proposal submission interfaces, and this can be disastrous if you don't familiarize yourself with the limitations of a particular funder's online submission process well in advance of your grant deadline.

For instance, many federal agencies, including the Institute of Museum and Library Services (IMLS), require applicants to submit their proposals using Grants.gov. In order to apply for a grant using Grants.gov you must first register, which can take as long as four weeks. This takes some advance planning on the applicants' part. Also, it is not uncommon for applicants to have technical difficulty submitting applications via Grants.gov. If this happens to you, you must have some extra time before the grant deadline to communicate with the funding agency to arrange for submitting your proposal another way.

Online proposals are similar to other kinds of proposals in that your first step is to look over the entire application before beginning to write the proposal. Writing an online proposal goes more smoothly if you print the guidelines and any forms in advance. After reading them carefully, write your text in a word-processing program (see Rule #18). The writing process is the same as for other kinds of proposals. When you are ready to submit your proposal, copy and paste your text into the online form, having

> **Rule #18**
> Never enter your proposal directly into an online application form without a backup. Always prepare the proposal in a word-processing program first, and then copy and paste it into the form.

done the grammar and spell check in advance. This way the online submission itself is very simple. You will have a copy of your proposal in the word-processing program just in case the submission was interrupted or the funder didn't receive your proposal.

Online applications differ from each other. Some look almost identical to a printed form, and others are a series of questions, each followed by a blank text box for you to complete. These can be frustrating, because sometimes you cannot see the entire application form at once. Forms that require you to fill in all the blank boxes before you can advance to the next page keep you from getting an overview of the whole application up front. If possible, figure out a way to print a copy of the entire online application or request one from the funder before you start to write.

If you are required to e-mail your proposal to the funder, there is a possibility that you will have more control over the presentation. Make sure to check application guidelines for requirements and specifications, such as proposal components, font and font size, margins and spacing, page length, and file format, for instance. You must adhere to guidelines in e-mail applications, too (see Appendix A.4 for an Online Application Example).

Full Proposals

With a full proposal you have the most control over how you present your case to the funder. Although you must include all the elements as defined in the application guidelines, you can usually make some parts longer and others shorter. This means you can customize a full proposal for your project more than you can with other kinds of proposals.

Full proposals are often used for government grants, they can range from 15 to 100 pages, and they may contain numerous sections that require considerable detail. Full proposals may contain as many as 11 different components; however, they are usually designed to extract the same information contained in the core proposal components outlined above—only in a way that suits the funder's expectations. You may need to rearrange the components or take parts of one and combine it into others to answer the funder's questions adequately. If you have the core proposal components in place, your project design is solid and your approach logical, and you have demonstrated need and made your case—you have what you need, so don't get unsettled when guidelines for a full proposal look confusing or unfamiliar at first. Take some time to read the application instructions carefully, and you will see that you may simply need to rearrange or rename what you have already prepared. The fun in writing this kind of proposal is that it can be more creative than the standard format.

No matter what kind of proposal you are writing, funders are usually asking for the same basic information. They may use different wording or prefer a different order; they may limit you to the number of words you can use; they may ask for different attachments and supporting documents; different signatures may be required; or specified forms must be used. Once you have gone through the grant process and written one solid proposal for a project, writing subsequent proposals for that same project will be relatively easy (see Appendix A.5 for a Full Proposal Application Example).

The Proposal-Writing Process

Proposal writing is a major undertaking, best approached by dividing it into manageable components. When you write the proposal components in a logical order, you can build one section upon the last to make a case for funding your project. Starting with the community profile, library profile, and organizational profile and then proceeding to the need statement allows you to think about and analyze your community, library, organization, and community needs over a period of time. Time is required during this phase of writing to iron out all the wrinkles, answer any questions you may have, and brainstorm alternative approaches before you begin to write your project description, evaluation plan, timeline, and budget.

When you allow yourself the time to write a proposal this way, it is more likely to flow effortlessly from one section to the next and to be compelling for the reader. Here is a suggested process for writing proposals:

1. Gather information about the library, community, and needs to be addressed.
2. Outline what you want to say before you start to write.
3. List all the sections required in the format specified in the guidelines.
4. Develop a schedule for writing, reviewing, completing forms, and getting signatures.
5. Request letters of support or draft memoranda of understanding from partners.
6. Write a first draft.
7. Revise and edit.

8. Recruit an outside reader.
9. Complete the final edits.
10. Complete forms and get signatures.
11. Package the proposal and make copies.
12. Submit the proposal.

When you go through the preliminary steps of the grant process before you write a proposal, you will have already established a system for grant work and incorporated it into your daily work. With this system in place, it will take less time to gather the basic information and data and to write the core components. Grant seekers with efficient systems, and those who have already completed needs assessments, planning, and project development, are able to simplify and shorten the proposal-writing phase.

Proposal writers need to be able to write well. Central to writing well is understanding your audience and keeping them in mind as you write. You must tell the audience what they need to know and at the same time be cognizant of grammatical, structural, and stylistic aspects of writing. State your ideas and concepts clearly, using concise sentences and understandable words. Your proposal does not have more authority if you use bigger words—it has authority because you deeply understand your topic and you have confidence in your project. Grant reviewers are usually assigned to read many proposals, so the easier yours is to read and the more quickly they can grasp your concepts, the more positive their response is likely to be to your proposal. Good writing will not disguise a bad program, but bad writing can result in an unfunded project.

Although the order of the information requested in a grant application or the ways components are defined by funders may differ, you should be able to adapt the basic proposal components to any grant. Every proposal will be different, specific to a particular funder and grant. Before starting to write, read some examples of the kind of proposal you plan to write: letter, form, online, or full.

You may want to customize your community profile, library profile, or organizational profile to a particular grant and funder. Focus on aspects of your community, library, and organization that speak to the grant you are applying for and the interests of the funder. This will mean refining and focusing the information in any general profiles you already have on hand.

Write a first draft, and then revise, revise, revise. When you are blocked or you are groping for a word or phrase, leave a blank and keep writing. For instance, if you find that you need more data as you write the need statement, weigh carefully whether to abandon the writing at this point to chase numbers. It may be better to keep writing for the moment and then go after the data on another day. Writing—even proposal writing—is a creative process. If you stop writing suddenly to attend to a task that uses a different part of your brain, it is unlikely that you'll be able to pick it up where you left off.

Set aside some generous blocks of time for writing. Don't try to write a proposal in between reference questions or otherwise fit it in sideways alongside all your other librarian duties. Librarians do many tasks of different kinds throughout the day, sometimes all at once. Draw the line at proposal writing, and give it the time and space it requires. If you are required to write proposals as part of your job, make it clear to your supervisor that you must be given the time for the grant process, including writing proposals.

Don't try to write an entire proposal in one sitting or in a few days. Allow plenty of time to flex, tweak, or adjust the project as you work. Sometimes, it is as you write and think through the logic that you discover inconsistencies. As long as the basic goals remain the same and the community needs are being met, consider your project as a living organism. Always check in with other team members, leadership, or administration if you see where to improve a project design as you write or if changes must be made to fill in some gaps.

Don't write by committee. Do have others read your proposal for clarity and accuracy; however, sending the proposal to committee members for editing or input can turn into a fiasco. One person must be responsible for writing the proposal and making the final decisions.

Do not send the same proposal to several different funders. This practice usually results in rejected applications. Customize your proposal to a particular funder's priorities.

The Nature of Proposal Writing

Regardless of the kind of proposal you are writing, proposals change as you work on them and develop or refine your ideas. Think of your proposal as a living, organic document. You will keep working on all your proposal components until the proposal is finished. Because the components all relate to each other, making an adjustment in one component usually means adjusting another one or more. For instance, after you write the need statement, you must revisit the library profile and community profile to fine-tune them so they support what you have developed in the need statement. After you write the project description, you will probably need to go back to the need statement (and maybe even the profiles, too) to tighten them up so they lead seamlessly to the project description. You want the proposal elements to flow easily from one right into the next. Together they must make logical sense and effortlessly build your case when read by reviewers. Proposals must be "easy reads." The information you are conveying must be cohesive and free of conflicting ideas or irrelevant concepts. You want reviewers to read your proposal and say, "That makes sense!" Reviewers who must flip back and forth through your proposal to make sense of it will eventually lose interest.

The nature of developing a need statement and project description usually involves more creativity than writing the community profile and library profile. As you develop your proposal, it is natural for new approaches or ideas to occur to you. To include these innovative elements, you must continue to work the entire proposal, from beginning to end, constantly moving through it to make sure all the parts together continue to make sense. Keeping your proposal consistent by linking one component to the next while at the same time inserting new ways of thinking can be challenging and fun. At the same time, managing this living document requires all your best writing and thinking skills. Persistence and patience will come in handy for this part of the proposal-writing process.

Follow Application Guidelines

You must read the application guidelines very carefully to determine the funder's definitions. Then adhere to their definitions (see Rule #7, p. 10). Sometimes funders use examples in their guidelines. Follow their examples, organize your components according to their definitions, and use their language for the purposes of submitting a proposal to that funder. Proposal writers who fail to recognize the difference in how funders define terms may be unsuccessful because they present the information incorrectly.

Writing the Library Profile

When you write a proposal you are building a case for why a funder should fund your technology project over all the others applying for the same grant. By starting with the library profile you set the stage or paint a background for your proposal. This component usually appears near the beginning of your proposal, and it is one of the easiest to write. A skillful and concise introduction to your library is especially important. The library profile introduces the funder to your library, and it also introduces the funder to your writing. The clarity of your writing and your skill in describing your organization will set the tone for your proposal and give the funder an idea of what is yet to come. This is your first opportunity to draw the reader into your story.

A library profile may already be written for your library. Because profiles are often needed for marketing purposes or for reports to your larger organization or the state, librarians keep them updated and ready to go. If you don't already have a library profile, you can usually find the information you need to write one pretty easily. A library profile will usually suffice on its own; however, if your library is part of a larger organization—such as a college or university library, association or museum library, or library that serves a nonprofit or school—an organizational profile of the larger organization and the role the library plays within the organization will give the funder a broader overview of your situation. Consider including an organizational profile in your proposal in addition to a library profile if describing your larger organization will lend credibility to your project or help define the people you serve. It is important to show that your larger organization supports you in implementing the proposed project.

Funders want to know about your library and why you are the best organization to implement your project. In the library profile tell them about your library's history and its development into the vital community information center that it is today. Mention your library's mission, vision, and goals to assure the funder that your organization fits with theirs. Highlight your achievements, primary programs, current budget, leadership, key staff members, and partners. Including numbers of people you serve broken down by age and other demographics can be compelling depending on your community and your project. If your library partners with other libraries, organizations, departments, or agencies, mention your partnerships and the projects where you partner and their role in providing library services and programs.

Take some time to adjust or customize your existing library profile so it relates to your project idea and the rest of your proposal. For instance, if you have implemented successful projects in the past like the one you are proposing, mention them here and document the difference they made for people in your community. Write a little more

121

about these programs and a little less about library programs and services that do not relate to the project you are proposing.

LIBRARY PROFILE EXAMPLE
Wonder Public Library
Wonder, New Mexico

- Library serves a community of approximately 7,300.
- Library is located in the Village of Wonder, Enchanted County, New Mexico.
- Library receives $50,000 annually from the Village of Wonder.
- Downturn in economy has meant recent budget cuts for Library.
- About 20 percent of community uses Library.
- Friends Group holds book sales to support children's programming.

History:
- Original building was built on Village land almost entirely by volunteers in 1979.
- Addition that now houses Children's Room was completed in 1993.
- In 2001, another addition provided a study area, computer lab, and office space.
- Latest addition, completed in May 2006, created a Young Adult Room.
- Additions were funded primarily by state and county funding and county bonds.

Staff:
- Library has one full-time director, one full-time children's librarian, and two part-time assistants.
- More than 60 volunteers keep the Wonder Public Library operating.
- Director and two staff members are certified by the New Mexico State Library.
- No professional development funds are received.

Collections:
- Adult circulating collection has approximately 10,000 items.
- Children's and Young Adult circulating collections have approximately 20,000 items.
- All Reference collections combined have approximately 1,000 items.
- Library has 65 popular magazine and five newspaper subscriptions.
- Approximately 75 percent of the library's collection is donations.
- Approximately 80 percent of collection is more than 25 years old.

Databases:
- Nine Infotrac databases are provided free of charge by New Mexico State Library.
- Database are available in the Library and remotely by registered patrons.

Computers and Internet:
- Internet access and word processing are available on seven computers for public use.
- Two additional computers for children offer games and educational software with no Internet access.
- Staff has five computers.
- All public computers are five years old or older.
- Wireless Internet access is available.

Programs:
Library provides Story Hours, Summer Reading Program, and Teen Gaming Night.

The Wonder Public Library profile presents profile information about a public library in an outline format with bulleted lists. The advantage to this approach is that it is easy for reviewers to read, and they will get a broad picture of your library relatively quickly without wading through a lengthy narrative. It will be simple for them to refer to if they have questions about the library as they continue to read the proposal. The disadvantage to this approach is that it is difficult to convey a personable tone using bulleted lists. Anecdotes and stories are not easily incorporated into this fact-based profile, and it is more challenging to make a connection with the reader using this format. For instance, this format is not conducive to highlighting special library accomplishments or your success with grants in the past; on the other hand, it is a clean and efficient way to convey the essential information about your library. This format may be more suitable for small libraries; however, it is important to consider the nature of the proposal and what the funder specifies in the application guidelines when deciding the format of the library profile for each proposal you write.

ORGANIZATIONAL PROFILE EXAMPLE
Unity College
Unity, New Jersey

Unity College is a community college located in Unity, New Jersey, that provides two-year degree studies, technical training, and basic skills classes for as many as 16,000 full-time and part-time students each quarter. It is the third largest college in the New Jersey State system of 30 community and technical colleges. Founded in 1927, Unity College received its first accreditation in 1937 and has been accredited by the Atlantic States Commission on Colleges and Universities since 1948.

Trends in the past 10 years have seen a wave of students who have jobs and family responsibilities in addition to their studies. A 50 percent increase in online courses has been necessary in recent years to meet the demand of these students who appreciate the convenience of virtual studies.

Vision:
Changing lives, building communities

Mission:
Unity College provides opportunities for diverse learners to achieve their educational and professional goals, thereby enriching the social, cultural, and economic environment of our region and the global community.

Values:
Caring, Civility, Hope, Integrity, Leadership

Strategic Directions:
As part of Unity College's strategic plan, five strategic goals have been identified. Three of those strategic directions are described below:

- **Focus on Learning:** The College will focus on learning as the foundation for decision making with respect to planning, technology, location, instructional methods, and successful outcomes. Learners will receive high-quality, innovative education and services that foster student success in achievement of their goals.

- **Expand Access:** The College will offer programs and services that are affordable and accessible to students of the community. Students will be provided flexible options for learning in locations that are accessible and resources that help make their education affordable.

- **Partnerships/Community Building:** The College will create and sustain meaningful and mutually beneficial partnerships that support the mission, vision, and goals of the College.

The Unity College organizational profile describes Unity College in an application submitted by the Library at Unity College. A library profile alone would probably not include enough information for a funder to understand the larger picture of the student population the library serves and the vision, mission, values, and strategic direction of the College. This mixed narrative and outline format provides the advantage of being easy to read and review while at the same time drawing the reader into the story of your proposal. This is an opportunity to establish that the organizational mission, vision, and goals are compatible with the funder's priorities and the library's plans. Trends among the students, faculty, and staff are appropriate here if this information supports the proposed project.

Writing the Community Profile

The community profile places your library or organization into a larger context. Describing the people your library serves is a good way to lay a foundation for the need statement, which usually comes next in the proposal. In building your case, it makes sense to tell readers about the nature of the people you serve before you identify the need your project will address.

In many cases the RFP, application information, or proposal guidelines will dictate what the funder wants to know about your community—for instance, poverty rate, high school graduation rate, mean age of students, number of minority families, or percentages of students who have special needs. In other cases, funders will leave it up to you which data to include. If this is the case, customize your community profile by first deciding what facts or statistics best support your project. For instance, if you are proposing a literacy project that uses technology, you might focus on a neighborhood or specific demographic in your community with a high incidence of illiteracy. If you are proposing a virtual learning website for your college library, focus on the numbers of students with computers and their preference for accessing information virtually. Information that is too generic or broad will not help you develop a winning argument for your project. In fact, if the community profile consists of information that does not relate to your project or your organization, the funder may question your entire proposal.

Community data includes hard data, or numbers, and soft data, or testimony and input from the people you serve. Use census numbers or data from your institution's research office, updated by news articles and statistics gathered by local businesses, the university public relations office and government agencies, and nonprofits serving specific populations. Universities often house business research departments that collect and analyze current data for your state, county, municipality, university system, or school district. Media coverage about the need or lack of service in your community, tuition rate hikes, student achievement, projections for the future, or population trends are other sources of community information that may support your project.

Use the most current data you can find, and make sure it is accurate. For instance, using the last census data for unemployment numbers will reveal that you are behind the curve. Especially if you are proposing a project to provide computer classes and online information for the rising unemployed population in your community, use the latest numbers from your state or city unemployment office and you will make a better case for your project.

Data is not hard to find. The hard work is sifting through all the data and deciding which data will make the best case for your project—and that takes time. Again, the purpose of profiling your community is to lay the groundwork for the need statement, which comes next in your proposal. You are building a case for funding your project one step at a time. Use data as your primary tool to state your case. Data, or facts, are very powerful at this stage in your proposal, because it is objective and qualifies as "proof" that your project is needed in your community. Creating a compelling community profile is a great way to attract the attention of a funder.

If a community profile is not requested as a separate component in the proposal you are writing, insert your community profile information at the beginning of the need statement. It is vital that you describe your community somewhere in your proposal.

COMMUNITY PROFILE EXAMPLE
Suffolk, New York

The City of Suffolk is home to approximately 120,000 people. Its 43 square miles are located along New York's Long Island coastline. Suffolk offers both urban and suburban areas, ranging from homes in wooded North Suffolk, to corporate downtown Suffolk Center, to the shoreline areas that envelop its popular parks and beaches. Located in Nassau County, New York, Suffolk is 25 miles from New York City. New York's capitol, Albany, is 100 miles to the north of Suffolk.

Suffolk provides a full range of public services, including its own police and fire departments, library, senior center, and parks and recreation department. The City has 11 elementary schools, six middle schools, and three high schools. Housing choices range from single-family homes to multiunit dwellings, with approximately 43 percent of the population living in renter-occupied housing units and 24 percent of the population living in apartment complexes with 20 or more units.

Demographic information shows that the community's population is diverse, with approximately 40 percent of the population being minority or mixed race and approximately 37 percent of the population being foreign born. Of the foreign-born population, approximately 76 percent are U.S. citizens. Approximately 44 percent of the population speaks a language other than English, and 22 percent of those who speak another language indicated that they speak English "less than very well."

According to 2010 census data, the per capita income in Suffolk is significantly lower than surrounding communities. Suffolk's per capita income was $34,987 as compared to Richmond ($82,049), Barrington ($77,519), and Hampton ($74,346).

Compared to the rest of the country, Suffolk's cost of living is 43.32 percent higher than the U.S. national average. Recent economic conditions in the United States have led to an increase in unemployment in the City. Two large employers, Access Technologies and SureFire Systems, have closed their doors in the past three years, leaving the unemployment rate in Suffolk at 15 percent. Recent job growth is negative, with jobs in the City decreasing by approximately 3.3 percent annually. Many unemployed citizens do not have computers at home, and they are unfamiliar with how to search for employment on the Internet. This makes it challenging for them to become employed by finding and applying for jobs online.

The Suffolk, New York, community profile gives an overall description of the community the library serves, including hard demographic data, geographic information, and average income comparisons with surrounding communities. The information at the end about unemployment is significant in this community profile, because the proposed project will train and support the unemployed population in this community to find and apply for jobs online. Here is where this applicant begins to draw the reader in to the project idea. The need statement, which comes next, will elaborate on the target population and their needs. This is an example of how to build each component upon the last.

Writing the Need Statement

One of the most critical points you will make in your proposal is demonstrating the need in your community that your project will address. You should always determine a need before you create a project or write a grant proposal. The funder wants to know why your project is important for your community, that it will make a difference, and exactly how it will improve people's lives. The need statement (sometimes called the "statement of need") objectively describes the need, or problem, in your community that your project will help alleviate. More importantly, this is where you present your arguments in a logical sequence to convince the funder how important it is for them to fund your project. The need statement is the "proof" you have that your project is needed, so it is important to base it on facts. Avoid making statements like, "We feel that the community would benefit from . . ." or "We think this would be a great asset to the community. . ." or "Community members would like . . ." without providing concrete evidence. The need statement does not have to be long and involved. Short, concise, and relevant information that captures the reader's attention and makes a good case for your project is all you need.

Begin by focusing on the data or information that led you to determine your project is necessary. There must be a compelling and logical reason why the project is important. When a funder reads your need statement they should clearly see why they should fund it. Start with the facts and then move to the solution. Your logic will show how your project will provide a solution, resulting in a change for your target audience. Support your logic with qualified research and evidence. Include data that is historical, geographic, quantitative, and factual. Use statistics and local human-interest stories as supporting examples. Creative storytelling techniques can be useful in demonstrating need and helps the funder to see your community members as real people with real needs. Using this technique can soften this section, which can become very dry if it consists of facts and statistics only.

Write from a positive perspective, focusing on the good outcomes that will result when the need is met or problem solved rather than from a negative or deficit-based perspective. Give the reader hope. The picture you paint in the need statement shouldn't be so grim that the situation seems hopeless. In that case the funder may wonder if an investment in your project will be money wasted. With such a negative outlook your ability to see your way through the problem may be in question.

Avoid circular reasoning. In circular reasoning, you present the absence of your solution as the problem. Then you offer your solution as the way to solve the problem. In other words, the lack of something (like computers, books, money, or qualified staff) is not the problem or need. The need is never for things. The need exists among the people of your community. Focus on people, not on things. Funders want to help people, not buy things.

NEED STATEMENT EXAMPLE
Online Management Course
for Librarians in New Mexico

Over the past year, approximately 24 library director vacancies have been created in public libraries across New Mexico. This represents 26 percent of the 91 public libraries in New Mexico. New Mexico statutes require library directors in communities over 3,000 who do not have a Master in Library Science (MLS) degree to become certified by passing a written examination. Many new directors filling these vacant positions will need to prepare for and pass the Public Library Director Certification Exam. The need for supporting library directors in acquiring the required competencies is particularly great in New Mexico, because 76 percent of library directors do not hold an MLS degree. Many do not have previous library experience. The success of these library directors in acquiring the required competencies is necessary to ensure the delivery of quality library services throughout New Mexico. The online training model developed by this project will be an efficient and cost-effective way to significantly augment the preparation of new library directors for success in acquiring the Management competency and passing the Certification Exam in this competency area.

At this time, preexamination study sessions are held regularly at the New Mexico State Library (NMSL) in Santa Fe and a Certification Exam Study Guide is available online; however, the NMSL does not offer online classes to assist directors in acquiring the required competencies. There are very few free classes available to library directors who want to prepare for Exam competencies online. Because of the distances between many rural New Mexican communities and Santa Fe, combined with insufficient staff reserves in the small, rural libraries to provide coverage, it is difficult for many directors from outlying libraries to travel to Santa Fe for the study sessions. There is a need for synchronous and asynchronous online training to support library directors without MLS degrees in New Mexico in becoming certified. This project will develop and deliver a course in Management that will assist new library directors without MLS degrees in preparing for success in acquiring this competency online and in passing the Certification Exam in this competency area.

Growing budget cuts, short staffing, and the economic recession's impact on the NMSL compound these insufficiencies in the public libraries. At this time the State Library Development Bureau's Continuing Education Program is operating without a budget. This project will ensure that the State Library has the ability to continue to offer a sufficient level of training opportunities for new library directors and their staff.

Online learning tools are becoming increasingly necessary especially during this economic downturn, which is exacerbated by New Mexico already being a large, sparsely populated state with a high poverty level. By introducing Blackboard and Wimba, the state's online course management and collaborative learning platforms, to new library directors, this project will broaden their ability to take additional online professional development courses and to encourage other library staff to follow their lead.

Guidelines for this proposal did not request a community profile; therefore, information about the target population is included in this needs statement. Once the population is described, the writer begins to build a case by elaborating on the needs that exist among the target population. The needs described are addressed with a solution meant to lead the reader to agree that the proposed project is the solution to meet the needs. This need statement mentions "growing budget cuts, short staffing, and the economic recession's impact" as factors; however, the lack of money and staff are not the primary need described in this statement. Be careful not to focus on the lack of money and things in your need statement.

127

Community Needs Assessments

Community needs assessments are a good place to get the facts for your need statement. Organizations usually conduct community needs assessments prior to strategic planning to determine what their communities really need, how well they are serving their communities, and what other services or resources they can provide in the future to serve them better. Identifying the needs and challenges of the people you serve will tell you how the library can help support them—whether it is to focus on literacy, improve access to electronic databases for students, teach job-seeking skills, provide educational support, reduce school dropout rates, provide a safe place for teens, or close the digital divide.

A community needs assessment involves collecting, analyzing, and synthesizing input from an entire community. It provides an objective look at data about the people you serve, and it is an invaluable tool to you as you write the need statement. Link the community needs assessment data with demographics about your community from the community profile.

Writing the Project Description

As you write your proposal components, you will inevitably be fine-tuning your library project. Conversely, as you continue to fine-tune your project, you must make sure the proposal components reflect every aspect of your project. To help keep your proposal synchronized and to help keep yourself on track, make a project outline (see Chapter 3, p. 39, for a Technology Project Outline Example) that includes the following information:

- Goals
- Objectives
- Outcomes
- Activities

As you know, proposals are living, organic documents, so this outline is subject to change. Keep it simple and easy to adjust. It will serve as your compass as you write your entire proposal.

The project description is the heart of the proposal. It describes the nuts and bolts of your project and ultimately explains how you are going to meet your goals and objectives by doing specific activities, step by step. It should not only explain what you intend to do but it should clearly address what you know about the funder's priorities. Whenever possible, make it clear to readers that your project matches the funder's concerns as much as your own.

Each section of the grant proposal must build from the previous section and lay the groundwork for the next. The project description, then, must derive from the need statement and set the stage for the evaluation plan. Describe the strategies you have selected to approach the community's needs. By relating your community's needs to project goals and objectives, and illustrating how doing the activities will achieve outcomes for your target population, you are leading the reviewer through the thought process you went through when you designed your project. The project description is sometimes known as the "approach" or "methodology," terms that clearly illustrate what you are expected to convey in this component.

Some funders specify the order in which they want you to present the information contained in the project description. Follow their instructions exactly. Whatever their order or specific instructions, in some way you should include:

- Significance or uniqueness of project (why this is the right project to meet the need)
- Goals (purpose of the project)
- Target audience (who will benefit)
- Outcomes (how the target population will benefit)
- Objectives (what you intend to accomplish in SMART terms)
- Activities (how you will make the project happen)
- Staff (who will do what)
- Partners (who else is working with you on the project)
- Sustainability (how the project will continue after grant is over)

Your ability to weave together the answers to these questions in a seamless and readable narrative is essential for a successful grant proposal. This is where your skill as a proposal writer is really put to the test.

Name your project or give it a title if you haven't done this already. Reviewers read many proposals, often one after the other, and you can make yours memorable by establishing a name with which they can associate your project. Keep the title short, descriptive of your project, and easy to remember.

Significance or Uniqueness

Begin by explaining why you are proposing this specific technology project to meet the community needs you have identified in the need statement. Acknowledge that you are aware of other solutions to the need, and show the funder why you have chosen this solution over others—or why your project is a particularly significant or unique solution. Note any research you have done about similar projects and how yours differs from, or builds on, earlier work. Funders are more inclined to fund projects that are well thought out, so this is your chance to demonstrate to them you have done just this. If yours is a model or demonstration project, describe how others will be able to replicate it, or how it can be adapted to other libraries and organizations in other communities. Show the funder that you are prepared and committed to implementing the project.

Goals

Goals state the purpose of your project. They are broad statements that describe the overall desired result of your project. A strong or bold statement of purpose—or project goal—at the beginning of the project description can grab the reviewer's attention, compelling them to read on.

Target Audience

Clarify who will benefit from your project, that is, the target audience. Include detailed information about them, such as their presence in the community, the estimated numbers to be served, how you will attract them to your project, and how you will involve them.

129

Outcomes

Outcomes are used to identify a change in behavior, attitude, skill, life condition, or knowledge among the people served by the project. They reflect the long-term impact a project is making toward solving a community problem or toward improving the lives of the target population. Most funders require you to state the outcomes of your proposed project, and many funders specify outcome-based evaluation (OBE). If you are required to implement OBE by a funder, you must first establish outcomes in your project description. The fact that you propose to buy computers, digitize historical materials, provide gaming for teens, or install a wireless network in the library is admirable, but the funder wants to know that these things will make a difference for people—and how they will make a difference.

Objectives

Once you have (1) introduced your project, (2) told the funder why it should fund the project, and (3) explained the goals, target audience, and expected outcomes, the next logical step is to identify how you intend to solve the problem or meet the need. The solution is expressed in terms of goals, objectives, and activities. Objectives are specific, measurable, achievable, realistic, and time-bound (SMART) terms that specify how you will achieve your outcomes and goals—they are the intellectual center of your proposal. Ask yourself what objectives will demonstrate that the outcomes or goals have been achieved. For instance, if an outcome is, "Mature adult community members will be more knowledgeable about using computers in the library," one objective might be that of all mature adult community members 25 percent will say they know more about using computers as a result of attending computer training in the library. Specific objectives measure program achievement, and they will dictate the nature of your evaluation plan.

Objectives are not to be confused with activities. Activities are your methods for achieving the goals and accomplishing the objectives. Objectives are also not to be confused with goals. Goals are identified as statements of the broad purpose of a program and are long-range desires or benefits. Objectives are more immediate or short range, and they are measurable.

Activities

This is where you tell the funder how the project will work, describing project activities in detail and indicating how the objectives will be accomplished. Explain how your project will proceed. Tell the funder what will be done in a logical order, including sequence, flow, and interrelationship of activities. Describe the precise steps you will follow to carry out each objective. Some proposals list activities under their corresponding objectives, and others explain activities in a narrative. If your project design is simple and you are applying to a small foundation, for instance, a narrative is a "friendlier" approach. Proposing complex projects to federal agencies usually warrants an outline or list approach. This information will be used later in the timeline.

Staff

The funder wants to know who will do what, so identify staff who will do project activities described in the activities section. Sometimes (especially when your project is complex) your project description will read better if you mesh the activities and staff sections together. In this case you will indicate who will do a task when you describe the task. Explain who will supervise or manage the project, any outside consultants you will be hiring, and other library staff who are participating in project implementation. You don't need to go into much detail here, but you do need to show the funder that you've thought through who will perform all aspects of the project. This information will be used later in the budget and the timeline.

Partners

Emphasize collaborations and partnerships. Your project can have a wider impact when more organizations are involved, and collaborating with other organizations is a beneficial way to share equipment, expertise, and resources. Mention partners in every section of your project description, including staff members participating from other organizations and the activities they will perform. Include salaries and benefits for these personnel in your budget, and indicate whether or not these positions are being offered as match.

Sustainability

Funders want to know that your project—or your efforts to meet a specific need in your community—will not cease when project funding comes to an end. Having partners and supporters and showing that you are investigating other sources of funding for the future, and including matching funds, proves your project isn't short term but one that is worth supporting because it will make a real difference in the long run. Include any ways that the project might leverage impact for other library goals or help meet other community needs in the future.

131

PROJECT DESCRIPTION EXAMPLE
Mobile Computer Classroom for Seniors

The Mobile Computer Classroom for Seniors project combines technology education, adult programming, and outreach that will enable seniors who are unable to attend regular computer classes at the Bellevue County Public Library by bringing the classroom to them. The Bellevue County Public Library currently offers some free basic computer classes for adults. Over 80 percent of students in attendance are seniors. One segment of the community that does not have equal access to technology education is seniors living in retirement communities. Bellevue County has a large retirement community at Kensington Gardens, a combination of independent and dependent homes for seniors. While Kensington Gardens offers a variety of on-site programs and transports its residents to events throughout the community, it lacks the ability to transport residents to smaller outings such as computer classes at the library. Many residents have expressed an interest in attending computer classes at the library; however, because of the lack of transportation they are not able to take advantage of this opportunity.

Project Goal:
The Mobile Computer Classroom for Seniors project will provide technology courses for seniors where they are in the Kensington Garden Retirement Community for the purpose of educating them to use computers to improve their quality of life.

(Continued)

PROJECT DESCRIPTION EXAMPLE *(Continued)*
Mobile Computer Classroom for Seniors

Target Audience:

Educational opportunities are plentiful in Bellevue County for young adults; however, there is a lack of affordable education for senior adults. Nearby Western Alabama University (WAU), located in Newville, offers adult and community education classes, but these classes are limited to residents of Newville. WAU charges tuition for all classes, including the noncredit community education courses. Furthermore, many of these classes are offered online, which assumes all residents who want to take classes not only have computers but also know how to use them to take online classes. If a senior wanted to take a class to learn about computers, taking an online class would not work. Furthermore, WAU accepts only online registration. This eliminates that portion of our population that does not know how to use computers.

Seniors have been left behind in the digital world. Dependence on computers is a relatively new part of our culture; only in recent years has the Internet had a daily effect on our lives. Seniors need equal access to technology education to level the playing field. Nowadays, a person applies for Social Security online, reads e-books on a computer or e-device, and purchases airline tickets and researches the latest information about health issues via the Internet. Without equal access to information, a person's quality of life decreases.

The most important part of education already exists among seniors, and that is the desire to learn. Surveys of current computer class attendees, requests from Kensington Gardens residents, and a community needs assessment conducted by the library in 2010 indicates that seniors in Bellevue County are in need of technology education. The Mobile Computer Classroom will allow us to reach many seniors whose transportation challenges prevent them from coming to the library for these classes.

Outcomes:

More seniors in the community will have the ability to learn about technology, enabling them to use computers, e-book readers, smartphones, and other technologies in their daily lives. Additionally, seniors who take classes through this project will say that learning about using technology has improved their quality of life. Seniors will know how to use the library's website, databases, and other tools and how to borrow e-books to improve their daily lives.

Objectives:

- By April 2012, the number of computer classes offered by the library will increase by 100 percent.
- By April 2012, the library will offer at least 12 off-site classes at Kensington Gardens Retirement Community by transporting the Mobile Computer Classroom for Seniors to Kensington Gardens.
- By April 2012, the library will use the mobile lab to increase on-site computer classes for seniors by 50 percent.
- By April 2012, computer class attendance and library computer usage will increase by 100 percent.

Activities:

The project manager will survey seniors in current and prospective computer classes and residents of Kensington Gardens to gain an understanding of their technology education needs. Results will be used to determine the specific focus of classes, approximate number of classes needed, and locations of classes. The project manager will also interview the director at Kensington Gardens to gain his input and determine any facility requirements for setting up the lab.

(Continued)

PROJECT DESCRIPTION EXAMPLE *(Continued)*
Mobile Computer Classroom for Seniors

After reviewing survey and interview results, the project manager will revise the current computer class curriculum to better meet the needs of seniors and then plan computer class schedules for on-site and off-site sessions. The project manager will work with the director of Kensington Gardens to schedule computer classes at the Retirement Community. The technology librarian will teach classes at Kensington Gardens, and the technology librarian and reference librarian will continue to teach the in-library classes. Teachers will transport the mobile lab to Kensington Gardens.

The project manager will evaluate the progress of the project and benefit to seniors by conducting surveys, gathering data, and conducting informal interviews with participants throughout the course of the project and by monitoring class attendance. He will solicit feedback from the director of Kensington Gardens.

A project assistant will maintain equipment, run periodic updates, be responsible for the safety of equipment, notify the network administrator about technical problems, coordinate with Kensington Gardens on technical issues, install and configure software on the laptops, and maintain the hardware.

Sustainability:
The Mobile Computer Classroom for Seniors project will continue as long as demand for computer classes exists. Utilizing the equipment from the grant, library staff can maintain classes with its current staff.

The Mobile Computer Classroom project description touches on most of the essential elements of this component; however, there is room for some fine-tuning in this example. You want the reader or reviewer to easily read this section to gain an understanding of your entire project design. Any superfluous or unrelated information will interrupt the flow. Although it is a good idea to include an introductory paragraph that bridges the reader from the need statement, you must take care not to continue to justify needs in this component. The information about seniors' transportation needs; classes at the nearby university being unsuitable for seniors without computer skills; and needs assessment results indicating seniors need technology training all belong in the need statement. Relocating this information will allow the writer to streamline the project description.

The project goal is a very good broad statement about what the project plans to accomplish. The target audience has been adequately described; however, one simple statement in the target audience section, such as, "The project will target senior adults living at the Kensington Garden Retirement Community and in Bellevue County, Alabama" would make this much clearer. The outcomes and objectives are very good. The outcomes describe how the seniors will gain new knowledge or skills and how their quality of life will change, and the objectives for the most part are SMART.

The activities are described in a chronological order that is easy to visualize, and it is clear who will perform each activity. The partnership between the library and the retirement community could be stressed more. Sustainability is addressed; however, a reviewer will wonder how staff can add this work onto their workload in the future without a cost. At this point, it would be interesting to take a look at the budget for this proposal to see if staff time is included as part of the project cost and if that cost is being requested in the grant. If so, a funder will wonder why they should fund staff now when staff can easily incorporate these duties into their jobs later at no extra cost.

As a funder I would like to know if the applicant has researched other projects like this and how the applicant plans to build on the lessons learned from others. This sounds like something that may have been done in other communities, and it would not be a good investment to repeat any past mistakes.

Writing the Evaluation Plan

Projects are undertaken to have an impact—to address a need in your community. How will you or your funder know if the project was a success? Evaluation plans show how you will track your progress and measure your success as indicated by progress toward achieving your stated objectives. They tell you where you can improve or adjust your project and allow you to better allocate resources during project implementation. The key to writing an evaluation plan is to first have objectives that are measurable—the two are intertwined.

There are different kinds of evaluations, and the form your evaluation plan takes will be different in each case. Decide on an evaluation approach that serves the project best and that will truly measure the success of your particular project. Your objectives themselves will determine the kinds of information you will need to collect for your evaluation. For instance, if an objective states that 50 percent more mature adult community members will know more about using computers as a result of the project, you could ask mature adults if they know more after they have attended a computer class that is part of your project. You could also conduct pre- and post-tests to determine this or have them take a simple survey upon completion of the class.

The evaluation component of your proposal might be one or two paragraphs or one or more pages, depending on the nature of your project. A funder may specify what kind of evaluation you must do. Some funders prefer that you conduct evaluations throughout your project (formative), and others want you to evaluate the project at its conclusion (summative). A funder may not require a formal evaluation at all. Some want monitoring reports only. It is up to you to read the guidelines, find out what is needed, and then decide how to write the evaluation plan for your project. Many funders regard a sound evaluation plan based on measurable objectives to be a sign of a proposal they are likely to fund.

It is essential that you describe your evaluation plan in a way that clearly indicates you are serious about assessing your project's potential for success. No matter what kind of evaluation you choose, you will want to describe how you will collect the data you need. There are two types of data to gather: qualitative and quantitative. Most sound evaluation plans include both types. Qualitative evaluation methods measure quality, and they include interviews, focus groups, questionnaires, observations, and surveys. Quantitative evaluation methods are more formal and numerical, measuring quantity. Quantitative means are used to generate statistics via methods like test scores or numbers of participants.

There are many ways to collect evaluation information and data. Evaluation tools or instruments can include questionnaires and surveys, interviews, documentation review, observation, focus groups, or case studies, for example. It is important to use the right evaluation tool to measure your results. Decide what measurement instrument is most appropriate to get the strongest data specific to your project objectives.

Questionnaires or Surveys

You can get lots of information quickly and easily from many people in a non-threatening way using questionnaires and surveys. People can complete them anonymously, they are inexpensive to administer, and you can administer them to many people. It is fairly easy to compare and analyze results from surveys and questionnaires. Information gathered from surveys is only as good as the questions you ask. The shorter a survey is, the easier it will be to complete and the more likely people are to complete them. Be sure to provide confidentiality to your survey participants.

Interviews

Use interviews when you want to fully understand someone's impressions or experiences or learn more about their answers in surveys or questionnaires. Interviews give you the opportunity to get the full range and depth of information, they give you the opportunity to develop a rapport with the interviewee, and you can be flexible with your questioning. This method provides subjective data, because it is based on opinions that may not reflect the true success of the program or service. It is a very time-consuming process, but it may yield future partners and new ideas. Interviews can add valuable information for outcome-based assessments, because they may reveal changes in a person's behavior, attitude, skill, life condition, or knowledge.

Documentation Review

Use documentation reviews when you want an impression of how your service or program is operating without interrupting it. This method is composed of reviewing statistics, memos, minutes, and so forth. Because this method does not measure changes in people's behavior, skills, knowledge, attitudes, condition, or life status, use it only as a supplement to instruments that do measure these things.

Observation

By observing a service or program, you can gather accurate information about how it actually operates, particularly about the process. With this method you view operations as they are actually occurring.

Focus Groups

Focus groups allow you to explore a topic in depth through group discussion. They can provide very honest and useful information, you can get reactions to an experience or suggestion, and you can gain an understanding of common complaints. Focus group members can be organized into manageable numbers. If the participants are comfortable, they may give very helpful feedback. This is an efficient way to get key information about a service or program, and you can quickly and reliably get impressions. This information is subjective, and it could be time-consuming to compile the data.

Case Studies

Use case studies to fully understand or depict a customer's experiences as a participant in your program or service input, process, and results. This is a powerful way to portray to outsiders the impact your project has had on individuals and may be the best way to convey something like change in condition of life. Case studies are very time-consuming, and they are difficult to collect, organize, and describe; however, they can provide powerful stories to convey to the "powers that be" the value of your library and the difference it can mean in people's lives.

Decide which method(s) is most appropriate to get the strongest data to measure a particular objective. When your project design has measurable objectives, the evaluation plan will become a natural extension of the objectives, and it will be relatively simple to complete. Evaluation plans are easier to read when they are presented in a table or outline format; however, if a particular funder specifies otherwise, follow its guidelines.

EVALUATION PLAN EXAMPLE
Carroll University Library E-book Project

1. Carroll University currently owns 500 e-book titles. The acquisitions librarian will track the purchases of all new titles added to the collection to ensure the e-book collection increases by 50 percent by the end of the project.
2. The Carroll Library currently tracks e-book usage. To evaluate this project, the use of new e-book acquisitions will be tracked separately. Usage statistics will be compared to determine the usage of new e-book acquisitions versus e-books already in the collection.
3. A survey of students, faculty, and staff who use the new e-books will ask them how they were aware of the new materials.
4. A survey conducted three months after project implementation will ask students who use e-books how they use these materials for their coursework.

The Carroll University Library E-book Project evaluation plan will work for a project that has objectives to match. Funders want to know that the evaluation plan will measure what you say you will do. For instance, if one objective is to increase the e-book collection by 50 percent by the end of the project, #1 will accomplish that. The surveys proposed in the evaluation plan (#3 and #4) do not necessarily measure progress toward a goal or objective; however, they will provide information that may help the applicant improve or adjust the project as it is being implemented.

Preparing the Budget

The budget depicts the cost of your project in dollars and includes the sum of all expenses from personnel, benefits, consultants, materials and supplies, rent, equipment, administrative costs, and travel costs, for instance. Budgets are detailed cost projections and should be accurate and well researched. Some funders provide budget forms that must be submitted with your proposal, while others leave it up to you to create a budget from scratch. It may be difficult to estimate some costs, but make your best effort. Take the time to obtain exact costs rather than estimating. You must be realistic to ensure that, if funded, you will have adequate funds to implement the project you are proposing. Do the math correctly, and work with your financial office or administrator who may have valuable knowledge they can share with you about cost projections.

It is often simpler to first prepare two budgets: a personnel budget and a non-personnel budget. Then combine them in your proposal for your total project costs. This is because they have different formats. Personnel budgets include full-time equivalent (FTE) calculations and benefits, and non-personnel budgets don't.

Personnel Budget

This budget consists of the salaries or a portion of salaries for everyone who will work on the project. Using your activities section from the project description, figure out the FTE required for each position working on your project, as follows:

1. Select one position, and determine the activities that position will do.
2. Determine the amount of time the position will be spending on these activities over the duration of the project and calculate the FTE.
3. Determine the salary for that FTE.
4. Calculate the cost of benefits on that salary and FTE.
5. Go through the same process for all personnel.
6. Calculate cost for consultants. Benefits will probably not apply, but taxes may.
7. Enter all personnel budget information in a table format.
8. Total all personnel costs.

Non-personnel Budget

This budget consists of costs for all items other than personnel. Develop a non-personnel budget for your project in a table format. Be as specific as possible. Break large categories down into smaller segments, such as brochure printing, paper costs, and newspaper ads, instead of "marketing." Rather than entering one number for technology expenses, specify what each computer, modem, and repeater will cost. If your project will require training on a new automated system, or ongoing maintenance or subscription costs, enter these items separately as well. When you are estimating technology costs, get several quotes. If your organization, municipality, school, or university requires purchases to be made through existing contracts, work within these guidelines. Do not try to obtain the cheapest price or find the best sales at your nearest big box store. These prices will not exist next week, not to mention when the grant is funded. Technology prices are expected to change from the time you write your proposal to the time of project implementation. Make your best estimate. Adjustments can be made after you are awarded the grant if necessary. Adjustments are easier to make when the non-personnel budget is itemized in detail. Total all non-personnel costs.

Create your project budget by combining the personnel budget and the non-personnel budget and adding the total costs from each to determine the total project cost. If you are not requesting the full amount, add a line at the end of the budget to indicate amount requested.

The Close the Gap @ the Library budget is a good example of a thoroughly researched budget for a technology project (see p. 138). It is clear that the applicant

137

Budget Example

CLOSE THE GAP @ THE LIBRARY
BUDGET

Item	Description	Amount Requested
5 public computers	Dell Optiplex 790 mini tower	@ $699 each = $3,495
1 public printer	Dell 3330 laser printer	$350
1 DSL modem	D-link 2540B DSL modem	$54
1 router	Netgear Wireless N router	$130
1 repeater	Hawking HWREN1 Hi-Gain Wireless 300 N range extender	$70
Public computer management software	Pharos SignUp for Public Library	$3,041
Antivirus software for 5 public computers	McAffee Total Protection for 5 computers	@ $179 each = $895
Computer protection and security software	DeepFreeze with 1-year support for 5 public computers	@ $40 each = $200
Internet service	Qwest DSL Internet service for 1 year	@ $75 per month = $900
DSL installation	1-time fee	$100
NON-PERSONNEL COSTS		**$9,235**

Position	Description	Amount Requested
Reference librarian and library assistant	WebJunction Network Essentials Class x 2	@ $100 each = $200
Computer technician	WebJunction Troubleshooting Computer Problems Tutorial	$100
PERSONNEL COSTS		**$300**
TOTAL PROJECT COST		**$9,535**

has done some work identifying specific items and pricing them. A funder wants to see that you understand what needs to be purchased and that you know how to select the right equipment. A budget that reflects this kind of detail regarding technology tells the funder more than what the project will cost. It says the applicant knows about technology. This adds strength to the proposal.

The personnel budget needs much more work. For instance, it shows funding is being requested for staff training only. As a funder, I would ask, "Who is going to do the work of installing the hardware and software and the work of implementing the project?" Funders are not impressed when you throw in your library staff for free. It is fine for the library or a partner to contribute a portion of personnel costs as match; however, a budget must reflect the actual cost for staff to do the work of the project.

Match and In-Kind

Provide information on other funding sources, financial commitments, or support that will be provided by your library or partners for this project. When others have already committed funds, personnel, equipment, space, or other items to a project, it is very important to include this information in your budget. When a funder sees that others are willing to assume a portion of project costs, it demonstrates the importance of your project to your library and community. This also indicates a degree of commitment from library administration and is a good predictor of future sustainability for your project.

Project the costs for office space, computers, personnel, or equipment contributed by your library, a partner, or another outside source. Contributions are called "in-kind" when they are noncash contributions. Match is a cash contribution made to the project cost by someone other than the funder. Make a column in your budget to reflect match or in-kind amounts.

Budget Narrative

Sometimes a funder requires a budget narrative (or budget justification), which means that in addition to the budget in table format you must explain how you have determined the costs. Essentially, the narrative explains in words exactly what appears in the budget. Don't include a budget narrative if it isn't required, because it usually doesn't add value to your proposal.

Creating the Timeline

Timelines are project-planning tools that are used to represent the timing of tasks required to complete a project. They are easy to understand and construct, they tell reviewers when activities happen, and they provide another way to see the project that supports the rest of your proposal.

There are many ways to construct a timeline; however, a table format with each activity taking up one row is common. Dates run along the top row, and heading columns represent days, weeks, or months—depending on the duration of your project. Checkmarks or horizontal bars marking the expected beginning and end of a task represent the time required for each task. Tasks are listed sequentially, at the same time, or overlapping each other. Include the personnel responsible for each activity. In

139

constructing a timeline, keep the tasks to a manageable number (no more than 15–20) so that the chart fits on a single page. If your project is complex, it may require subtasks and subcharts.

The Online Course for New Library Directors project timeline (see p. 141) includes main project activities and shows when the activity will be performed and by whom. Funders can easily see how your project will progress through time for the duration.

Writing the Executive Summary

The executive summary is the last proposal component you will write, and it is the most important. Here you provide readers with an encapsulated version of your entire proposal, giving them a full overview of what is to follow.

The executive summary is the first thing the reviewers see, and it forms their first impression of your proposal. Funders determine from your executive summary whether or not the proposal is within their guidelines. This is your best marketing tool and may be your only chance to interest a funder in your project. To make a good impression and draw the reader into the body of your proposal, craft this section very carefully. It is considered the most challenging component to write, because you must summarize, in a persuasive and logical fashion, the most important points you have made in all the other components of your proposal. At the same time you must capture the readers' attention and convince them that your project deserves full consideration and close attention.

By the time you are ready to write the executive summary, you have a thorough understanding of exactly what your project is all about and all its various aspects. As you have learned by now, the project evolves, is adjusted and tweaked, and takes shape while you are designing it—and even sometimes while you are writing your proposal. If you write your executive summary too early, you will end up having to write it over again to reflect the changes you have made as you design your project and write your other proposal components.

Usually a one-page summary of your entire proposal, the executive summary includes a sentence or two on each proposal component. It is meant to read quickly, giving the funder or reviewer a good sense of the applicant, the need, the project, goals and objectives, approach, and budget. Often reviewers must write a summary of your project along with their comments for presentation to a review panel. Ideally, the reviewers are able to use your executive summary as a basis for their proposal review. Thus, if you write a quality executive summary, you will make the reviewers' job easier. Larger funders may use the executive summary as a way to screen applications or select which applications to forward to the next step in the grant review process. If your proposal isn't well summarized in the executive summary it could mean the difference between advancing to the next level or not. Yes, even after all this hard work, you can ruin your chances for success by submitting a poorly written executive summary.

Funders often specify how long the executive summary should be. Be certain to adhere strictly to their guidelines and include the following:

- Brief descriptions of your community, library, organization, or school and your library's capacity to implement and administer the project

Timeline Example

Online Course for New Library Directors

PROJECT TIMELINE

.... Project Month ....

Activity	Staff Responsible	1	2	3	4	5	6	7	8	9
Determine Management competencies	CEC	✓								
Determine course objectives and content	CEC, PM	✓								
Attend Blackboard and Wimba training	T		✓							
Develop course content, lesson plans, activities, and assignments	CEC, T			✓	✓					
Develop and incorporate methods to determine students' success	PM, CEC, T	✓	✓	✓	✓	✓	✓			
Set up online course in Blackboard	T						✓			
Plan and set up Wimba event	T						✓			
Market class to new directors	CEC							✓		
Recruit and register students	CEC							✓		
Conduct course and assist students	T								✓	
Assess students' knowledge	CEC, T								✓	
Project evaluation	PM	✓	✓	✓	✓	✓	✓	✓	✓	✓
Reporting	PM						✓			✓
Ongoing meetings/ communication	PM, CEC, T	✓	✓	✓	✓	✓	✓	✓	✓	✓

CEC = continuing education coordinator; PM = program manager; T = trainer.

141

- Brief statement about the community need that the project will address
- Short description of the project, including goals, objectives, activities, who will staff the project, the approach, who will benefit, how will they benefit, how and where will it operate, how you will evaluate the project, and the duration of the project
- How the project meets the funder's goals or priorities
- Partners and their roles
- Sustainability
- Overall cost of the project, amount of the request, any match or in-kind contributions, and other funders supporting the project and for how much

From your proposal components, extract the most important information about your project and use it to highlight the strength of your project and your library in the executive summary. Tell the reader what you are going to do and why, why the project is important, why you are the organization to do it, and what you want them to do. Place more emphasis or devote more space to those elements that are weighted more heavily in the scoring process, if you have that information. (Federal applications often indicate how many points each section is worth.) Arrange the information so that it is easy to read and makes logical sense. Use bullets and, if appropriate, use bold subheadings to name sections of your executive summary as a visual aid.

Because this is the last component you will write, and it is the most challenging, the tendency is to rush through it at the last minute and fail to recognize its significance. Many proposal writers resort to vague generalizations, and others try to include every detail of their project idea. The best approach is to select the most significant facts that best convey your idea and present them in a readable format.

Sometimes a funder requests an abstract rather than, or in addition to, an executive summary. Abstracts are shorter than executive summaries, usually one or two paragraphs. Abstracts are more challenging to write, because you are trying to convince the reader of the project's importance in much less space.

Preparing the Appendix

Throughout the proposal-writing process, you will be gathering materials that could be used in the appendix (or attachment) component of your proposal. Your task is to select those materials that best support your proposal and build credibility. Include only those items that are germane to your proposal. The appendix can include:

- Studies, research, tables, or graphs
- Résumés or CVs for key personnel
- List of board members
- Auditor's report or statement
- Letters of support or endorsement
- Memoranda of understanding
- Copy of library brochures or other library publications
- Photos or architect's drawings
- Library's current budget

- Organizational chart
- Press articles that relate to your library, project, or community need
- Articles about another project yours will build on
- Library's technology plan

Read the grant guidelines very carefully to determine if you are allowed to include an appendix in your proposal and how long it can be—or how many attachments you can include. If this is not specified in the guidelines, contact the funder for instructions. Number the pages in the appendix separately, and, if it is extensive, include a separate table of contents or list of attachments on the first page of the appendix for easy review.

Whether the funder examines the attachments carefully or glances at them briefly, an appendix can provide you with an advantage when your proposal is being compared to a competitor's. Be selective, because too much material can hurt your application. Sometimes a funder specifies certain attachments only. If you think including something will support your proposal and it is not on the funder's list of accepted attachments, contact the funder for guidance. Otherwise, follow the guidelines.

Other Possible Proposal Components

Title Sheet
A title sheet or cover sheet makes an attractive presentation and includes the name of your project, your library's name and address, the date, and the name and address of the funder in a pleasing design.

Table of Contents
Similar to a table of contents in a book, this organizes your proposal for reviewers and makes it easy for them to locate specific information. Usually reserved for larger proposals, they include all components and the pages where they are found.

Cover Letter
A cover letter is your first opportunity to impress the funder. It should be easy to read, compelling, and interesting. It includes a project summary with goals and outcomes as well as the community needs the project will address. Indicate how your project addresses the funder's priorities, and include a short description of your organization, the amount you are requesting, and your contact name, address, e-mail, and phone number.

The cover letter gives you an opportunity to connect with the funder on a personal and professional level. Address the cover letter to the contact person specified by the funder in the proposal guidelines. If you have previously contacted this person to clarify the appropriateness of your project for the grant, or to ask questions about the guidelines, address them personally in the cover letter. Keep the cover letter short, to the point, and cordial.

Write a cover letter to accompany most foundation proposals. Keep it brief, one page or less, and make sure that it does the following:

- States the purpose of the proposal in one sentence, including the amount requested
- Connects personally to the reader
- Relates the proposed project to the funder's priorities and interests
- Provides background on your library and why you should receive the grant
- Includes your contact information
- Is printed on your library's letterhead

When you are applying for a government grant and there is a cover page on your proposal, it isn't necessary to add a cover letter. If application guidelines instruct you to omit the cover letter, always follow the instructions.

The Proposal Example on pages 145–156 includes some of the proposal components discussed in this chapter. Comments throughout the proposal will help give you some insight about what works in the proposal and suggestions on how to improve the proposal.

Packaging

The physical preparation of your proposal and its assembly will be handled differently for each individual grant application. Check the guidelines for the funder's specific requirements for the proposal package and follow them. Federal proposals do not offer many options for you to customize the "look" of your proposal; however, many foundation and corporate funders leave the packaging up to you. Electronic submissions usually allow very little leeway to personalize your proposal package. Remember to adhere to the application guidelines. Don't be tempted to make an attractive package when the funder wants plain text.

When you have the option to package a proposal in your own style, make it look familiar and friendly to the reader. Use a type style and layout to match the funder's publication preferences. Follow standard graphic design principles to present your proposal in a visually pleasing way, highlighting the proposal's structure, hierarchy, and order. A well-designed proposal makes even complex information look accessible, helps reviewers find the information they need, and establishes your organization's credibility.

Make copies for yourself and any extra copies the funder requires. Don't bind your proposal unless the funder specifies this, because the first thing most funders do is unbind any bound proposals so they can copy them for reviewers.

Submitting

One last time, go through your checklist to make sure you have met all the funder's application requirements. Then submit your proposal by e-mailing it, clicking on the "Submit" button, or sending it in the mail. Make sure you keep a copy of the proposal for yourself, and get a confirmation delivery or tracking number for your package.

Set Yourself Up for Success

- Do the preliminary steps in the grant process before you begin to write a proposal. One of the biggest problems in grant work is starting your grant work

(Continued p. 157)

Proposal Example

Visual Literacy:
Development and Implementation of Artistic Strategy
and Best Practice for Improving Visual Literacy
in Middle School Students

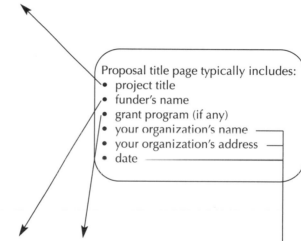

Proposal title page typically includes:
- project title
- funder's name
- grant program (if any)
- your organization's name
- your organization's address
- date

Submitted to the We Give Technology Grants Foundation
Community Education Grants Program

by

Farmington Aztec Cuba Middle School
21665 State Route 44
Farmington, NM 87000
August 18, 2011

(Continued)

145

Proposal Example *(Continued)*

Farmington Aztec Cuba Middle School
21665 State Route 44
Farmington, NM 87000
August 18, 2011

We Give Technology Grants Foundation
116 Z Street
New York, NY 10000

Dear Mr. Funder:

I am writing to respectfully request that the We Give Technology Grants Foundation consider our grant application. The goal of our grant project is to improve student visual literacy: the ability to interpret, analyze, and construct meaning from pictures. The primary objective of the proposed project is to raise student scores in regard to historical photographs on the 2014 New Mexico State Social Studies Exam. A long-term benefit would be that students continue to apply the learned artistic strategy to other visuals in their lives whether it is for school, personal interest, or when reading the newspaper. It has been said that "a picture is worth a thousand words," but imagine if you were able to interpret a picture with less than a dozen words.

A team including my art, social studies, and language arts teachers and myself developed this project. Collaboratively, we hope to increase the achievement of our seventh and eighth grade middle school students at Farmington Aztec Cuba (FAC) Middle School. As the library media specialist, it is my mission to collaborate with teachers to integrate and teach information literacy skills in the curriculum. These transferable information skills and strategies help students with their lifelong information needs, intellectual growth, and achievement. This mission is closely aligned with the first goal of my school board: "Faculty, students, parents, staff, and community will work together to achieve high levels of student learning necessary for success in the twenty-first century." The purpose of the We Give Technology Grants Foundation closely relates to the school's goal and the goal of the Visual Literacy project, because the Foundation supports creativity, achievement, and transformation of secondary education.

I thank you in advance for considering our proposal. Funding will mean middle school students will learn a new skill that they can use well beyond eighth grade. I will follow up with you in the next two weeks to answer any questions you may have and to learn if there is a possibility of our proposal meeting your funding goals. Should you have any questions in the meantime, please feel free to contact me.

Sincerely,

Sue Brand, Library Media Specialist
(505) 555-1212 x13
suebrand@fac.edu

> Clearly communicates the project's goal, primary objective, and outcome in the first paragraph.

> Personable and inviting tone invites reviewers to continue reading.

> Collaborations, aligned missions, and common goals with school, students, parents, and community are essential.

> Aligns Foundation's priorities with purpose of the proposed project.

> Follow-up plans indicate your commitment.

> Including complete contact information makes it easy for funders who have questions.

> Missing from this cover letter are (1) dollar amount requested and (2) duration of the project.

(Continued)

Proposal Example *(Continued)*

> Good one-page summary providing essential facts.

Executive Summary

In today's digital world, young people are constantly bombarded with images. Most of these images are designed for quick interpretation so that the person seeing the image draws meaning from it immediately. The younger generation has adapted to this rapid pace of society. However, when presented with the challenge to look at art or study historical pictures, students have trouble relating to the picture and pulling meaning from it. They go with their first impression and often apply no methodology for breaking down the picture into parts that can be analyzed for meaning.

> Establishes purpose of the project.

The focus of the Visual Literacy project is to teach students an artistic strategy that can be applied to looking at art and then be able to transfer this strategy when studying history. Farmington Aztec Cuba (FAC) School District is a small rural district in northwestern New Mexico that consists of five buildings and serves approximately 3,500 students. The funding from this grant would enable FAC to further its goal of "achieving high levels of student learning necessary for success in the twenty-first century" by providing students with a strategy for deciphering visuals that can be used on the 2014 New Mexico Social Studies (NMSS) Exam and beyond. Another outcome of this grant would be increased technology use by students: improved navigation skills, ethical use of information, and digital citizenship. These are skills that students can build on as they move through the upper grades and into society. We believe that this project and our mission meet the funding goals of the We Give Technology Grants Foundation. The project is designed to boost student achievement, and the addition of updated materials and technology will help to provide more learning opportunities for our secondary students, transforming their education.

> Would benefit by clarifying project goals, objectives, and activities here.

> Mentions outcomes for students.

> Aligns applicant's mission with funder's mission.

We respectfully request $102,970.06 from the We Fund Technology Grants Foundation to help fund this project. The total cost for implementing this project is $105,370. The majority of grant funds will be used to procure print materials and technology equipment. Print materials include updating the library art and historical fiction collections and developing a new visual collection containing art posters and historical photographs. Technology equipment encompasses outfitting the Library Media Center, art classroom, and social studies classrooms with interactive whiteboards, including arm-mounted projectors for showing and writing on visuals and two laptop carts for students to utilize in the classrooms for online searching, project work, posting to the project wiki, and online discussion.

> States total project cost and amount requested.

> Mentions specific materials and equipment the grant will fund.

The teachers, district administration, and I are excited about the prospect of partnering with you. Thank you for considering our request.

> The duration of the project has not yet been mentioned. This basic information must be mentioned early in the proposal for reviewers to be able to put the scope of the project and the amount requested into perspective.

(Continued)

Proposal Example *(Continued)*

Community Profile

The Farmington Aztec Cuba (FAC) School District is located in a rural area of northwestern New Mexico, approximately 150 miles from Albuquerque. Much of the workforce travels up to 75 miles to Farmington for employment. Several families own and work agricultural and livestock farms in the area. Oil and gas drilling are major enterprises. Our adjoining neighbor, the Ute Mountain Indian Reservation, including Sun Burst Casino, employs many area residents. Median household income for the area is $23,987. Three elementary schools feed into the middle school from the two surrounding towns of Aztec and Cuba and several of the smallest towns in New Mexico. A little over 300 students are enrolled at FAC Middle School (309 in 2009–2010), which is composed of seventh and eighth grades. In the 2009–2010 school year, 56 percent of students were eligible for free or reduced-price lunch.

> Provides a good overview of the community.

> Last two sentences could be relocated to the organizational (or school) profile.

Library and Organizational Profile

The Library Media Center is a shared facility connecting the two middle and high school buildings. The collection of approximately 28,000 items serves both populations. Two full-time librarians and one library aide staff the library. The Library Media Center supports the curriculum of the school, and the library media specialists have the vital role of teaching students information and technology skills. At present, the library has limited technological resources. Because of increasing integration of technology in the curriculum to meet the National Technology Education Standards (NETS) and to prepare students for the twenty-first century, we are finding that the 20 computers in the library and two labs across the hall, which serve grades 7–12, are in use most of the school day. Because of heavy use and scheduling, it is not uncommon for computers to be unavailable when a class or student needs them. It is the mission of the District Technology Planning Team (DTPT) that "All students, teachers, and staff will have equal access to appropriate technology to function and develop successfully." The District has provided equal access, but, with declining state budgets and increased technology demands of the curriculum, there are not enough computer stations available for our current student enrollment. This affects student productivity, learning, and achievement.

> Including the library's history, accomplishments, or status of the art and historical fiction collections would enhance this library profile.

> Information about needs belongs in the need statement.

To fulfill the purpose of the Visual Literacy project, middle school students will need to have computers accessible to them and areas of the library collection will need to be updated. Enhancing the library's art and historical fiction collections, as well as creating a visual/poster collection, will provide students and teachers access to resources that complement classroom instruction. Providing interactive whiteboard technology and laptop carts in the classroom will support the DTPT mission mentioned earlier and the online portion of the project: searching for information, visuals, ethically using visuals, posting to the wiki, and learning digital citizenship and etiquette. All of these skills are a substantial component of the NETS and continue to be implemented by teachers in the district in all curriculum areas.

> Because this paragraph explains what the project will do, it belongs in the project description.

(Continued)

Proposal Example *(Continued)*

Need Statement

To promote student achievement and success, we are seeking funds to implement the Visual Literacy project. This project will address the need of students to be able to visually interpret a picture. On the 2010 New Mexico State Social Studies Eighth Grade Exam, there were two questions where students displayed a poor ability to evaluate historical pictures to determine time period and place. (See Appendix B.) Only 47 percent of students correctly answered a question involving a newspaper photograph of the Lusitania from World War I. On another question regarding the Great Depression, 57 percent of students answered a question correctly when provided with a picture from the Dust Bowl era. Students need to learn a strategy, or a method, to help them decipher and study a picture, break it down, and pull some meaning from it.

> To enhance the need statement include information about why visual literacy is important, its relevance to digital citizenship, and using pictures ethically.

> Using data in a need statement is a very powerful way to demonstrate need.

Project Description

The primary goal of this project is to improve student visual information literacy: the ability to interpret, analyze, and construct meaning from pictures (or learn a strategy to interpret art by well-known artists and then apply the strategy to historical photographs). Introduction of the strategy employing artistic elements of description, elements of art, and principles of design to interpret art will be taught in seventh grade. All seventh grade students in art class will then study techniques of various well-known artists using the Getting to Know series of books. Students will select an artist and complete the "Space Project" by analyzing one piece of art and replicating an art technique. (See Appendix C.) To support this curriculum the library will have on display various art posters for students to submit their interpretations. The librarian will add these to a project wiki for all students to view.

> Mention the project's goal at the beginning of the project description.

The project will then continue in eighth grade. Students will transfer what they have learned about deriving meaning from art and apply it to historical photographs. They will practice this in social studies class. Their assignment will be to locate and choose a picture from U.S. history using the Library of Congress American Memory website, interpret it, and add it (or supply a hyperlink to it, depending on copyright) to the project wiki. Students will also be required to post two comments on a submission by their peers.

> Describing project activities in chronological order outlines the strategy, approach, or methodology.

During the two-year project, language arts teachers will include one historical novel per year as a required choice for a book report. This will help students gain background knowledge, other than textbook information, of various time periods in U.S. history. A complete listing of activities and staff involved are provided within this proposal on the timeline chart.

> Mention project duration near the beginning of the proposal, that is, in the cover letter and executive summary.

Objectives:

By completion of the project in June 2014:
1. Student scores in regard to historical photographs on the 2014 New Mexico State Social Studies Eighth Grade Exam will increase 75 percent.

> These are excellent SMART objectives; however, this proposal would read more smoothly if the objectives followed the goal.

(Continued)

Proposal Example (Continued)

2. Of eighth graders who participated in this project, 75 percent will say that the use of a strategy employing artistic items (description, art elements, and principles of design) has increased their confidence and ability to interpret artistic items and historical photographs.
3. Of students who participated, 75 percent will say that the project has raised their awareness of plagiarism/ethical use of images.
4. Of students who participated, 75 percent will say that the project has raised their awareness of digital citizenship.
5. Of students who participated, 75 percent will say that the project has increased their confidence and ability to navigate websites (Library of Congress American Memory database, project wiki, etc.).

Outcomes:
- Students will gain confidence in their ability to interpret visuals (i.e., art, historical photographs).
- Students will know how to use a strategy employing artistic items, such as description elements (foreground, background, medium, title, artist, and when created); elements of art (line, shape, form and volume, space, color, value, and texture); and principles of design (pattern and repetition, variety, emphasis, harmony and unity, balance, contrast, proportion, rhythm and movement) to interpret art and historical photographs.
- Students will increase their technology skill of navigating the Internet and Library of Congress American Memory database, using digital pictures ethically and responsibly.
- Students will acquire the technology skill of using visual pictures ethically (provide credit for them in the form of a Works Cited to avoid plagiarism).
- Students will develop digital citizenship by writing and typing their interpretation, posting it to the project wiki, and commenting on two submissions by their peers.
- Student access to technology will be increased.

> The first six are very good outcomes for students.

- The art section of the library collection will be increased by approximately 65 titles.
- The historical fiction section of the library collection will be increased by approximately 100 titles.
- A collection of approximately 45 reproduced art posters and historical photographs will be created and available for use to support the Visual Literacy project.

> The next three are objectives, not outcomes.

Although the grant timeline is two years, the project will continue on with the next class of seventh graders, eventually reaching every student in the district. The learned artistic strategy will build on sixth grade knowledge and is a skill that students can take with them to use in the upper grades in any subject, and beyond. The library media specialist will supervise and manage the project but will partner, support, and work closely with the art, social studies, and language arts teachers. This group will make up the Visual Literacy project team (see Appendix F, Key Staff) that will be instrumental in carrying out the project and managing the grant.

> Funders want to know your project is sustainable.

(Continued)

150

Proposal Example *(Continued)*

Evaluation Plan

The project will be evaluated both quantitatively and qualitatively. Qualitative data will come from the 2014 New Mexico State Social Studies Eighth Grade Exam, while qualitative data will come from teachers and students. Teachers will evaluate the project through observation of students completing the assignments, student grades, and classroom participation. This will be discussed at grant team meetings. Students will be provided the opportunity to give feedback in the form of an online survey or questionnaire at the completion of the project.

Objective/Outcome	Evaluation Method/Tool
Student scores in regard to historical photographs on the 2014 New Mexico State Social Studies Eighth Grade Exam will increase 75 percent.	Scores on the 2014 New Mexico State Social Studies Eighth Grade Exam will be used.
Of eighth graders who participated in this project, 75 percent will say that the use of a strategy employing artistic items (description, art elements, and principles of design) has increased their confidence and ability interpret artistic items and historical photographs.	Students will complete an online survey/questionnaire at the conclusion of the project, including the opportunity for comments/feedback on the project.
Of students who participated, 75 percent will say that the project has raised their awareness of plagiarism and ethical use of images.	Students will complete an online survey/questionnaire at the conclusion of the project, including the opportunity for comments/feedback on the project.
Of students who participated, 75 percent will say that the project has raised their awareness of digital citizenship.	Students will complete an online survey/questionnaire at the conclusion of the project, including the opportunity for comments/feedback on the project.
Of students who participated, 75 percent will say that the project has increased their confidence and ability to navigate websites (Library of Congress American Memory database, project wiki, etc.).	Students will complete an online survey/questionnaire at the conclusion of the project, including the opportunity for comments/feedback on the project.

This evaluation plan is very well done. It explains how each objective will be measured and what evaluation tools and methods will be used.

151

(Continued)

Proposal Example *(Continued)*

Budget

Personnel Budget

Personnel	Match	Amount Requested
Five project team members (three social studies teachers, one art teacher, one library media specialist) @ $40/hr each meet for (six) 2-hour meetings = 60 hours.	$2,400.00	
Library media specialist @ $40/hr administers grant, coordinates project, sets up wiki, and maintains progress/ updates = 54 hours.		$2,160.00
Total Personnel Budget	**$2,400.00**	**$2,160.00**

> A funder is usually encouraged by a match. This shows your commitment to the project.

> A funder wants to know that staff benefits are included. A separate column for benefits or indicating cost of benefits in the calculation would make this clear.

Non-Personnel Budget

Item	Match	Amount Requested
Five Promethean boards 378 DLP with arm-mounted projector and integrated speakers		$3,199.00 × 5 = $15,995.00
Five wall mounts for 378 board		$980.00 × 5 = $4,900.00
Rails for (five) 378 boards @ $130 each		$650.00
One art teacher laptop		$999.99
One cart for art teacher (Bretford presentation cart with 4″ casters and power)		$228.42
Two Bretford Basics 30 computer intelligent laptop carts @ $1,673 each		$3,346.00
Sixty laptops for four carts @ $999.99 each		$59,999.40
Two laser printers (HP2055dn), one per laptop cart @ $406.99 each		$813.98
Two wireless access points (Apple Airport Extreme Base Station) @ $197.50 each		$395.00
One set of *Getting to Know* books for art room		$310.31

> The strength of this budget is in the breakdown of technology costs. This shows a funder that the applicant has thought carefully about what the project needs to accomplish and they have done their research.

(Continued)

Proposal Example *(Continued)*

Non-Personnel Budget *(Continued)*

Item	Match	Amount Requested
New materials for art section of library		$5,000.00
Print and poster holder for housing art and historical photographs (Brodart)		$171.95
New historical fiction materials for library		$5,000.00
New art posters and historical photographs depicting U.S. history for library		$4,000.00
Total Non-Personnel Costs	**0**	**$100,810.06**

Project Budget

	Match	Amount Requested
Total Personnel Costs	$2,400.00	$2,160.00
Total Non-Personnel Costs		$100,810.06
Total Project Cost	**$2,400.00**	**$102,970.06**

Timeline

The timeframe for the project spans over the two years students are at the middle school. Students have the same social studies, language arts, art, and library media specialist teachers over these two years because grades seven and eight have <u>looped contact</u>. Students have social studies and language arts classes every day but art only for a quarter each year. The Library Media Center operates on a flexible schedule and accommodates classes based on their needs, and/or the library media specialist visits the subject classroom to provide information skills instruction.

Avoid jargon.

This information is more suited to the project description.

Who, What	Year 1 (seventh graders)				Year 2 (eighth graders)			
	First Marking Period	Second Marking Period	Third Marking Period	Fourth Marking Period	First Parking period	Second Marking Period	Third Marking Period	Fourth Marking Period
Library media specialist collaborates with art teacher to order art books, process materials, and add them to the collection. Year 1.	←→							

This timeline is outstanding. It is clear who is going to do what and when. Funders can see the entire project at a glance.

(Continued)

Proposal Example *(Continued)*

Timeline *(Continued)*

Who, What	Year 1 (seventh graders)				Year 2 (eighth graders)			
	First Marking Period	Second Marking Period	Third Marking Period	Fourth Marking Period	First Marking Period	Second Marking Period	Third Marking Period	Fourth Marking Period
Library media specialist collaborates with language arts teachers to order, process, and add historical fiction books to the collection. Year 1.	←→	→						
Library media specialist collaborates with art teacher and social studies teachers to order art posters and historical photograph posters, processes them, and develops new poster collection for visual literacy. Year 1.	←→	→						
Library media specialist orders and processes all technology equipment. Year 1.		←→	→					
Art teacher introduces strategy employing artistic elements of description, elements of art, and principles of design to interpret art. Year 1.	←			→				
Art teacher oversees students studying techniques of various well-known artists using *Getting to Know* series. Students will select an artist and complete "Space Project" (analyzing one piece of art and replicating an art technique). Year 1.	←			→				

(Continued)

154

Proposal Example *(Continued)*

Timeline *(Continued)*

Who, What	Year 1 (seventh graders)				Year 2 (eighth graders)			
	First Marking Period	Second Marking Period	Third Marking Period	Fourth Marking Period	First Marking Period	Second Marking Period	Third Marking Period	Fourth Marking Period
Language arts teacher oversees students' language arts classes reading at least one historical novel each year (U.S. history) for book report to gain historical background knowledge. Year 1 and Year 2.			⟷			⟷		
Library media specialist oversees bulletin board in Library hallway with an art picture that students can add their opinions/interpretations of the piece using the artistic items of description, elements of art, and principles of design. Post final results and comments to a wiki. Year 1.	⟷							
Library media specialist, social studies teacher, and art teacher teach students to access the Internet and the Library of Congress website. They select and interpret a U.S. historical picture. Year 2.						⟷		
Library media specialist and social studies teacher oversee students ethically posting their interpretation of historical photograph to the wiki, include their interpretation, and comment on two submissions by their peers. Year 2.							⟷	

(Continued)

155

Proposal Example *(Continued)*

Timeline *(Continued)*

Grant team meets six times to plan (develop U.S. historical photograph interpretation project, grading rubric, warm ups/bell ringers, a model project, surveys, etc.) and communicate about progress.	Meeting one (Sept.–Nov.)	Meeting two (Dec.–Feb.)	Meeting three (Mar.–May)	Meeting one (Sept.–Nov.)	Meeting two (Dec.–Feb.)	Meeting three (Mar.–May)
	✕	✕	✕	✕	✕	✕

First marking period = September through Mid-October.
Second marking period = Mid-October through January.
Third marking period = February through Mid-April.
Fourth marking Period = April through June.

Year 1—The art teacher will be working with the seventh graders and teaching them the strategy for evaluating art and practicing on a well-known piece of art. They will study an artist and try to replicate the artist's technique. In addition, students will read a historical novel as one of their language arts book reports to acquire background knowledge of U.S. history.

Year 2—Students will work with historical photographs and select one to interpret. They will ethically post the historical photograph to a wiki with their interpretation, inviting other students to comment. Each student will comment on two submissions by their peers. In addition, students will read a historical novel as one of their language arts book reports to increase their background knowledge of American history.

These activities belong in the project description where they will further clarify the approach or methodology.

Appendices:
A. Letters of Administrative Support
B. Data from the 2010 New Mexico Social Studies Eighth Grade Exam
C. Art "Space Project" Curriculum
D. Photos of Library and School Building
E. Library Budget
F. Profiles of Key Staff
G. List of Board Members
H. Organizational Chart

The appendices are very thorough, providing supporting documentation for the need statement; qualifications of staff; commitment from administration; and a view of the school, library, and curriculum.

Source: Adapted from a proposal by Amy Austin.

with proposal writing. The grant process involves making the commitment, planning, designing projects, organizing teams, understanding sources, and doing the research before it is time to select the right grant and write the proposal.

- Embrace a "proactive" approach to grant work by starting the process early. Spend time to complete the preliminary steps of grant work before you identify a funder and begin writing a proposal. Proactive grant seekers devote smaller amounts of time to the process throughout the grant-seeking process. They do not start with writing a proposal.

- Avoid a "reactive" approach, which is to start with finding an RFP and writing a proposal. Reactive grant seekers devote inordinate amounts of time writing proposals because they have to go back and do the preliminary steps while they are racing against a deadline.

- Follow the directions and guidelines carefully. They will tell you what you must include in your proposal. This can be as simple as following an outline, or it can be very complex, prescribing font size, margin size, line spacing, kind of binding, and much more. Arrange your proposal in the format specified by the funder. This applies to both paper and electronic submissions. Federal agencies will reject a proposal that does not adhere to every detail specified in the guidelines—including incorrect font size. If you have questions, contact the funder.

- Be open to developing several approaches as you design your project and write your proposal. Extricate yourself from the notion that a single project idea is the only way to address the need you have identified. Project designers and proposal writers who think this way miss opportunities to learn about alternative ways to solve a problem.

- Avoid writing general proposals. A general proposal, written to submit to multiple funders, lacks specificity and is not sufficiently targeted to a funder's priorities. Shotgun approaches result in a high number of rejections and establish your library in a negative light with funders.

- It's all about people, not things. Ground your projects in meeting the needs of your community. A technology grant is never about buying technology. Avoid writing about what the library needs or focusing on the lack of something, like computers. By definition, everyone who applies for a grant lacks something. This is not a compelling reason for a funder to give you a grant.

- Complete a community needs assessment, and have your strategic plan and technology plan in place prior to writing a proposal. Identify a specific need and target population before you begin to write.

- Have someone from outside your library read your proposal before you submit it. Ask them if they understand what you are proposing.

- Keep your basic proposal components on file and updated.

- Continuously form partnerships and collaborations.

- Keep it simple.

- Do the math correctly.

- Write SMART objectives.

Proposal Writing Tips

1. Follow all instructions, grant guidelines, and format requirements.
2. Organize your thoughts and identify the central point of your proposal before you start to write.
3. Outline what you want to say in the format required by the funder.
4. Display confidence and capability by presenting your project with the belief that it will be successful.
5. Be proactive.
6. Keep it simple.
7. Revise and edit. Read and reread.
8. Avoid jargon, including "librarian-ese."
9. Explain or clarify acronyms.
10. Use the active voice to convey that you own the project and that you will be doing the work.
11. Avoid flowery or exaggerated language.
12. Keep research and data up to date.
13. Demonstrate your ability to achieve the stated objectives. Your proposal must show that you will be able to successfully implement the project.
14. Be persuasive, but reinforce your claims with plans.
15. Be specific and include strong goals, measurable objectives, and outcomes.
16. Be concise and to the point. Elaborate only to provide necessary depth and detail.
17. Emphasize collaboration and partnerships throughout your proposal.
18. Build a concise, logical case for your project.
19. Write your executive summary, abstract, or summary last.
20. Check your budget to make sure costs are reasonable and current and the math is right.
21. Plan in advance for letters of support.
22. Watch trends in funding and incorporate a forward-thinking approach.
23. Enlist draft reviewers.

Summary

Writing a proposal is similar to sales or marketing in that you are trying to convince a funder to support your project. Your proposal tells the story of your community, your library, and your community's needs; it describes your project and your approach and how your project will make a positive and even life-changing impact on the lives of people in the community you serve. Good proposal writing follows the principles of good writing in general.

Additional Resources

Browning, Beverly A. 2005. *Grant Writing for Dummies*. Hoboken, NJ: Wiley.

———. *Perfect Phrases for Writing Grant Proposals: Hundreds of Ready-to-Use Phrases to Present Your Organization, Explain Your Cause, and Get the Funding You Need*. New York: McGraw-Hill.

Clarke, Cheryl A. 2001. *Storytelling for Grantseekers: The Guide to Creative Nonprofit Fundraising*. San Francisco: Jossey-Bass.

Ezell, Tom, Carole Nugent, Sergio González, Creed C. Black, and Rhonda Ritchie. 2000. *The Grantwriter's Start-Up Kit: A Beginner's Guide to Grant Proposals*. San Francisco, CA: Jossey-Bass Publishers.

Geever, Jane C. 2004. *The Foundation Center's Guide to Proposal Writing.* 4th ed. New York: The Foundation Center.

Gitlin, Laura N., and Kevin J. Lyons. 2008. *Successful Grant Writing: Strategies for Health and Human Service Professionals.* New York: Springer.

Hale, P.D. 1997. *Writing Grant Proposals That Win.* Alexandria, VA: Capitol.

Hall, Mary S., and Susan Howlett. 2003. *Getting Funded: The Complete Guide to Writing Grant Proposals.* 4th ed. Portland, OR: Portland State University.

Harris, Dianne. 2007. *The Complete Guide to Writing Effective & Award Winning Grants: Step-by-Step Instructions.* Ocala, FL: Atlantic.

Koch, Deborah. 2009. *How to Say It—Grantwriting: Write Proposals That Grantmakers Want to Fund.* New York: Prentice Hall.

Margolin, Judith B. 2008. *The Grantseeker's Guide to Winning Proposals.* New York: The Foundation Center.

Miller, P.W. 2000. *Grant-Writing: Strategies for Developing Winning Proposals.* Munster, IN: Patrick W. Miller & Associates.

Miner, Jeremy T., and Lynn E. Miner. 2008. *Proposal Planning and Writing.* Westport, CT: Greenwood.

Reif-Lehrer, L. 2004. *Grant Application Writer's Handbook.* Boston: Jones and Bartlett.

Smith, Nancy Burke, and Judy Tremore. 2008. *The Everything Grant Writing Book: Create the Perfect Proposal to Raise the Funds You Need.* Avon, MA: Adams Media.

Smith, Nancy Burke, and E. Gabriel Works. 2006. *The Complete Book of Grant Writing: Learn to Write Grants Like a Professional.* Naperville, IL: Sourcebooks.

Thompson, Waddy. 2007. *The Complete Idiot's Guide to Grant Writing.* Indianapolis: Alpha Books.

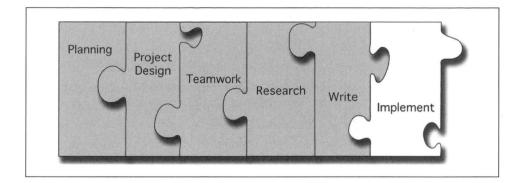

Chapter 9

Implementing Your Technology Project

After submitting your proposal, you will likely have a wait ahead of you. Funders have varying grant review processes that may be swift or lengthy. The grant guidelines or application package should give you a timeframe, letting you know when you can expect to hear from funders about whether or not they have funded your project. This is the busiest time for most funders, so, although you may be anxious to hear from them, remember that you are just one of many applicants whose proposals they are reviewing. Although it is acceptable to contact funders about their receipt of your application, refrain from calling or e-mailing them during the review process about how close they are to making a decision. As you can imagine, funders could become annoyed at receiving too many "Are we there yet?" calls. They will let you know when they have made a decision about which projects to fund.

Winning a Grant

After all the hard work you and your grant team have put into planning and proposal writing, there is no better news than to be notified that your library has been awarded a grant. If you are a grant winner, congratulations on your success at securing funding that will allow you to provide a library service or program that will make a difference in your community! Now you know you can implement a technology project to meet a community need, where previously inadequate funding would have made this less likely. The obstacle is no longer inadequate funding, so it's time to get to work. First, here are a few things to do that will help pave the way for a smooth implementation.

Thank the Funder

Write a brief letter or note on behalf of your library and grant team expressing thanks to the funder for supporting your technology project. Assure the funder that you are anticipating a successful project that will meet specific needs in your community. Tell the funder you will stay in touch and that the funder can expect to receive regular reports on your progress.

Identify a Project Manager

One person must take responsibility for implementing the project, ensuring that the work is done and the resources are available, evaluating project progress, and achieving project goals. There must be one "go to" person who is ultimately responsible for all project management decisions and answering to administration, the funder, and your community. There is no substitute for a project manager who is a strong leader and who is accountable for the success—and challenges—of the project and its implementation from start to finish.

Inform the Grant Team and Administrators

Inform your grant team about their success, and congratulate them for a job well done. Tell your administrators, department heads, mayors, principles, directors, and grants offices to keep them in the loop and give them some good news to spread around. In these tough economic times everyone likes to share the good news about a newly acquired grant. Honor your team's hard work by celebrating with them along with your administrators, leaders, partners, and supporters. It is always important to acknowledge the people whose hard work made your proposal a success and to spread the good news to everyone in your organization.

Get "Buy-In" and Commitment

It is essential that you have a commitment from the organization—including leadership and administration—to support your technology project right from the beginning of the grant process. Now, at the implementation stage, it is good practice to contact these top-level players about your first steps and remind them about the project plan. Confirm with them that they endorse the purpose of the project and that you have their commitment and support, including making available any resources you require from the organization. Often these are very busy people; however, it is important to keep them informed and remind them that you rely on their support. If you need their support in the future, you will want them to remember you and your project and exactly what your project is working to accomplish for the people you all serve. Never take their commitment for granted. Be visible.

Let all library staff know about your success and remind them about the project, that it was created from the library's plans, how it will meet a need in the community, and that it will make their jobs easier. Everyone who will be affected by project implementation and the use of technology to accomplish project goals must be "on board." If staff members have doubts about using new technology or the change involved, listen carefully to them and invite their input. They may have insight on some aspect of the project that will make your life easier in the long run, or they may make you aware of a "missing piece." You are more likely to gain support from staff, create team players, and successfully implement your project when you are a good listener.

In the beginning stages of a technology project, there is a phase called "information discovery." When projects involve technology it usually means a change in processes for staff. Before changes are implemented it is important to know what staff are currently doing and to discuss with them what this will look like after project implementation. Some staff who will be affected may not have been intimately involved in project planning or the grant process. They must be brought up to speed. Find out what they are currently doing in their day-to-day tasks, what the processes are, and how they communicate. The idea is to identify where the project will improve their work processes and to plan integration of new technology seamlessly into their established work processes. The ultimate goal is to enhance library services and programs using technology to benefit the community—not to disrupt the work of unsuspecting staff members.

Inform Your Community

Once everyone in your library and organization has heard the good news, and you have confirmed you have their support, check in with the funder about making an announcement to the community. The funder may want you to sign a contract or agreement about the use of grant funds before announcing it to the public. Once your funder clears you to announce your success, send a press release to the local paper and media; your school district or college or university public relations office; municipal offices; state and regional library associations; and your state library. Make an announcement in the library's newsletter and on your library's webpage.

Review the Budget

First verify that the amount you were awarded is the amount you requested in your proposal. Funders sometimes fund only partial projects. If you received less than full funding, verify with the funder the scope of work it is funding. Review salaries and benefits costs, consultant costs, rent, supplies, and other expenses that may have changed since you submitted your proposal.

You can be almost certain that the technology costs in your budget have changed. This is to be expected, because technology prices have most likely fluctuated since you created the budget for your proposal. Because technology itself is a moving target, technology budgets can be a challenge to manage. New versions of hardware and software are constantly coming on the market, and you will want to purchase the newest technology for your project. Just because you specified and accurately priced technology for your budget six months ago when you prepared your proposal does not mean you must purchase what is now outdated technology. Carefully look at the technology and equipment costs, broadband costs, and software costs in your budget and recalculate this part of your budget based on current technology and prices.

Contact the funder immediately to address any discrepancies in the budget. A funder that has awarded you a technology grant will expect to hear from you. If costs have risen or new technology is available, the funder may ask you to readjust those specific items in your budget to total the same dollar amount of the grant. It is possible that a funder may fund the entire project for the higher amount. If you find that your project will cost less than you proposed, get the funder's approval to use the excess funds to support your project in other ways. Be clear and specific about what those other ways are prior to contacting the funder. Funders are not likely to fund your project at the higher amount if you aren't sure how you will spend the excess funds.

Contact the Funder

Call the funder contact or program officer to get reacquainted or introduce yourself if you haven't already spoken with the person. Confirm that the funder has your name and correct phone, fax, and e-mail. Report that you are available if there are any questions and ask any questions you may have. Begin to develop a working relationship with your contact because he or she can be very helpful to you as you begin project implementation and throughout the life of your project.

Clarify the Terms of the Grant and Reporting Requirements

Make sure you understand the terms of the grant. If you need clarification, now is the time to ask. There may be a grant contract to sign stipulating the conditions of the grant and how the funds are to be spent. Be sure you are comfortable with the conditions of the grant contract before you or an authorized official sign it, then sign and return it as soon as possible.

Familiarize yourself with the funder's reporting requirements so that you gather the right information, you are ready to prepare your reports when they are due, and you send them to the funder on time. Insert these dates into your project timeline. Some funders require one final evaluation at the conclusion of the project, while others require periodic reports throughout the life of the project. Clarify what kind of information the funder wants to see in your reports. Minimally include all information gathered from the evaluation plan included in your proposal. Here are some things that funders may request in a progress report:

- Extent the project goal was achieved
- Summary of outcomes achieved for people
- Activities completed
- Report of expenditures
- Survey results
- Adjustments in project design
- Lessons learned
- Future plans for the grant project
- Anecdotes or interviews of project participants
- Publications or presentations about the grant project
- Honors or awards received as a result of the grant

Implementing the Project

After completing these preliminary tasks, you will want to move ahead very quickly to implement the project. It has likely been a long time since you identified a community need, designed a project, and wrote the proposal. Starting a new technology initiative can be daunting; however, you are at an advantage having just completed the grant process. You are prepared to confidently begin implementation, because the process has already led you through the following important steps:

- Securing a commitment from the organization to support your project
- Planning a project that meets specific community needs

- Designing a project that is built around goals, objectives, outcomes, and activities that arise from your library's strategic plan and technology plan
- Fostering partners and collaborators
- Developing a project timeline, evaluation plan, and budget
- Acquiring funding for the project

New technology projects differ from other kinds of library projects in that they are more likely to involve significant changes in processes, systems, and staff roles. Because there are many facets of technology projects that can be challenging, they must be managed closely. For example, implementing technology in the library may mean working with organizational or municipal IT staff, new vendors, and technology contractors. You may be issuing RFPs and hiring consultants to work on the project. Having a good knowledge about organizational politics, knowing the appropriate department heads, and having an ability to nimbly navigate your way through institutional processes can be valuable assets.

Solid strategies for implementing technology projects begin with well-executed community needs assessments, strategic plans, and technology plans. It is truly amazing how knowing your community's needs, understanding your library's plans, and having confidence that the project design is a product of your library's plans that will benefit the people in your community can set the stage for a smooth project implementation and keep you on track when you face the inevitable challenges or distractions.

The following are some steps to take as you begin project implementation.

Step 1: Name the Project

If you haven't already named your project, name it now. A project with a name encourages ownership and fosters pride in the work being done. A name will solidify the project in the minds of project staff, other library staff, administrators, city leaders, school personnel, students, teachers, and employees. Without a name, the project may blend—or even disappear—into all the other work being done in the library. Libraries are busy places with many activities going on, and you want your technology project to stand out.

Step 2: Create a Home for Your Project

Establish a "home" or physical space for project personnel to work in close proximity to each other. Give your project the recognition it deserves by defining a place for it to thrive. People need to have a place to work—one that encourages them to communicate easily with each other as they make the project come to life. A dedicated physical space encourages teamwork and good communication and promotes project "ownership."

Step 3: Hire Personnel

If the project requires new staff members or consultants, post or advertise these positions as soon as possible. In many organizations the hiring process can take some time. If you are hiring consultants or contractors, consider issuing an RFP for the scope of work you need accomplished.

165

If you are adding new project responsibilities to the jobs of existing library personnel or IT staff, meet with these people right away to clarify their new responsibilities and review their time commitment to the project. If there have been personnel changes since you submitted the proposal, introduce new personnel to the project and clarify their roles. Make sure they understand your expectations and adjust project responsibilities based on their individual strengths. Address current responsibilities that will be assumed by others for the duration of the project. Include these other staff members in the discussion. It is never acceptable to add project responsibilities to a staff member's job without compensation.

When you first identified project personnel for the purposes of writing a grant proposal, it was possible that some people agreed to be listed as project personnel without thinking too much about what that would entail. Things change and circumstances may have influenced a person's interest in participating. Check in with all project personnel to make sure they are committed to working on the project and that they understand what is expected of them.

Step 4: Create the Team

It is essential to have the "right" people on the project team. All project personnel must believe in the importance of the project, know the goals, understand the community needs being met, and believe that the project will improve people's lives. Integrate organizational IT staff into the team even if your organization doesn't typically do this. IT staff who will do the work of the project must be as committed to the project as other staff members. Part of being committed is being part of the team.

Create a resilient team, one that can weather adversity and stay productive through the difficult patches. Hire team players, people who complement each other, who are reliable, motivated, and resilient. Foster an environment of mutual respect and facilitate communication.

Step 5: Focus on the Vision

Librarians who are focused primarily on meeting community needs are more likely to implement successful technology projects than librarians who are focused on the technology itself. Keep your eye on how the project will make a difference for people in your community rather than acquiring technology for the sake of acquiring technology.

Create a project vision that is tied to outcomes for people. When it comes to technology projects it is easy to become consumed by the details or distracted by the new technology. Team members often concentrate on their tasks and the jobs at hand, losing sight of the big picture—or the value for the customer. Remind them about the connection between what they are doing and the project goals. Remember what you are trying to achieve. The project is not about installing servers and routers; buying new computers, iPads, or video gaming equipment; digitizing materials; or providing e-books. It is about enhancing access to information for people or enabling people to use information that will make a difference in their lives. Focusing on the vision will help you and team members make decisions that will contribute to the actualization of the vision.

Step 6: Establish a Baseline for Evaluation

Begin implementing the evaluation plan for your project as soon as you receive funding. After securing funding and before your project is implemented, you must establish a baseline or starting point against which you will measure your success. Your proposal's evaluation plan articulated how you will evaluate your project, beginning with how you will establish a baseline for measuring your progress. You might do an assessment of current knowledge among the beneficiaries of your project, establish the state of technology in your library, conduct a preproject survey, or update the community needs assessment to establish an accurate baseline. If the needs assessment took place many months ago, take into account any recent changes in your community's population demographics. Where you start the evaluation depends on the nature of your project and the objectives specified in your project design. Reread the objectives and the evaluation methodology in your proposal, and start working on this aspect of your project right away. Remember to include information the funder requires in the progress reports.

Step 7: Issue RFPs for Technology

If your project involves purchasing extensive technology, hardware or software, electronic products, digitization equipment, or computer systems, issue RFPs for these products. You may have found out as you developed the budget for your proposal that database vendors or library automation system vendors, for instance, are not likely to reveal the "cost" of their products without knowing more about your specifications. This is because there are many ways to customize products for libraries, and each customized product is priced differently. When you create an RFP for exactly what you want, vendors will respond only to your specifications. This will save you time and provide a way for you to compare "like" products. You will be in the driver's seat, and the selection process will go more smoothly.

Step 8: Purchase Equipment, Materials, and Supplies

Technology projects by definition mean that you will be acquiring technology. When you were first notified that your project was funded, you reviewed the budget and notified the funder about any price fluctuations. You may have signed an agreement about the use of funds that included a revised technology budget. Issue purchase orders or place orders for equipment and technology immediately before the prices fluctuate again. At this time, also make any other purchases that are necessary for project upstart in the way of supplies, equipment, and materials.

Step 9: Update the Project Timeline

All project tasks must be defined prior to implementation. Using the timeline from your proposal, update the activities by including each detailed step, specific personnel responsible for each activity, and inclusive dates for every activity. Change generic timeframes on your timeline such as "Month 1" to specific dates. Post the timeline in a prominent place in the project work area where project personnel will see it daily. At the beginning implementation stages there may be some future activities that are vaguely defined. Brief statements and general timeframes can be more clearly defined

167

later when you are more familiar with how the project is progressing. The timeline provides the essential structure for project implementation and formally states the scope of work. It is a tool that allows time and personnel cost estimates, scheduling and resource requirements, and assimilates change. Share timeline updates with all team members, and review the timeline in team meetings throughout project implementation.

Step 10: Provide Staff Training

Prepare team members and library staff for implementation with the necessary training and support. This is especially important when new technology is involved. Employing technology will not be productive if staff are not proficient in its use. Most commercial library product vendors provide training as part of the purchase price. Ensure that all library staff who will be affected attend training.

Step 11: Monitor the Project

An essential part of project implementation is monitoring progress or the degree to which you are reaching project goals and objectives. You must start this as soon as you begin to address community needs by measuring the change from the baseline data established earlier.

Step 12: Maintain Flexibility and Adaptability

Although it is important to implement the project as it has been presented to the funder, it is equally important to remain flexible and adaptable when unexpected events arise. Use the project design as a guide for project implementation, not as a "master" or unchangeable document. It is not necessary—it can even be detrimental—to stick to every minute detail of your project plan when things are going awry. Instill this capability in your team so that when something is not working they will trouble-shoot the problem with open minds rather than continuing to do what isn't working simply because that is what the plan dictates.

Summary

Once you have the implementation phase in place, it is a matter of managing the project through to completion. Before you forget all about the grant process, life goes back to "normal," and your job reverts to what it was before you went through it, it is essential that you pause to review and debrief the grant process. It only makes sense to use your experiences to prepare for the next round of grant applications. There is no better time to purposefully take a look at how it went and make a concerted effort to improve and build grant work into your job as a librarian.

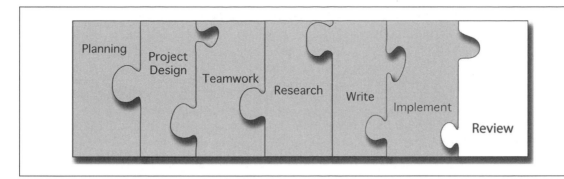

Chapter 10

Reviewing and Continuing the Grant Process

Whether you are already implementing a project that was funded or you are ready to continue the grant process for a project that still needs funding, your next step is to review the grant process you just completed. The purpose is to identify where you excelled, what you can do to improve, what steps in the process need more attention, and what you would do exactly the same way the next time around. As you debrief and review you will see how to weave grant work into your job as a librarian. By doing this, grant work will become second nature and success at winning grants will follow.

The grant process does not stop when you hear back from a funder. It continues as long as you are seeking grant funding—and in this economic climate it is a wise librarian who continues seeking grants and alternative funding to provide library services, programs, and projects.

Debrief and Review

Shortly after hearing from a funder about whether or not your project was funded, take some time to meet with your grant team to discuss the entire grant process. There is no better time to look back at how it went than after you have just received word from a funder about whether or not your project was funded. The process is still fresh in your minds, and this is the best time to review lessons learned so you can apply them to future grant work.

It usually takes experiencing the process once—from the commitment and planning stages through submitting the proposal—before you can really understand how it works. Reviewing the process at this point will give you an opportunity to look objectively at the process at a time when your team is not actually experiencing the process. In this "neutral" space you will be able to look back and see where you can make improvements or adjustments for the next time around.

Share openly with each other about what went well and what didn't go so well. The point is to learn lessons you can apply to the process going forward, not to lay blame or focus on what has already happened. Establish some ground rules for the debriefing meeting, especially if the process was challenging or didn't go so well for your team. There is always something to learn by debriefing and reviewing that will help you improve on the process. Remember to document what the team decides to do differently the next time, and pass this document on to the next grant team for its first meeting.

After debriefing and reviewing, it is important to continue with the grant process. You and your team have gained momentum. Don't let it disappear. Now that you have your strategic plan in place, your community profile and needs assessment have been updated, and you have discovered and designed several projects, the process will likely go more smoothly and be less time-consuming.

When Your Project Is Not Funded

If your project is not funded, contact the funder and ask for feedback on your proposal. When reviewers read proposals, they take notes and write comments that are used to determine which projects they recommend for funding and which ones they do not. Often the comments will tell you where you went wrong, where you can make improvements, where you did not make yourself clear, and where you were successful. Sometimes you can find out how many submissions there were and where your proposal was ranked among them. Although some funders do not release comments, reveal rankings, or provide feedback, it is worthwhile to ask because you can learn a great deal from the reviewers' feedback. Remember to remain objective and stay positive. Reviewers must pay attention to the smallest details to separate the proposals they will fund from the others. Although some comments may seem trivial to you, they indicate how the reviewers decided which projects to fund. Don't disregard them or minimize them; rather, learn from them.

Maintain a healthy perspective about a rejection. You may have written an outstanding proposal, but if the funder had funds to award only a few proposals, even some excellent ones had to be denied. A funder with more resources might have funded your proposal. Keep trying.

Many funders will provide a list of the projects they funded, and some make abstracts or executive summaries of the winning proposals available online. It is well worth your time to look at the successful projects, because this could give you a clearer understanding of a funder's priorities or give you some insight into why your proposal wasn't funded. Here are some common reasons why proposals are rejected:

- The applicant did not follow the guidelines or application instructions.
- The format specified by the funder was not followed.
- The project did not match the funder's priorities and interests.
- The grant request was not within the funding range.
- The goal or purpose of the project did not relate to community needs.
- The proposal was disorganized, unclear, or difficult to understand.
- The proposal was poorly written.
- The proposal did not make a good case.
- There were math errors in the budget.

- Items in the budget (including technology) did not relate to the project.
- Personnel to do the work were seriously underestimated or did not appear in the budget.
- Personnel in the budget were not reflected in the project design.
- There were no partners or collaborators.
- The evaluation plan was not well thought out.
- The evaluation plan did not measure project objectives or outcomes for people.
- The project wasn't sustainable.
- There was no evidence that the organization or community supported the project idea.

Continuing the Grant Process

By experiencing all the steps in the grant process you have already done the hard work of preparing the groundwork for new grant opportunities that come your way. You now have an updated community needs assessment, community profile, organizational profile, strategic plan, technology plan, and project design. You can make grant work part of your job by staying informed about your community's needs, keeping your plans up to date, updating your proposal components, continuing to do the research, participating in professional development and continuing education, fostering partnerships and building relationships, joining fundraising groups, and volunteering to be a grant reviewer.

Keep Plans and Assessments Up-to-Date

The grant process is always aligned with your library's plans, including the strategic plan, technology plan, and resulting project plans. So, when you update your strategic plan or technology plan, or you are aware of new community needs, you must build these changes into your existing project plans or create new ones. When you update and review all your plans continuously, as changes occur in your community, this becomes a matter of course—a normal part of your job. Creating strategic plans and technology plans, performing needs assessments, and designing project plans can be overwhelming when you do this every three to five years or so. When done on an ongoing basis, updating plans is not such a daunting task. When you keep your plans up to date, you are always ready to apply for a new grant opportunity.

Update Proposal Components

Certain proposal components can be updated along with the library's plans. The statement of need can be adjusted as your community needs assessment is updated. You may have several statements of need, depending on your particular community and the various projects you have planned. Your community profile, often part of the statement of need, can be updated as your municipality, college or university, school, or organization changes and information about its residents, students, employees, or people served is updated. When new census data is released, incorporate this information into your community profile and statement of need. Collect any current articles about your community's status that may not be reflected in census data.

171

Regularly update your organizational overview as you would your résumé. Add new achievements, events and programming, leadership, board members, and key staff members. Keep articles from local newspapers and library newsletters about events at your library and honors or awards. Update your vision, mission, and budget figures. Anecdotes, success stories, and endorsements from satisfied customers and partners or collaborators can keep this component fresh and current.

Continue to Do the Research
Stay up to date with new grant opportunities by subscribing to the *Library Grants Blog* and to e-mail alerts and RSS feeds at Grants.gov and individual government agencies. Frequently check websites of foundations, corporations, and government departments that fund projects like yours.

Participate in Professional Development and Continuing Education
There is always more to learn about grants and proposal writing, so take tutorials, classes, and webinars whenever you have the opportunity. Here are some possibilities:

- Go to your local community foundation for workshops on their resources, researching grant opportunities, or preparing grant proposals.
- Attend information sessions given by foundations in your area.
- Take Foundation Center tutorials, online classes, webinars, and classroom training on proposal writing, proposal budgeting, and funding research.
- Watch for free webinars on grants for libraries at TechSoup and WebJunction.
- The Grantsmanship Center offers an intensive five-day Grantsmanship Training Program.
- Look to your state library for workshops or guidance on grant research, proposal writing, or how to apply for LSTA and other funding.
- Federal agencies often offer free regional informational sessions and workshops on upcoming funding opportunities.
- Attend workshops on grants research, proposal writing, and project planning at your state, regional, or national library association conference.

Foster Partnerships and Build Relationships
It is best to create and nurture partnerships when you are not under pressure to write a proposal on a tight application deadline. Continuously work on these relationships as a matter of course. Make a point of meeting people outside your organization, leaders in the community, and key people in agencies or businesses that are doing activities that relate to the projects you have planned. Put some effort into working together with organizational IT staff whenever you have the opportunity, and work on maintaining positive relationships with these people. Find common areas of interest, and find out where your mission and theirs have commonalities. Also, make a point of building relationships with potential funders. If you have already received a grant, recognize your funder by using its name and logo on project materials, distribute press releases, and spread the word in your newsletter and on your library's website. Invite the funder to special events, and recognize the funder at your annual

award program. Thank funders and keep them updated about the progress of your project.

Join Fundraising Groups and Associations

Join your state or local fundraising groups and associations. You will meet others in your community who are experienced fundraisers and proposal writers, and you may be invited to workshops about grants and proposal writing or talks by local funders. You will have the opportunity to network and join a supportive group with others like you who are searching for grants and writing proposals. Groups like this can offer advice and support in the grant process.

Be a Grant Reviewer

Volunteer to be a grant reviewer. You can learn a lot about the grant process and how to build stronger proposals while also building relationships with funders. Sometimes requests for grant reviewers are issued by government agencies and foundations using an online form.

Summary

Now you have all the information you need to start the grant process on your own. If you need any ideas to motivate you or help you with creative project ideas, spend some time reading the next chapter on successfully funded technology projects. Remember to customize your project designs to your community and your library.

Chapter 11

Technology Grant Success Stories

To give you some inspiration and to motivate you to seek funding opportunities for your library technology projects, here are some examples of successfully funded library technology projects. These projects were developed to meet specific needs in communities and address the priorities of particular funders. No two communities have the same needs, nor do they require the same library services and programs. Likewise, no two funders have the exact same priorities or interests. Starting with the needs among the people in your community and your library's plans, use these success stories to brainstorm project ideas that apply to your library, and think about funder possibilities that might be appropriate for your technology project.

Government-Funded Technology Projects

@CCESS CENTER: The Public Library of the Future
Toledo–Lucas County Public Library
Toledo, Ohio

175

The Toledo–Lucas County Public Library (TLCPL), in partnership with a wide array of community-serving institutions in the region, proposes a much-needed expansion of public computer access for Toledo residents through its @CCESS CENTER project. The @CCESS Center project plans to renovate and expand an existing library computer center and add a mobile unit to provide broadband access and training. Both the expanded library computer center and the mobile unit will provide one-on-one instruction in basic computer skills, Internet use, job search, e-mail account management, and healthcare and preventative care awareness. The library also proposes to provide classes for small business owners and those interested in starting a small business. Proposed class topics include writing a business plan, business finances, health and safety regulations, and starting your own small business, as well as a key course, Retooling Your Life, which plans to teach patrons about job searches, interviewing skills, educational opportunities, and public benefits.

Grant Amount: $2,163,655

Funder: National Telecommunications and Information Administration (NTIA) Broadband Technology Opportunities Program (BTOP) for Public Computer Center Project

Funder Priorities:

- to provide access to broadband service to consumers residing in unserved areas of the country;

- to provide improved access to broadband service to consumers residing in underserved areas of the country;
- to provide broadband education, awareness, training, access, equipment, and support to: (i) Schools, libraries, medical and healthcare providers, community colleges and other institutions of higher learning, and other community support organizations; (ii) organizations and agencies that provide outreach, access, equipment, and support services to facilitate greater use of broadband services by vulnerable populations (e.g., low-income, unemployed, aged); or (iii) job-creating strategic facilities located in state or federally designated economic development zones;
- to improve access to, and use of, broadband service by public safety agencies; and
- to stimulate the demand for broadband, economic growth, and job creation.

Community Need: The City of Toledo is the eighth poorest city in the United States with an unemployment rate that has doubled from December 2006 and has an underserved population that needs twenty-first century education and retraining to improve job and life skills. The number of Toledo residents with home high-speed Internet access is lower than its surrounding Lucas County where only 55 percent of residents have broadband service. The demand for public access computers at the TLCPL far exceeds our ability to provide.

Technology Used: The technology strategy proposed includes a mobile computer lab for the @CCESS CENTER; increasing WAN bandwidth to 20 Mbps; replacing network electronics in the Kent Branch; moving MDF and upgrading data infrastructure to CAT 6; building a fixed computer lab consisting of 12 student PCs, instructor station, large LCD displays, Smartboard overlay, production software, Internet access, and online curriculum content and databases; expanding public computers to 109 units; deploying adaptive technologies; and building a mobile computer lab.

Target Audience: Larger Toledo population will be served in the @CCESS CENTER. Cybermobile will serve people in senior centers, housing units, health and social service facilities, and after-school youth sites.

Partnerships and Collaborations: City of Toledo; Lucas County, Ohio; Advocates for Basic Legal Equality, Inc.; Area Office on Aging of Northwest Ohio, Inc.; Lucas County Workforce Development Agency; Lucas Metropolitan Housing Authority; Neighborhood Health Association, Inc.; Owens Community College; Buehrer Group Architecture & Engineering Inc.; St. Vincent Mercy Medical Center; ProMedica Health System; The Andersons; Continental Security; Brooks Insurance Company; Buckeye Cable System; Fifth Third Bank; KeyBank; Library Legacy Foundation; Torrence Sound Equipment Co.; Library Design

Keys to Success:
- Start with a fine, experienced, cooperative team.
- Don't try to apply for a grant on your own.
- Your application must meet the grant requirements.

- Read the fine print.
- The grant must be a good match between what the grantor wants and what the grantee can deliver.

Challenges:

- Timeframes for reporting may be tight. Plan ahead.
- Prepare for paperwork overload.

Advice:

- Attend/participate in all orientations, webinars, and training sessions offered by the funder. They are invaluable.
- From my limited experience, federal government staff is wonderful. They are experienced professionals who want you to be in compliance and successful. They give excellent tips, share excellent models, and put you in contact with resourceful people.
- Make sure that all your financials add up. Double-check all figures with a calculator.
- When in doubt about the meaning of things, ask. Don't guess.
- If you have to file more than one report, be sure that financials and major points agree in all of them.

Contact: Margaret Danziger, Deputy Director

Project Application, Award Documents and Reports Website:
http://www2.ntia.doc.gov/grantee/toledo-lucas-county-public-library

Further Reading: Library Public Computer Center projects funded by BTOP at http://www2.ntia.doc.gov/computercenters

Septimus D. Cabaniss Papers Digitization Project
W.S. Hoole Special Collections Library
University of Alabama Libraries
Tuscaloosa, Alabama

A model demonstration project for low-cost digitization and web delivery of manuscript materials, the Septimus D. Cabaniss Papers Digitization Project (see Figure 11.1) digitized a large and nationally important manuscript collection related to the emancipation of slaves. The model was designed to enable institutions to mass-digitize manuscript collections at minimal cost, leveraging the extensive series descriptions already available in the collection finding aid to provide search and retrieval. Digitized content for the collection is linked from the finding aid, providing online access to 31.8 linear feet of valuable archival material that otherwise would not be available on the web. Software and workflows were developed to support the process of web delivery of material regardless of the current method of finding aid access.

Grant Amount: $35,758

Funder: National Historical Publications and Records Commission (NHPRC) Digitizing Historical Records Program

Figure 11.1. Septimus D. Cabaniss Papers Digitization Project Website

HOOLE LIBRARY
Gorgas - Bruno - McLure - Rodgers - UA Libraries

Septimus D. Cabaniss Papers Digitization Project

🖶 **Printer-friendly version**

The University of Alabama Libraries' Digital Services Department was awarded a grant by the National Historical Publications and Records Commission to digitize the papers of Septimus D. Cabaniss, a Civil War era attorney, noteworthy for his role as executor of the estate of a wealthy plantation owner who sought to manumit and leave property to his slaves. The grant funded project lasted 14 months, beginning in January 2010 and ending in February 2011.

Project Purpose and Significance

The purposes of this project were to scan and make available online the complete Septimus D. Cabaniss papers (1815-1889, 31.8 linear feet) in an efficient and cost effective manner, demonstrating and testing a simple and straightforward model. This model will enable other institutions to digitize large quantities of materials at a minimal cost, and still provide effective search and retrieval, as well as context of content for scholars. While we present our digital collections via Acumen, we are providing open source software to enable other institutions to implement this model regardless of the delivery system used for EAD finding aids. More information can be found on our **wiki page**.

The online finding aid serves the primary point of entry to the online material. This provides users with the same context, provenance, and order as encountered by a researcher perusing the analog materials in the reading room. Additionally, this workflow provides quick and

Funder Priorities: The NHPRC funds projects that use cost-effective methods to digitize nationally significant historical record collections and make the digital versions freely available online. Projects must make use of existing holdings of historical repositories and consist of entire collections or series. The materials should already be available to the public at the archives and described so that projects can reuse existing information to serve as metadata for the digitized collection. To make these projects as widely useful as possible for archives, historical repositories, and researchers, the applications must demonstrate:

- the national significance of the collections or records series to be digitized;
- an effective workflow that repurposes existing descriptive material rather than creating new metadata about the records;
- reasonable costs and standards for the project as well as sustainable preservation plans for the resulting digital records; and
- well-designed plans that evaluate the use of the digitized materials and the effectiveness of the methods employed in digitizing and displaying the materials.

Community Need: Easier and more cost-effective way to access digital collections

Technology Used:

- We used the Acumen Digital Library Software (open source: http://sourceforge .net/projects/acumendls/; in action here: http://acumen.lib.ua.edu/).

- We developed our own workflow support software, which is also available open source (from our wiki: http://www.lib.ua.edu/wiki/digcoll/index.php/Cabaniss), to enable others to follow our low-cost model of digitization regardless of their EAD finding aid delivery method.
- Hardware used included the Phase One Capture Back overhead scanner and Epson flatbed scanners.
- Software for optimization included Photoshop.

Target Audience: Researchers, students, faculty, other digital libraries

Keys to Success:

- Pay careful attention to the granting agency's specifications and interests.
- Extensively document the importance of the content to be digitized, including target audiences and letters of support.
- Plan. For instance, (1) map out processes and test them to verify that they work; and (2) gather reasonable time and cost estimates.

Challenges:

- Finding a nationally important manuscript collection that was processed enough for digitization, without rights restrictions or immediate preservation needs
- Obtaining documentation of, or proving, the importance of little-known collections
- Finding time to develop and test the methodology (software, processes, workflows) to support the proposal

Lessons Learned:

- Start preparing long before the grant announcements come out.
- Use previous successful grant applications and previous grant announcements as guides.
- You will spend far more time on the grant as a PI (principal investigator) than you expect. From 3 to 5 percent of your time is *not* enough!

Advice:

- Plan every detail, and test your plan, looking for points of failure and measuring time and costs.
- Make sure your project manager is capable and responsible and has all the support he or she needs.
- Prepare for the unexpected. Use the slowest measures you have for the time it will take, as this will allow time to make up for problems encountered.

Contact: Jody L. DeRidder, Head, Digital Services, the University of Alabama Libraries

Project Website: http://www.lib.ua.edu/libraries/hoole/cabaniss

Grow Your Business
Orange County Library System
Orlando, Florida

The Orlando area had a boom in the technology arena that employed 53,000 people; however, at the same time the region had a technology deficit. Workers needed basic

179

and technical skills, and employers needed training opportunities for non-English speakers. The Grow Your Business Project (see Figure 11.2) proposed to create new training classes and deliver them in multiple ways in three languages: English, Spanish, and Haitian-Creole. Grow Your Business provided two computer training tracks: a Small Business Track for employers and small businesses and a Job Seekers Course Track for employees and job seekers.

Grant Amount: $185,000

Funder: Institute of Museum and Library Services (IMLS) Leadership Grant

Funder Priorities: National Leadership Grants support projects that have the potential to advance museum, library, and archival practice. The Institute also encourages grant proposals that promote the skills necessary to develop twenty-first century communities, citizens, and workers. Proposals should address key needs and challenges that face libraries, museums, and archives. Successful proposals will be innovative responses to these challenges and will have national impact.

Community Need: Workers need basic and technical skills, and employers need training opportunities for non-English speakers.

Technology Used: Computers, software, projection equipment, and sound equipment for training; 12 laptops, one application server, software, LCD projector, and wireless printer for mobile lab

---

Figure 11.2. Grow Your Business

GROW YOUR BUSINESS
With the Orange County Library System

Public Technology Training Curriculum

Here at the Orange County Library System, we believe in offering the best technology training to our patrons and to the community. Through an IMLS grant, we have developed two curriculums to meet the needs of small business owners and job seekers/improvers. The Grow Your Business curriculum is offered through in-person training, self-paced online tutorials, and live online instruction.

Please contact us if you are interested in learning more about our technology training program - Including purchasing course booklets ($3/ea.), temporary viewing access to online tutorials, and how to sit in on a live online class.

Small Business Course Track

OCLS has mapped out course tracks to help you meet your goals and interests in small business. Classes include building a business plan, creating a businsess website, marketing strategies and more.

Job Seekers Course Track

OCLS mapped out course tracks to help you meet your goals and interests in improving your job skills. Classes include enhancing your software skills, bookkeeping, database development and more.

Several classes are also offered in Spanish and Haitian-Creole. You can find a complete list of our technology training classes. A full list of self-paced online tutorials in English, Spanish, and Haitian-Creole is also available. Check our class calendar to find what live online classes are being offered.

ORANGE COUNTY LIBRARY SYSTEM
Orlando, Florida

Target Audiences: Employers, small businesses, employees, and job seekers

Partnerships and Collaborations: Our project started with us seeing a report published by Workforce Central Florida on the state of the workforce in Central Florida and the need for technology training opportunities. We approached Workforce Central Florida to talk further about training needs and what we could offer. Their feedback was part of our successful proposal, and we continued to collaborate with them throughout the grant project. We coordinated presentations to their staff so they could refer their clients to our training and held some orientation classes at their facilities to introduce the library to their clients.

Keys to Success: Meet a genuine need in the community that is identifiable to other communities. We built on something we knew we were successful at and could provide a unique offering to meet the identified need. A lot of preplanning and coordination between multiple departments occurred during the proposal-writing process. Communication is always key in a large undertaking that involves several people and steps. Each department that would be involved in the project contributed to the proposal.

Have a project that is sustainable—even several years after the grant we still provide training. We continue to get feedback on how valuable software skills are to job seekers. People tell us how much they appreciate getting good quality training for free in a comfortable environment.

Challenges: One of the biggest challenges was getting to the people we wanted to serve. Traditional marketing wasn't enough. We had to go directly to the people to show that we had a quality product and also that we truly wanted to help the Spanish and Haitian-Creole speaking communities gain technology skills and were willing to do it in their native languages. Allowing staff the time to make personal connections to develop word-of-mouth referrals was very important and brought scheduling and time management issues with it.

Another big challenge was determining how to measure success. A couple of staff members completed training in outcome-based evaluation, and that really helped us to focus on how we could evaluate our project.

It was a challenge to get the business community to understand the quality of training that the library can offer. Because it was "free" and offered at the library people thought that it probably wasn't very good. Staff had to work hard to show people that the library was dedicated to providing quality training.

Lessons Learned: Be prepared to adjust/adapt as your project progresses. You can make changes along the way as you learn new things and start getting results—whether the results were good or bad.

We experimented with course scheduling, classroom formats, methods of offering digital training, marketing, and so forth to meet the needs of our audience. Training must take multiple forms and requires a personal touch/connection between the student and the training.

Small successes are still success, especially when those small steps build into larger accomplishments.

Think outside of the box regarding community outreach. Staff used nontraditional ways of communicating with community members. One example was taking the mobile lab to a large Haitian-Creole church to train people where they were.

Schedule courses according to people's needs. Courses must be convenient for people to attend. For instance, offer options where community members can progress through several levels at a faster pace.

Advice: Believe in your project. Our project proposal was not successful the first time we applied, but we believed so strongly in it that we took the feedback given and addressed the concerns when we reapplied the following year.

Know the grant that you are applying for, and follow the instructions exactly. Each grant has its own requirements, and some funders like a lot more detail than others. Keep thorough notes to make project tracking and reporting easier.

Be willing to ask questions. Communicate, communicate, communicate. If you keep people informed there will be fewer issues, quicker solutions, and sometimes results beyond your expectations.

Contact: Jo Ann Sampson, Project Director

Project Website: http://www.ocls.info/gyb/curriculum/

IMLS Project Profile Website: http://www.imls.gov/profiles/Jul09.shtm

Virtual Library of Cherokee Knowledge

The Cherokee Nation proposes to establish the Virtual Library of Cherokee Knowledge, providing the Cherokee citizens and the interested public access to a comprehensive digital repository of authentic Cherokee Knowledge related to the Nation's epic history, language, traditions, culture, events, and leaders. It is a historically important project that will provide electronic viewing of many of the tribe's most significant documents and materials from the 1830s forward, many of the items never before available for public study and research. The tribe's archives contain thousands of important papers, writings, and manuscripts from the their most recent chiefs as well as hundreds of other manuscripts, books, photographs, oral histories, and artifacts that document the epic history of the Cherokee people. This project enables the tribe, through the consultation with professionals in the fields of digitization and historical documentation, to establish the foremost virtual library and database available in the world on modern Cherokee history and culture, to once and for all gather their records in one centralized location for cultural preservation in perpetuity. Once online, the database will offer a critically important educational program to encourage cultural literacy and develop technological capabilities of the citizens of the Nation.

Grant Amount: $150,000

Funder: Institute of Museum and Library Services (IMLS), Native American Library Services Enhancement Grant

Funder Priorities: Enhancement Grant projects may enhance existing library services or implement new library services, particularly as they relate to the following goals in the updated IMLS statute (20 U.S.C. §9141):

(1) Expanding services for learning and access to information and educational resources in a variety of formats, in all types of libraries, for individuals of all ages in order to support such individuals' needs for education, life-long learning, workforce development, and digital literacy skills;

(2) Establishing or enhancing electronic and other linkages and improved coordination among and between libraries and entities, as described in 9134(b)(6), for the purpose of improving the quality of and access to library and information services;

(3) (A) Providing training and professional development, including continuing education, to enhance the skills of the current library workforce and leadership, and advance the delivery of library and information services; and

(B) Enhancing efforts to recruit future professionals to the field of library and information services;

(4) Developing public and private partnerships with other agencies and community-based organizations;

(5) Targeting library services to individuals of diverse geographic, cultural, and socioeconomic backgrounds, to individuals with disabilities, and to individuals with limited functional literacy or information skills;

(6) Targeting library and information services to persons having difficulty using a library and to underserved urban and rural communities, including children (from birth through age 17) from families with incomes below the poverty line (as defined by the Office of Management and Budget and revised annually in accordance with section 9902(2) of title 42) applicable to a family of the size involved;

(7) Developing library services that provide all users access to information through local, state, regional, national, and international collaborations and networks; and

(8) Carrying out other activities consistent with the purposes set forth in section 9121.

Grant Application: http://www.imls.gov/applicants/samples/Cherokee%20Nation.pdf

Scores Digitization Project

Sibley Music Library
Eastman School of Music
Rochester, New York

The Sibley Music Library proposes to support its continuing efforts to digitize music scores in the public domain. The project provides free online access to rare and unique scores that are no longer protected by copyright, are not widely held by other libraries, and are not digitized elsewhere. To date, Sibley Music Library has digitized more than 11,000 public domain scores and books. The new grant will support the digitization of 9,500 additional scores from May 2011 through September 2012. Sibley is particularly rich in late nineteenth- and early twentieth-century (i.e., public domain) scores, including solo, chamber, orchestral, vocal, and operatic music.

Grant Amount: $300,000

Funder: National Endowment for the Humanities (NEH) Preservation and Access Award

Funder Priorities: NEH especially encourages applications that address the following topics:

183

- Digital Preservation: how to preserve digital humanities materials, including born-digital materials, for which there is no analog counterpart;
- Recorded Sound and Moving Image Collections: how to preserve and increase access to the record of the twentieth century contained in these formats; and
- Preventive Conservation: how to protect humanities collections and slow their deterioration through the use of sustainable preservation strategies.

Project Website: http://digitalscores.wordpress.com/

Dupree, Timber Lake, and Eagle Butte Upper Elementary Schools
Cheyenne River Reservation, South Dakota

This grant enabled librarians from these three Cheyenne River Reservation schools to attend the annual South Dakota Library Association Conference and the American Association of School Librarians Conference. All three of the school libraries have extended their hours to provide services beyond the traditional school day. They also plan to update or enhance their automation systems and purchase new library materials. Some of those purchases included library books, Accelerated Reader (AR) quizzes, digital Playaways, laptop and desktop computers (both replacements and additional units), digital cameras, TV sets, and DVD players.

Grant Amount: $286,000

Funder: U.S. Department of Education Improving Literacy through School Libraries

Waterville Public Schools
Waterville, Maine

Library media centers in Waterville schools will acquire new books, software, more staff hours, and updated equipment and software. At Waterville Senior High School, the grant purchased a MacBook Cart and 25 MacBooks, ten desktop computers to accommodate classes and student research in the Learning Center and Circulation Room, ten MacBook floater laptops, an inventory scanner, updated desktop computers for two offices, CQ Researcher and Science Online databases, approximately 600 new books, and seminar training for two staff members. The grant has provided school library media centers with subscriptions to online databases such as netTrekker, Science Online, BrainPop, Culturegrams, and CQ Researcher. These databases address a broad range of reading levels to raise student achievement and provide access to high-quality online information selected to support the curriculum.

Outdated computer workstations in the library media centers have been updated to expand access to networked reading skills software, the electronic card catalog, and online resources. These improvements include 14 desktop computers and four laptops for student use; and three desktops and two laptops for library staff use; two mobile laptop carts to transport 50 laptops in two schools; portable barcode scanners for inventory and collection development; and portable barcode scanners for all K–12 schools for inventory and collection development.

Professional development for library staff and the purchase of reading motivation materials are also included.

Grant Amount: $243,646

Funder: U.S. Department of Education Improving Literacy through School Libraries

Project Reach
Marmaduke School District
Marmaduke, Arkansas

The goal of Project Reach is to improve literacy skills for 780 students pre-K–12. Four objectives guide and inform the project.

Objective 1: Purchase new collections of print and nonprint materials: The library collections of the district are sorely out of date and are lacking in appropriate materials to promote literacy and academic success. Collection additions will include modern reference materials, updated nonfiction titles, and engaging fiction.

Objective 2: Technology: Project Reach will replace obsolete technology with modern computer systems that will encourage students to learn through enhanced Internet connections. The addition of color printers, scanners, and digital cameras will promote creativity and imaginative student projects. Online resources will encourage students to use databases and conduct quality research. Interactive video conferencing equipment will support resource networking and the school curricula as well as facilitate professional development.

Objective 3: Professional development: Training will focus on early literacy instruction and improve methods of collaboration and coaching between the LMSs (library media specialists), their aides, and teachers. Library consultants from the University of Arkansas will provide a fresh perspective on modern library media center operations.

Objective 4: Increased access will result in a 75 percent increase in the use of the LMC (library media center) during nonschool hours. The library media center will be open after school, on weekends, and for six weeks during the summer and will sponsor the "Wired Bunch" (tech group) as well as reading camps that will maintain and increase literacy skills during the summer months.

Grant Amount: $492,671

Funder: U.S. Department of Education Improving Literacy through School Libraries

Washington County Digital Library
Pacific University Library
Forest Grove, Oregon

Washington County has many organizations, including cultural/historical societies, public libraries, museums, and academic libraries, that are collecting or housing materials (including photographs) about the county's history. The use of these fragile materials is limited because they are not centrally organized and they are difficult to access. Washington County Museum and Pacific University Library, in collaboration with libraries and historical societies throughout the county, propose to build a unified digital collection with libraries and historical images related to this region, to be called the Washington County Digital Library. Our goal is to bring this vibrant visual history to our citizens. This project will greatly increase public access to the visual history of Washington County, using technologies and standard practices that support the broader efforts within the state and region to share and preserve local history.

Grant Amount: $107,325

Funder: LSTA from Oregon State Library

Technology Used: Two scanning workstations with computers and photo scanners; two external hard drives; photo imaging software, Photoshop, and Dreamweaver; collection management system and hosting

Target Audience: Researchers, teachers, students, historians, authors, genealogists, librarians, and the general public

Partnerships and Collaborations: Washington County Museum

Project Virtual Vision
Traurig Library, Naugatuck Valley Community College
Waterbury, Connecticut

Naugatuck Valley Community College's growing population of students and community patrons with visual and learning disabilities need full access to library services in order to improve their academic and information literacy skills. Project Virtual Vision will supplement and update antiquated equipment with current software and adaptive technology to create a well-equipped, well-supported study space. Extensive training will afford patrons enhanced, one-on-one consultations with reference staff. The library will also spearhead the formation of a campus-wide advisory board to address accessibility issues and help ensure that users are aware of the equipment and the project.

Grant Amount: $10,748

Funder: LSTA from Connecticut State Library

FAIR @ Your Library
West Hartford Public Library
West Hartford, Connecticut

FAIR @ Your Library will enable persons with disabling conditions fuller, easier, and more independent access to library resources. People with visual, hearing, and mobility impairments face special challenges when trying to access the library's collections, services, and programs. The library will acquire assistive technology products and software, promote the use of these specialized products through focused publicity and collaboration with community agencies, expand staff awareness and sensitivity to a more diverse group of library users, and train staff and library users in the use of these new resources.

Grant Amount: $17,020

Funder: Connecticut State Library LSTA Funding

Assistance for Job Seekers in Lakeshores Library System
Lakeshores Library System
Waterford North, Wisconsin

The Lakeshores Library System proposes to assist those seeking employment by providing two mobile computer labs, materials, and job skills training. We will be working closely with the Racine County Workforce Development Office and the Walworth County Job Center to provide training for library staff and volunteers to effectively work with job seekers on résumé writing, job searching, and other topics. The Volunteer Connection office in Elkhorn will collaborate with libraries to provide trained volunteers to staff the mobile labs in instances where libraries are unable to provide staff time for the labs. Lakeshores Library System member libraries will provide space and wireless access to the mobile computer labs according to an established schedule. Job seekers will be able to use their local library to conduct job searches, take aptitude tests, complete applications, and perform other online activities without the usual time restrictions imposed on libraries' computer time. The mobile labs will each include six laptops downloaded with Microsoft Office, WinWay Resume software, and CIPA-compliant filtering software. Besides the laptops, the mobile labs will include a wireless printer and projector for training purposes. Availability of the mobile labs will be heavily publicized in the local media in both counties throughout the length of the project. Other activities will include a continuing education workshop for Lakeshores member library staff and trustees on providing assistance to job seekers and creating a link on the Lakeshores webpage to assist job seekers and trainers.

Grant Amount: $17,960

Funder: Wisconsin Division for Libraries and Technology LSTA Funding

Purchasing Laptops for the Marinette Jail to Utilize OWL
Marinette County Library System
Marinette County, Wisconsin

Over the past four years, the Marinette County Jail has made significant strides in the way of inmate education and literacy, with their dynamic staff and passion to make a difference. It is my goal to partner with the jail, purchasing laptops and corresponding materials and supplies to train the inmates and jail staff on the library databases and then allow them to independently access these databases from within the walls of the jail. Whether this be the LearnATest database for résumé building, GED testing, or basic skills, the Tumble books database for beginning readers, or eBooks for access to expensive paper materials the jail can't normally afford, we can give access to so much information for just the price of a computer. This is the perfect time for the library to get the information we have to one of the most information-poor subsets of our community—the jail inmates. I'm confident that this grant will go a long way toward decreasing recidivism while increasing literacy and the relationship the library has with its patrons. We need to actively get the library to those who need it the most, which oftentimes are those who do not come into the library at all. I think we can break the cycle of crime by actively stepping up and doing everything we can to give

187

these inmates the resources they need when they come out of incarceration. It is my belief that this can only help them on their way to becoming productive citizens that the community can be proud of.

Grant Amount: $5,205

Funder: Wisconsin Division for Libraries and Technology LSTA Funding

My Life, My Library
St. Paul Public Library
St. Paul, Minnesota

My Life, My Library is a partnership between the Saint Paul Public Library and the Saint Paul Neighborhood Network (SPNN) to create video segments that highlight various library services in several languages. Six topics will be covered, ranging from The Library Is Always Free to Finding a Job. For each topic, a 5–15 minute video segment, as well as a 2–3 minute web segment will be created. SPNN will run the video segments, and the web segments will be available through the library website. In addition, DVDs will be recorded that can be used by new customers at libraries and will be distributed to partner agencies serving limited English proficiency groups.

Grant Amount: $50,000

Funder: Minnesota State Library LSTA Funding

Privately Funded Technology Projects

Virtual Learning Commons
York University Libraries
Toronto, Ontario, Canada

The Virtual Learning Commons is a pan-university e-learning resource intended for all York University students, providing online assistance on a range of critical skills and academic literacies. This project provides a 24/7 online alternative to the new Learning Commons @ Scott Library and will take a similar holistic and integrated approach to supporting academic literacies. The focus of the resource is on helping students to complete assignments, initially focusing on the three core areas of research, writing, and learning skills. These three themes are interwoven, because they are inter-related and recursive processes. The resource is modular to allow students to use it flexibly. This approach also allows faculty to embed individual modules within their own online learning environments (such as Moodle). The resource employs a variety of media including video, audio, and interactive components in order to provide students with flexible learning options. The design is such that any part of the resource can be modified, removed, or expanded to facilitate ongoing development, ensuring that the elements remain relevant to students over time.

Grant Amount: $500,000

Funder: York University Vice President Academic and Provost

Funder Priorities: To advance innovation and change in the areas of: Teaching and Learning and the Student Experience, including those that support accessibility, community engagement, and the development of academic partnerships. Projects that helped advance the priorities of the University Academic Plan and White Paper (E-learning, Experiential Education, Community Engagement, and the Student Experience) were given more attention.

Community Need: Students' need for research, writing, and learning skills; and assistance in developing critical skills and support in achieving academic literacies.

Technology Used: The technology used includes video equipment (video camera), sound equipment (portable audio recorder), computing equipment (server, laptop, desktop), audio software, video software, and e-learning suite software (Captivate). The technology will help us meet a need among students who are not able to study on campus and make use of resources available in the physical learning commons.

Target Audience: This project was proposed to help students 24/7 when they are off campus, primarily undergraduate students because they are least familiar with the research and writing process. Secondarily, the project will be useful to graduate students in their project and thesis preparation. Also, faculty and staff will be able to use the resource in their teaching and advising roles.

Partnerships and Collaborations: The Libraries collaborated with the Writing Department and Learning Skills Services (CDS) at York University. Both departments were integral to the development of the concept of the project as well as the grant proposal. In the roll out of the project they will be responsible for content creation and will serve on the advisory board as well as the steering committee.

Keys to Success: Our proposal was successful because it addressed all of the criteria outlined in the call for proposals and was endorsed by letters of support from each of the departments (Libraries, Writing, and Learning Skills). The budget was accurate (not inflated) and was clearly tied to the objectives of the project. The proposal was also closely tied to the University Academic Plan as well as University Strategic Priorities.

Challenges: The most challenging aspect of writing the technology component of the proposal was the fact that the project required hiring a web designer, educational consultant, and audio/video engineer. Because we could not hire these professionals before applying for the grant we were left guessing what hardware and software they would want to work with.

Lessons Learned: Next time I would start the grant-writing process a little earlier as it was a bit of a scramble getting all of the pieces together, including the signatures. Also there was some disagreement in the grant proposal advisory group regarding the balance between expressing the project in the language that the project funder would understand versus staying true to the original philosophical concept.

Advice: My advice to other grant seekers is to: (1) Clearly outline your project's objectives and outcomes, and match those to the grant funder's philosophy/priorities/strategic plan. (2) Be sure that your grant proposal addresses all of the components outlined in the call for proposals. (3) Become familiar with your funder, and include in your proposal people or equipment to which they already have access (i.e., employing graduate students).

Contact: Sarah Coysh, E-learning Librarian

Playaways
Lakeview Elementary School Library
Trophy Club, Texas

As a librarian, the enjoyment I feel when I watch students get excited about reading is indescribable. Unfortunately, many students lose this excitement as the years go on. Reading for pleasure gets replaced with many other daily activities, and lifelong reading and learning become unimportant to students. I've even read comments from students who think that reading is just a waste of their time!

In addition, students who are struggling readers because of a variety of factors (dyslexia, English as a second language, etc.) often get discouraged. Fifteen years of teaching has taught me that they must practice their reading to improve, but it can be such a tiring struggle for them.

Studies have shown that using audiobooks is a great way to motivate and help reluctant and struggling readers. They can also be great for readers who are ready for more challenging texts, though. In this way, Playaways can be beneficial to every student at Lakeview, no matter what their reading level or attitude is. They are already tuned in to technology, so it's also very comfortable for them.

This grant will enable the Lakeview Elementary School Library to create a strong collection of Playaway units that can be updated and built on in coming years. In addition, this grant will allow us to purchase hardback copies of each of the books recorded on the Playaways. Students can check these books out with the units to read along (see Figure 11.3).

Grant Amount: $3,847

Funder: Northwest Education Foundation

Funder Priorities:

- Provide resources to enable all students to work at their highest potential
- Attract, support, and recognize teachers for innovative efforts and exemplary teaching
- Team with the school district to build community awareness and confidence in our schools
- Involve the community in ensuring a quality education for the leaders and workers of tomorrow

Community Need: Alternative way to read for struggling readers

Technology Used: 53 Playaways, earbuds, extra batteries, and extra battery covers

Target Audience: Students K–5

Figure 11.3. Playaways

Keys to Success:

- Making the grant schoolwide so that it services all levels of readers from K–5, English Language Learners (ELL), and Gifted students, reluctant readers, struggling readers, and so forth, as well as including some math and music Playaways, such as multiplication rap and children's songs
- Including some professional Playaways that teachers could use, such as *Overcoming Dyslexia* by Sally Shaywitz (Knopf, 2003)

Challenge: Being sure that the grant committee understood what Playaways were and finding research to back up how beneficial they can be

Lesson Learned: The headphones are difficult to manage. I tried checking them out to students, but it's hard to track on paper and would be cumbersome in our automated checkout system. In the future parents will be asked to provide headphones for our laptop carts that can be used for Playaways, too.

Advice:

- Serve the widest audience possible. That was a selling point according to the feedback I received.

- Have parents fill out a permission form before their kids can check out a Playaway, because they are expensive to replace. I put that in my grant to let the committee know that I had thought ahead.

Contact: Gailanne Smith, Librarian

Project Website: http://www.nisdtx.org/Page/14627

Technology Upgrade
Flint Public Library
Flint, Michigan

During the grant period, the Flint District Library will enhance and expand its services to both adults and children by replacing some technological systems, including the automated catalog and check-out, telephone and voicemail, and pay-for-print and library card systems. In addition, the library will create a children's computer-assisted literacy station in each of its four locations.

Grant Amount: $425,000

Funder: Charles Stewart Mott Foundation

Funder Priorities: Underlying all of our grant-making programs are certain values that provide a basis for the interrelatedness of our grant making:

- We believe that learning how people can live together most effectively is one of the fundamental needs of humanity. In so doing, people create a sense of "community," or belonging, whether at the local neighborhood level or as a global society.
- Building strong communities through collaboration provides a basis for positive change. As we have found, the most effective solutions often are those devised locally, where people have the greatest stake in the outcome.
- Strong, self-reliant individuals are essential to a well-functioning society. Moreover, individuals have a critical role to play in shaping their surroundings.
- There is a fundamental need to promote the social, economic, and political empowerment of all individuals. All individuals should have the right to work and pay their own way, the right to an education, the right to better themselves, and the right to a clean and healthy environment. Therein, society must respect individual, human, and civil rights, and those rights should be protected by law.
- At the same time, such rights carry with them responsibilities, and it is incumbent upon us to encourage citizen participation. All individuals have an obligation not only to seek out but also to seize opportunities that make them a vital part of solving problems, to work toward self-sufficiency, and to help foster social cohesion.
- Also fundamental to any grant making is leadership. Clearly, leadership springs from the needs and values of people; likewise, leadership can inspire the aspirations and potential of others. It is our practice to seek out and support leadership in all the projects and programs we support.

- Finally, respect for the diversity of life is integral to our work in all areas. The ultimate quality of life is tied inextricably to maintaining a sustainable human and physical environment.
- Through our programming, we endeavor to enhance the capacity of individuals, families, or institutions at the local level and beyond. We hope that our collective work in any program area could lead to systemic change.
- Foundation mission: To support efforts that promote a just, equitable, and sustainable society.

Community Need: The residents of the city of Flint and Genesee County rely on free high-speed wired and wireless Internet access and computer literacy training provided by the Flint District Library. To continue to meet these needs the Flint District Library required additional funding.

Target Audience: Residents of the city of Flint and Genesee County

Sample Kinds of Grant Applications

Appendix A.1. Letter Proposal Example

Ms. Stella A. Milo, Library Science Instructor
South Dakota Community College
25497 Eagle Street
Pierre, SD 12296

November 23, 2009

Ms. Dixie Smith, Executive Director
Jolie Foundation
13224 Long Way
New York, NY 10000

Dear Ms. Smith:

I am pleased to submit my proposal, *Online Management Course for New Library Directors in South Dakota*, for consideration by the Jolie Foundation. In partnership with the South Dakota State Library (SDSL), the South Dakota Community College (SDCC) Library Science Program is proposing a model project to develop and deliver an online course in Management for new library directors who do not have a formal education in library science. This course will assist directors in preparing for the Management competency and for passing the Management portion of the South Dakota Public Library Director Certification Exam. The Jolie Foundation will be particularly interested in this project because the Foundation is interested in improving library services for all citizens of our state, which is also the intent of this project.

The need for this project is particularly great in South Dakota because of the large number of library directors without MLS degrees (76 percent), many without previous library experience; the distances between rural communities and Pierre where the Exam Study Sessions are held; insufficient staff reserves in small rural libraries to provide coverage while directors are attending out-of-town Study Sessions; and the inability of budgets in small rural libraries to cover directors' travel expenses to Pierre. The current economic downturn, including SDSL's recent funding cuts and staff shortages, has made addressing the growing need for synchronous and asynchronous online training for new library directors more important than ever.

As an alternative, accessible, effective, innovative, and cost-efficient way for new library directors to prepare for the Management competency and used as a model to develop future online training for library directors and other staff in South Dakota, this project will contribute significantly to improved library services in communities throughout our state. Teaching the basics of librarianship to library directors who have not had the advantage of a formal education in library science or previous experience in libraries will significantly improve library services in our smallest, most rural, and poorest communities.

(Continued)

Appendix A.1. Letter Proposal Example *(Continued)*

The goal of this project is to contribute to the improvement of library services in South Dakota communities served by new library directors who do not have MLS degrees, and possibly no previous library experience, by assisting them in preparing for the Management competency and to pass the Management section of the Certification Exam. Directors who are competent managers are more likely to lead libraries that deliver higher-quality library services.

This project will have an immediate impact in the following ways:

- New directors will have an alternative way to acquire this competency that will not require travel to Pierre.
- An online course offers increased opportunities for discussion, sharing experiences, networking, and relationship building.
- More in-depth exploration of a competency is possible in a course lasting more than one day.
- Participants will have the ability to practice new skills as they learn them.
- Coursework can be done in participants' own time when it is most convenient for them.
- Time and cost to travel to Pierre for a study session will be saved.
- Library directors unable to travel to study sessions because of time, money, or staff constraints will have an equal opportunity to succeed.
- Library directors can spend more time in their libraries while preparing for the Exam.
- This alternative online way to prepare for the Certification Exam will honor different learning styles.

This project has the potential to effect changes in public library services in South Dakota in the following ways:

- This model project will address the growing need for synchronous and asynchronous online training to support not only new library directors but also all current and future library directors without MLS degrees in South Dakota to successfully pass the Certification Exam. Lessons learned in implementing this project will pave the way for the NMSL to develop a full complement of online classes on additional competencies for library directors who are preparing for the Certification Exam.
- In the future, additional continuing education courses offered by the NMSL will use this model to deliver a variety of training to all library staff in the state in order to improve the services offered by public libraries so they can respond to the growing needs of library clientele and the changing role of libraries in community life. The increased training capabilities of the NMSL will have a long-term positive effect on the quality of library services in our state.

(Continued)

Appendix A.1. Letter Proposal Example *(Continued)*

- The development of online classes will broaden the ability of all library staff to learn to use online tools so they can pass the skill on to clientele and thus improve public library services.
- More library directors in communities under 3,000 may elect to become certified voluntarily given an online option. This will result in improved library services in the smallest, poorest, most rural communities that have the greatest need.

Project evaluation methods to determine the degree of success will include:

- Of participants who complete the course, 85 percent will indicate through an online survey that the project had the anticipated immediate impact.
- Of participants who complete the course, 85 percent will demonstrate the Management competency as defined by the SDSL.
- Of the new library directors who demonstrate competency in the course, 100 percent will pass the Management competency section of the Certification Exam. This will be determined by analyzing participants' Certification Exam results.
- Of participants who complete the course, 85 percent will indicate in interviews that their knowledge about Management has increased from taking this course; they have gained management skills by taking this course; and they would take more online classes to prepare for the Certification Exam.
- The development of another course based on this model by the SDSL will indicate the degree of this project's success.

This project is a partnership between SDCC and the SDSL. The SDSL has been offering the highest-quality service to South Dakotans since 1934. The Library assists not only residents and state employees but also more than 110 public libraries and branches. SDCC serves the greater Pierre citizenry and houses one of the highest-ranking Library Science Programs in our state. Key project personnel are Eunice Crawford, Continuing Education Coordinator at SDSL, and Stella A. Milo, a Library Science Instructor at SDCC for 25 years.

The SDCC and the SDSL are requesting a $5,000 grant from the Jolie Foundation to fund this $7,956 project to which the SDSL and SDCC will generously contribute $2,956 of staff time and resources and the use of Wimba and Blackboard, the statewide online training platforms.

Please do not hesitate to contact me at (555) 666-1234 or samilo@sdcc.edu if you have questions or would like to discuss any aspect of this proposal with me.

Sincerely,

Stella A. Milo

Appendix A.2. Form Application Example: LSTA Technology Grant Proposal

TENNESSEE DEPARTMENT OF STATE
Tennessee State Library and Archives
LIBRARY SERVICES AND TECHNOLOGY ACT
FY 2010 TECHNOLOGY GRANT PROPOSAL

Library: _____

Mailing Address: _____

City: _____ ZIP: _____

REGION/INDEPENDENT/METRO: _____

Library Director or Project Contact: _____

Telephone: (_____)_____ e-mail: _____

County(ies)/City to Be Served: _____

Congressional District(s) to Be Served: _____

Population Characteristics of the County or City to Be Served
Use data located at http://quickfacts.census.gov/qfd/index.html

County pop. (2008 estimate): _____ Percentage change since 2000 (+/–): _____

RACIAL CHARACTERISTICS

White persons	%
Black persons	%
American Indian, Alaskan Native persons	%
Asian persons	%
Native Hawaiian or other Pacific Islander	%
Two or more races	%
Hispanic or Latino origin	%
White, not Hispanic	%

AGE DISTRIBUTION

Population under 5 years	%
Population under 18 years	%
Population 65 years and over	%

ECONOMIC CHARACTERISTICS

Housing units, 2007	
Median household income, 2007	%
Persons below poverty, 2007	%

EDUCATION

High school graduates	%
Bachelor's degree or higher	%

(Continued)

199

Appendix A.2. Form Application Example: LSTA Technology Grant Proposal (Continued)

FY 2010 TECHNOLOGY GRANT PROPOSAL

LIBRARY: _____

REGION/METRO/INDEPENDENT: _____

*Amount requested should be 50% of total cost of item.

Grant Category	List name/brand of item. Attach additional pages if necessary.	*Amount requested
Wireless Networking (wireless equipment, routers, net-cards)	**(See recommendations.)**	
Computer Peripherals (printers, scanners, monitors, drives, etc.)		
Network Servers/ Hardware		
Library Management Software (including upgrades, additional modules for current systems)	**(Annual maintenance/license fees not eligible.)**	
General Software (children's, office, filtering)	**(Annual maintenance/license fees not eligible.)**	
DESKTOP PCs	**(See minimum specifications.)** _____ × $500.00 **(NUMBER)**	
NOTEBOOKs/ LAPTOPs	**(See minimum specifications.)** _____ × $600.00 **(NUMBER)**	
	TOTAL AMOUNT REQUESTED The library must provide and expend an equal or greater amount of local dollars.	

(Continued)

Appendix A.2. Form Application Example: LSTA Technology Grant Proposal *(Continued)*

CERTIFICATIONS

For this LSTA grant proposal to be considered for funding, the library must meet requirements for items in the certification table below.

➤ If this LSTA grant request **does not** include funding for computers to access the Internet, or computer software or peripherals installed on computers accessing the Internet, compliance with Item 1 is not required.

➤ Option B on FOLLOWING CIPA FORM allows LSTA funding for requests which do not support Internet access. **If you check NO on Item 1, you must submit the CIPA Form with Option B checked.**

****

I certify that the applicant public library is compliant with the following:

[check Yes or No]

		YES	NO
1	Children's Internet Protection Act (Complete enclosed Internet Safety Certification)		
2	Title VI, Civil Rights Act of 1964		

(ITEMS 3 & 4 ARE NOT REQUIRED FOR METROPOLITAN AND INDEPENDENT LIBRARIES)

		YES	NO
3	Library Service Agreement		
4	Maintenance of Effort		

_____

Signature of Library Director   **Date**

_____

Signature of Board Chairperson or Authorizing Authority   **Date**

(Continued)

Appendix A.2. Form Application Example: LSTA Technology Grant Proposal *(Continued)*

(CIPA FORM)
LIBRARY SERVICES AND TECHNOLOGY ACT
TECHNOLOGY GRANTS 2010
INTERNET SAFETY CERTIFICATION
FOR LSTA APPLICANT PUBLIC LIBRARIES

APPLICANT LIBRARY: _____

As the duly authorized representative of the applicant library, I hereby certify that (*check EITHER A or B*):

A. ☐	The recipient library has complied with the requirements of Section 9134(f)(1) of the Library Services and Technology Act and has in place the following policies, as provided by 20 U.S.C. Section 9134(f)(1): (i). A policy of Internet safety *for minors* that includes the operation of a technology protection measure with respect to any of its computers with Internet access that protects against access through such computers to visual depictions that are: (1) obscene; (2) child pornography; or (3) harmful to minors; and the library is enforcing the operations of such technology protection measure during any use of such computers *by minors*; and (ii). A policy of Internet safety that includes the operation of a technology protection measure with respect to any of its computers with Internet access that protects against access through such computers to visual depictions that are: (1) obscene; or (2) child pornography; and the library is enforcing the operation of such technology protection measure during any use of such computers.
B. ☐	The requirements of Section 9134(f) of the Library Services and Technology Act do not apply to the recipient library because no funds made available under the LSTA program will be used to purchase computers used to access the Internet or to pay for direct costs associated with accessing the Internet for a public library that does not receive discounted E-Rate services under the Communications Act of 1934, as amended.

_____
Signature of Authorized Representative

_____
Printed Name of Authorized Representative

_____
Title of Authorized Representative

_____
Date

(Continued)

Appendix A.2. Form Application Example: LSTA Technology Grant Proposal *(Continued)*

SUBSTITUTE W-9 FORM
REQUEST FOR TAXPAYER IDENTIFICATION NUMBER AND CERTIFICATION

---

1. Please complete general information:

Library Name _____ Phone (_____)_____

Address _____

City _____ State _____ ZIP Code _____

---

2. Circle the most appropriate category below: (please circle only one)

1) Individual (not an actual business)

2) Joint account (two or more individuals)

3) Custodian account of a minor

4) a. Revocable savings trust (grantor is also trustee)
   b. So-called trust account that is not a legal or valid trust under state law

5) Sole proprietorship (using a social security number for the taxpayer ID)

6) Sole proprietorship (using a federal employer identification number for taxpayer ID)

7) A valid trust, estate, or pension trust

8) Corporation

9) Association, club, religious, charitable, educational, or other non-profit organization (for entities that are exempt from federal tax, use category 13 below)

10) Partnership

11) A broker or registered nominee

12) Account with the US Department of Agriculture in the name of a public entity that receives agricultural program payments

13) Government agencies and organizations that are tax-exempt under Internal Revenue Service guidelines (i.e., IRC 501(c)3 entities)

---

3. Fill in your taxpayer identification number below: (please complete only one)

1) If you circled number 1–5 above, fill in your Social Security Number.

___ ___ ___ - ___ ___ - ___ ___ ___ ___

2) **If you circled number 6–13 above, fill in your Federal Employer Identification Number (EIN).**

___ ___ - ___ ___ ___ ___ ___ ___ ___

---

4. Sign and date the form:

Certification—Under penalties of perjury, I certify that the number shown on this form is my correct taxpayer identification number. If I circled category 13 above, I also certify that my agency or organization is tax-exempt per Internal Revenue Service guidelines and not subject to backup withholding.

Signature _____ Date _____

203

Appendix A.3. Common Grant Application Form

ANY STATE COMMON GRANT APPLICATION FORM

The Common Grant Application (CGA) can be used for all types of proposals: special projects, capital, and general operating support. Please note that there are some differences in the information required, depending upon the type of request.

A list of the funders who have agreed to accept this form is below. Please keep in mind that every funder has different guidelines, priorities, application procedures, and timelines. Contact each funder before starting the Common Grant Application Form to ensure that they accept the CGA and that all their requirements will be met.

Information about individual grant programs is available from each funder.

GENERAL INSTRUCTIONS

- The application has three parts. Be sure to complete each part.
- Type all proposals (minimum 10 point).
- Provide all of the information in the order listed.
- All questions relative to the request must be completed fully.
- Submit only one copy with numbered pages; do not bind or staple.
- Do not include materials other than those specifically requested at this time.

For specific questions about the Common Grant Application, please call 111-222-3456.

Grantmakers That Accept the Common Grant Application Form

The following funders have agreed to accept the Common Grant Application Form. Other funders, not listed, may also accept the Common Grant Application Form. *Before sending an application to any funder, be sure to check for their specific requirements.*

(Continued)

204

Appendix A.3. Common Grant Application Form *(Continued)*

ANY STATE COMMON GRANT APPLICATION FORM
PART ONE: GRANT AND ORGANIZATION INFORMATION

Grant Request

Total Amount Requested: $_____

Funder applying to: _____ Date Submitted: _____

Name of Project: _____

Duration of Project: from _____ to _____ When are funds needed? _____

Nature of Request: ☐ capital ☐ project ☐ operating ☐ program ☐ endowment

      ☐ other _____
              please list

In what geographical location will the funds be used? _____

_____

Organization Information

Name: _____

Address: _____

City: _____ State: _____ ZIP: _____

Phone number: _____ TTY: _____ FAX Number: _____

E-mail: _____ Federal ID #: _____ Date of Incorporation: _____

Chief Staff Officer (Name & Title): _____

    Phone number: _____

Contact Person (Name & Title): _____

    Phone number: _____

Board Chairperson (Name & Title): _____

    Phone Number: _____

Dates of organization's fiscal year: _____

Organization's total operating budget for past year _____ and current year _____

Please list the organization's staff composition in numbers:

Paid full-time _____ Paid part-time _____ Volunteers _____ Interns _____ Other _____

Total staff (both professional and volunteer) _____

(Continued)

Appendix A.3. Common Grant Application Form *(Continued)*

ANY STATE COMMON GRANT APPLICATION FORM
PART ONE: GRANT AND ORGANIZATION INFORMATION *(Continued)*

Organization Information *(Continued)*

Has the governing board approved a policy which states that the organization does not discriminate as to age, race, religion, disability, sexual orientation, sex, or national origin?

☐ Yes   ☐ No

If yes, when was the policy approved? _____

Does the organization have federal tax exempt status?   ☐ Yes   ☐ No

If no, please explain on separate sheet.

_____

Population Served

Please check the **primary** service category of organization (check only one):

☐ Arts/Culture ☐ Health ☐ Human Services ☐ Civil/Economic Development ☐ Education

☐ Environment ☐ Other (specify) _____

Provide percentages and/or descriptions of the populations the organization serves:

_____ African American   _____ Caucasian   _____ Native American

_____ Asian American   _____ Hispanic/Latino

_____ Other _____
                                please list

_____

Authorization

Has the organization's chief executive officer authorized this request?   ☐ Yes   ☐ No

An officer of the organization's governing body (such as a board member) must sign this application:

**You will have to print out this form and sign the application for submission.

The undersigned, an authorized officer of the organization, does hereby certify that the information set forth in this grant application is true and correct, that the Federal tax exemption determination letter attached hereto has not been revoked, and the present operation of the organization and its current sources of support are not inconsistent with the organization's continuing tax exempt classification as set forth in such determination letter.

Signature_____

Print Name/Title _____ Date _____

Remember to enclose all required support materials with the application (see Part Three).

Appendix A.3. Common Grant Application Form *(Continued)*

ANY STATE COMMON GRANT APPLICATION FORM
PART TWO: GRANT PROPOSAL NARRATIVE

Please provide the following information in the order presented below. Note that some sections are not required for general operating support. Refer to the glossary of terms (last page) as needed when preparing the narrative. Use no more than five pages, excluding attachments.

Organization Information and Background

- Provide a brief summary of the organization's mission, goals, history, programs, major accomplishments, success stories, and qualifications.

- Show evidence of client & community support.

Project/Program Description (NOT required for general operating requests)

- Abstract: Briefly describe the proposed program, how it relates to the organization's mission, capacity to carry out the program, and who will benefit from the program.

- Explain the significance of the program and why the organization is qualified to carry it out.

- Describe the expected outcomes and the indicators of those outcomes.

- Document the size and characteristics of the population to be served by the program.

- Outline the strategy/methodology and timeline to be used in the development and implementation of the program.

- What is the plan to involve the population you intend to serve in the design?

- How does this program enhance the existing services in the community?

Evaluation

- Briefly describe the evaluation process and how the results will be used.

- Explain how the organization will measure the effectiveness of the program.

- Describe the criteria for success.

- Describe the results expected to be achieved by the end of the funding period.

Funding Considerations

- Describe plans for obtaining other funding needed to carry out the project/program or organizational goals, including amounts requested of other funders.

- If the project/program is expected to continue beyond the grant period, describe plans for ensuring continued funding after the grant period.

- List the top five funders of this project (if applying for a program grant) or organization (if applying for general operating support) in the previous fiscal year, the current year, and those pending for the next fiscal year.

(Continued)

Appendix A.3. Common Grant Application Form *(Continued)*

ANY STATE COMMON GRANT APPLICATION FORM
Part Three: Required Attachments

Submit the following attachments (in the order listed) with the completed proposal:

1) Complete list of the organization's officers and directors.

2) The organization's actual income and expense statement for the **past** fiscal year, identifying the organization's principal sources of support.

3) The organization's projected income and expense budget for the **current** fiscal year, identifying the projected revenue sources.

4) The organization's most recent audited financial statement including notes and IRS Form 990.

5) Copies of the IRS federal tax exemption determination letters.

6) Program Budget (multi-year if applicable). *NOT required for general operating requests.*

7) Grantee Report (if previously funded).

NOTE: This is the end of the Common Grant Application Form. Make sure you have completed **each** section of all **three (3)** parts of the application. A glossary is included on the last page for your reference. Please contact 111-222-3456 if you have any questions about the application form. You must contact funders directly with questions about their guidelines, funding priorities, specific application procedures, and deadlines.

Appendix A.4. Online Application Example: NN/LM Technology Improvement Award Application

National Network of Libraries of Medicine
Technology Improvement Award Application

Submit the completed application and supporting documents attached to an e-mail addressed to grants@xxx.xxx. Include "TI" and your LIBID in the subject line of the e-mail. Note: Fields will expand as you type.

1. Today's Date (mm/dd/yy)

2. LIBID

3. Name of institution or organization

4. Project manager name

5. Mailing address

6. E-mail address (e.g., manager@project.org)

7. Daytime telephone number (e.g., 555-555-5555)

8. Fax number (e.g., 555-555-5555)

9. Project title

10. Summary of Project

11. Please describe the problem or situation that led to the need for purchasing new equipment/technology.

12. What group will you reach with this project?

13. Please describe the equipment/technology to be purchased with the award and how it will be used.

(Continued)

Appendix A.4. Online Application Example:
NN/LM Technology Improvement Award Application *(Continued)*

14. Please describe what you plan to accomplish by using this technology. What are the expected outcomes of the project?

15. What is the schedule for the project? Provide a list of tasks in chronological order and indicate timeline for each task.

16. Provide a list of the key personnel and describe each person's responsibilities on the project. Please send résumés for key personnel via e-mail.

17. Additional comments or information

18. Please supply a budget for up to $4,900. Use the following categories: Equipment, Software, Communication Technologies, Installation, Training, and Other. For IT and computer hardware (Equipment) under $3,000, submit catalog pricing; for items $3,000 or more, submit three (3) vendor quotes preferably valid for 60 days. If your institution has a single vendor or sole source agreement, please provide a letter stating this. Send the quote information or catalogue page(s) or sole source letter via e-mail to grants@xxx.xxx.

19. Please provide a brief narrative justification for each category in your budget.

20. Total amount requested (maximum of $4,900)

Appendix A.5. Full Proposal Application Example: Grants.gov

| Save & Submit | Save | Print | Cancel | Check Package for Errors |

GRANTS.GOV™

Grant Application Package

Opportunity Title: Small Grants to Libraries: King James Bible

Offering Agency: National Endowment for the Humanities

CFDA Number: 45.164

CFDA Description: Promotion of the Humanities_Public Programs

Opportunity Number: 20110405-LJ

Competition ID:

Opportunity Open Date: 02/07/2011

Opportunity Close Date: 04/05/2011

Agency Contact:
Division of Public Programs
National Endowment for the Humanities
Room 426
1100 Pennsylvania Avenue, NW
Washington, D.C. 20506
202-606-8269

> This electronic grants application is intended to be used to apply for the specific Federal funding opportunity referenced here.
>
> If the Federal funding opportunity listed is not the opportunity for which you want to apply, close this application package by clicking on the "Cancel" button at the top of this screen. You will then need to locate the correct Federal funding opportunity, download its application and then apply.

This opportunity is only open to organizations, applicants who are submitting grant applications on behalf of a company, state, local or tribal government, academia, or other type of organization.

* Application Filing Name:

Mandatory Documents

Move Form to Complete

 =>

Move Form to Delete

 <=

Mandatory Documents for Submission
Application for Federal Domestic Assistance-Sho
Supplementary Cover Sheet for NEH Grant Program
Attachments

Open Form

Optional Documents

Move Form to Submission List

=>

Move Form to Delete

<=

Optional Documents for Submission

Open Form

211

Instructions

(1) Enter a name for the application in the Application Filing Name field.

- This application can be completed in its entirety offline; however, you will need to login to the Grants.gov website during the submission process.
- You can save your application at any time by clicking the "Save" button at the top of your screen.
- The "Save & Submit" button will not be functional until all required data fields in the application are completed and you clicked on the "Check Package for Errors" button and confirmed all data required data fields are completed.

(2) Open and complete all of the documents listed in the "Mandatory Documents" box. Complete the SF-424 form first.

- It is recommended that the SF-424 form be the first form completed for the application package. Data entered on the SF-424 will populate data fields in other mandatory and optional forms and the user cannot enter data in these fields.

- The forms listed in the "Mandatory Documents" box and "Optional Documents" may be predefined forms, such as SF-424, forms where a document needs to be attached, such as the Project Narrative or a combination of both. "Mandatory Documents" are required for this application. "Optional Documents" can be used to provide additional support for this application or may be required for specific types of grant activity. Reference the application package instructions for more information regarding "Optional Documents".

- To open and complete a form, simply click on the form's name to select the item and then click on the => button. This will move the document to the appropriate "Documents for Submission" box and the form will be automatically added to your application package. To view the form, scroll down the screen or select the form name and click on the "Open Form" button to begin completing the required data fields. To remove a form/document from the "Documents for Submission" box, click the document name to select it, and then click the <= button. This will return the form/document to the "Mandatory Documents" or "Optional Documents" box.

- All documents listed in the "Mandatory Documents" box must be moved to the "Mandatory Documents for Submission" box. When you open a required form, the fields which must be completed are highlighted in yellow with a red border. Optional fields and completed fields are displayed in white. If you enter invalid or incomplete information in a field, you will receive an error message.

(3) Click the "Save & Submit" button to submit your application to Grants.gov.

- Once you have properly completed all required documents and attached any required or optional documentation, save the completed application by clicking on the "Save" button.
- Click on the "Check Package for Errors" button to ensure that you have completed all required data fields. Correct any errors or if none are found, save the application package.
- The "Save & Submit" button will become active; click on the "Save & Submit" button to begin the application submission process.
- You will be taken to the applicant login page to enter your Grants.gov username and password. Follow all onscreen instructions for submission.

(Continued)

Appendix A.5. Full Proposal Application Example: Grants.gov *(Continued)*

View Burden Statement

OMB Number: 4040-0003
Expiration Date: 7/30/2011

APPLICATION FOR FEDERAL DOMESTIC ASSISTANCE - Short Organizational

* 1. NAME OF FEDERAL AGENCY:

National Endowment for the Humanities

2. CATALOG OF FEDERAL DOMESTIC ASSISTANCE NUMBER:

45.164

CFDA TITLE:

Promotion of the Humanities_Public Programs

* 3. DATE RECEIVED: Completed Upon Submission to Grants.gov   **SYSTEM USE ONLY**

* 4. FUNDING OPPORTUNITY NUMBER:

20110405-LJ

* TITLE:

Small Grants to Libraries: King James Bible

5. APPLICANT INFORMATION

* a. Legal Name:

b. Address:

* Street1:   Street2:

* City: County/Parish:

* State: Province:

* Country: USA: UNITED STATES   *** Zip/Postal Code:**

c. Web Address:

http://

* d. Type of Applicant: Select Applicant Type Code(s):   *** e. Employer/Taxpayer Identification Number (EIN/TIN):**

Type of Applicant: *** f. Organizational DUNS:**

Type of Applicant: *** g. Congressional District of Applicant:**

* Other (specify):

6. PROJECT INFORMATION

* a. Project Title:

* b. Project Description:

c. Proposed Project: *** Start Date:**   *** End Date:**

(Continued)

Appendix A.5. Full Proposal Application Example: Grants.gov *(Continued)*

APPLICATION FOR FEDERAL DOMESTIC ASSISTANCE - Short Organizational

7. PROJECT DIRECTOR

Prefix:	* First Name:	Middle Name:

* Last Name:	Suffix:

* Title:	* Email:

* Telephone Number:	Fax Number:

* Street1:	Street2:

* City:	County/Parish:

* State:	Province:

* Country:	* Zip/Postal Code:
USA: UNITED STATES	

8. PRIMARY CONTACT/GRANTS ADMINISTRATOR

☐ Same as Project Director (skip to item 9):

Prefix:	* First Name:	Middle Name:

* Last Name:	Suffix:

* Title:	* Email:

* Telephone Number:	Fax Number:

* Street1:	Street2:

* City:	County/Parish:

* State:	Province:

* Country:	* Zip/Postal Code:
USA: UNITED STATES	

213

(Continued)

Appendix A.5. Full Proposal Application Example: Grants.gov *(Continued)*

APPLICATION FOR FEDERAL DOMESTIC ASSISTANCE - Short Organizational

9. * By signing this application, I certify (1) to the statements contained in the list of certifications** and (2) that the statements herein are true, complete and accurate to the best of my knowledge. I also provide the required assurances** and agree to comply with any resulting terms if I accept an award. I am aware that any false, fictitious, or fraudulent statements or claims may subject me to criminal, civil, or administrative penalties (U.S. Code, Title 218, Section 1001)

** I Agree ☐

** The list of certifications and assurances, or an internet site where you may obtain this list, is contained in the announcement or agency specific instructions.

AUTHORIZED REPRESENTATIVE

Prefix:	* First Name:	Middle Name:

* Last Name:	Suffix:

* Title:	* Email:

* Telephone Number:	Fax Number:

* Signature of Authorized Representative:	* Date Signed:
Completed by Grants.gov upon submission.	Completed by Grants.gov upon submission.

(Continued)

Appendix A.5. Full Proposal Application Example: Grants.gov *(Continued)*

OMB Number: 3136-0134
Expiration Date: 6/30/2012

Supplementary Cover Sheet for NEH Grant Programs

1. Project Director   * Major Field of Study

2. Institution Information   * Type

3. Project Funding

Programs other than Challenge Grants ($)

Outright Funds	
Federal Match	
Total from NEH	
Cost Sharing	
Total Project Costs	

Challenge Grants Applicants Only ($)

Fiscal Year #1	
Fiscal Year #2	
Fiscal Year #3	
Fiscal Year #4	
Total from NEH	
Non-Federal Match	
Total	
Matching Ratio	to 1

4. Application Information

* Will this proposal be submitted to another NEH division, government agency, or private entity for funding?   ☐ Yes   ☐ No

If yes, please explain where and when:

* Type of Application   ☐ New   ☐ Supplement   If supplement, list current grant number(s).

* Project Field Code

(Continued)

215

Appendix A.5. Full Proposal Application Example: Grants.gov *(Continued)*

ATTACHMENTS FORM

Instructions: On this form, you will attach the various files that make up your grant application. Please consult with the appropriate Agency Guidelines for more information about each needed file. Please remember that any files you attach must be in the document format and named as specified in the Guidelines.

Important: Please attach your files in the proper sequence. See the appropriate Agency Guidelines for details.

1) Please attach Attachment 1	Add Attachment	Delete Attachment	View Attachment
2) Please attach Attachment 2	Add Attachment	Delete Attachment	View Attachment
3) Please attach Attachment 3	Add Attachment	Delete Attachment	View Attachment
4) Please attach Attachment 4	Add Attachment	Delete Attachment	View Attachment
5) Please attach Attachment 5	Add Attachment	Delete Attachment	View Attachment
6) Please attach Attachment 6	Add Attachment	Delete Attachment	View Attachment
7) Please attach Attachment 7	Add Attachment	Delete Attachment	View Attachment
8) Please attach Attachment 8	Add Attachment	Delete Attachment	View Attachment
9) Please attach Attachment 9	Add Attachment	Delete Attachment	View Attachment
10) Please attach Attachment 10	Add Attachment	Delete Attachment	View Attachment
11) Please attach Attachment 11	Add Attachment	Delete Attachment	View Attachment
12) Please attach Attachment 12	Add Attachment	Delete Attachment	View Attachment
13) Please attach Attachment 13	Add Attachment	Delete Attachment	View Attachment
14) Please attach Attachment 14	Add Attachment	Delete Attachment	View Attachment
15) Please attach Attachment 15	Add Attachment	Delete Attachment	View Attachment

Resources

Appendix B.1. Rules of Grant Work

Rule #1   Grant work starts with planning.

Rule #2   Grants are about people, not about money or things.

Rule #3   Technology grants fund projects that meet your community's information needs using technology.

Rule #4   Designing the technology project and proposal writing are closely linked.

Rule #5   Grant work is a team effort.

Rule #6   Grant work requires support from your organization and leadership.

Rule #7   Always follow the application directions and funder's guidelines.

Rule #8   Grant work is a continuous process. It does not stop when you hear from the funder about success or rejection.

Rule #9   Your community's needs will guide you from the strategic planning phase all the way through the entire grant process.

Rule #10   If a library project does not meet a community need, you should not be doing it.

Rule #11   To be successful at grant work it is necessary to share the responsibilities with others.

Rule #12   It doesn't make sense to duplicate efforts—especially when it comes to technology projects.

Rule #13   Library leadership and the organization must commit to providing the resources and support required to do grant work.

Rule #14   Identify a funding source that is interested in supporting the goals and purpose of your project and improving the lives of your target population.

Rule #15   Use grant resources that focus on the goal or purpose of your project or on your target population. Do not limit your research to resources that include only grants for technology.

Rule #16   Begin by searching broadly. Your broad search results will guide you in narrowing your search to eventually pinpoint the right grant for your project.

Rule #17   Developing working relationships with potential funders is part of the grant process.

Rule #18   Never enter your proposal directly into an online application form without a backup. Always prepare the proposal in a word-processing program first, and then copy and paste it into the form.

Appendix B.2. Federal Government Funding Sources At-A-Glance

Department of Agriculture, U.S.	Rural Utilities Service (RUS) Telecommunications Programs • Broadband Initiatives Program (BIP) • Community Connect Grant Program • Distance Learning and Telemedicine Program (DLT) • Farm Bill Broadband Loan Program • Telecommunications Infrastructure Loan Program
Department of Commerce, U.S.	National Telecommunications and Information Administration (NTIA) • Broadband Technology Opportunities Program (BTOP)
Department of Education, U.S.	Office of Elementary and Secondary Education (OESE) • Improving Literacy through School Libraries Program • School Support and Technology Programs (SSTP) • Enhancing Education through Technology (Ed-Tech) Program Office of English Language Acquisition, Language Enhancement, and Academic Achievement for Limited English Proficient Students (OELA) Office of Innovation and Improvement (OII) • Ready to Teach Program • Star Schools Program Grants Office of Postsecondary Education (OPE) • Technological Innovation and Cooperation for Foreign Information Access Office of Special Education and Rehabilitative Services (OSERS) • Assistive Technology Program • Technology and Media Services Program Office of Vocational and Adult Education (OVAE) • Preparing America's Future
Department of Health and Human Services (HHS), U.S.	National Library of Medicine (NLM) • Information Resource Grants to Reduce Health Disparities National Network of Libraries of Medicine (NN/LM) • Technology Improvement Award
General Services Administration, U.S.	Computers for Learning Program
Institute of Museum and Library Services (IMLS)	Library and Services Technology Act (LSTA) Grants to States Program Learning Labs in Libraries and Museums National Leadership Grants Native American Library Services Enhancement Grants Sparks! Ignition Grants for Libraries and Museums
National Endowment for the Arts	Access to Artistic Excellence
National Endowment for the Humanities	Digital Humanities Start-Up Grants Humanities Collections and Reference Resources Grants National Digital Newspaper Program
National Historical Publications and Records Commission (NHPRC)	Digitizing Historical Records Program Electronic Records Projects Program

219

Appendix B.3. Technology Grant Resources At-A-Glance

Federal Government Resources	*Catalog of Federal Domestic Assistance* Grants.gov Individual Federal Agency Websites *Federal Register* *Primary Source* TGCI *Federal Register* Grant Announcements
State and Local Government Resources	State Library Agencies State Humanities Councils, Arts Councils, Cultural Services Agencies, and Departments of Education State and Local Funding Directories

Private Foundation Resources	Foundation Center Cooperating Collections
	Foundation Center Digital Grant Guides
	Newsletters and Periodicals
	Directories
	  • *Annual Register of Grant Support*
	  • *Big Book of Library Grant Money 2007: Profiles of Private and Corporate Foundations and Direct Corporate Givers Receptive to Library Grant Proposals*
	  • *Celebrity Foundation Directory*
	  • *Everything Technology: Directory of Technology Grants*
	  • *Foundation Directory, Foundation Directory Part 2, and Foundation Directory Supplement*
	  • *Foundation Directory Online*
	  • *Foundation Grants Index*
	  • *Foundation Grants for Preservation in Libraries, Archives, and Museums*
	  • *Foundation Reporter*

Corporate Resources	*Corporate Giving Directory* *Corporate Giving Online* *Corporate Philanthropy Report* *National Directory of Corporate Giving*
Club and Organization Resources	Michigan State University Service Clubs and Civic Organizations That Provide Funding
Professional Association Resources	American Association of School Librarians Awards & Grants American Library Association Awards, Grants & Scholarships Association of College and Research Libraries Public Library Association Special Libraries Association Grants and Scholarships

Index

About the Author

Pamela H. MacKellar (http://www.pamelamackellar.com/) is an author and library consultant with 30 years of experience in libraries, including over 10 years of management experience. She has conceived, planned, generated funding for, and implemented new library programs including a community technology center for people with disabilities in Albuquerque, New Mexico. Pam has had success in preparing winning proposals to the U.S. Department of Education, the Institute of Museum and Library Services, the National Network of Libraries of Medicine–South Central Region, the Bill & Melinda Gates Foundation, the Beaumont Foundation, the Albuquerque Community Foundation, and the MacArthur Foundation. Pam received the 2010 Loleta D. Fyan Grant in partnership with the New Mexico State Library for a project titled "Online Management Course for New Library Directors in New Mexico," which developed a free online course in management for new library directors without master's degrees in library science in New Mexico communities. She has completed the Grantsmanship Center's Grantsmanship Training Program, and she has served as a field reviewer, reading and evaluating grant proposals from libraries seeking state and federal funding.

Pam co-authored *Winning Grants: A How-To-Do-It Manual for Librarians with Multimedia Tutorials and Grant Development Tools* (Neal-Schuman, 2010) and *Grants for Libraries: A How-To-Do-It Manual for Librarians* (Neal-Schuman, 2006), and she authored *The Accidental Librarian* (Information Today, 2008; http://www.accidentallibrarian.com/). She has co-authored articles on grants for libraries, she co-authors the *Library Grants Blog* (http://librarygrants.blogspot.com/), she has designed a web tutorial on grants for librarians, and she has presented workshops and classes on such topics as grants for libraries and nonprofits and removing obstacles to create opportunities for librarians.

Pam holds a master's degree in library science from the State University of New York at Albany, a bachelor's degree in fine arts from the State University of New York at New Paltz, and a certificate in graphic design from the University of New Mexico Department of Continuing Education. She makes artist books and has exhibited them in juried shows nationally. Pam lives in New Mexico with her husband and one cat.